PENGUIN BOOKS

CRY OF PAIN

Mark Williams was born in 1952 and educated at Stockton-on-Tees Grammar School and St Peter's College, Oxford. Between 1979 and 1982 he was Lecturer in Applied Psychology at the University of Newcastle upon Tyne and from 1983 to 1991 was Research Scientist at the Medical Research Council's Applied Psychology Unit in Cambridge. Since 1991 he has been Professor of Clinical Psychology at the University of Wales, Bangor. His other books include *The Psychological Treatment of Depression* and, with F. Watts, C. MacLeod and A. Mathews, *Cognitive Psychology and Emotional Disorders*.

Professor Williams is married and has one son and two daughters.

CRY OF PAIN

Understanding Suicide and Self-harm

MARK WILLIAMS

PENGUIN BOOKS

PENGUIN BOOKS

Published by the Penguin Group
Penguin Books Ltd, 27 Wrights Lane, London w8 5tz, England
Penguin Books USA Inc., 375 Hudson Street, New York, New York 10014, USA
Penguin Books Australia Ltd, Ringwood, Victoria, Australia
Penguin Books Canada Ltd, 10 Alcorn Avenue, Toronto, Ontario, Canada m4v 3b2
Penguin Books (NZ) Ltd, 182–190 Wairau Road, Auckland 10, New Zealand

Penguin Books Ltd, Registered Offices: Harmondsworth, Middlesex, England

First published 1997
1 3 5 7 9 10 8 6 4 2

Set in 10.25/12pt Monotype Baskerville
Typeset by Rowland Phototypesetting Ltd, Bury St Edmunds, Suffolk
Printed in England by Clays Ltd, St Ives plc

CONTENTS

LIST OF TEXT FIGURES

LIST OF TABLES

ACKNOWLEDGEMENTS

A number of people have helped with this book at various stages. I am grateful to Isaac Sakinofsky of the Clarke Institute of Psychiatry in Toronto, and to David Clark of the Center for Suicide Research and Prevention, Chicago, for help in obtaining up-to-date statistics from North America. My colleague Leslie Pollock has been helpful in keeping me abreast of developments within the WHO database. Keith Hawton kindly made available details of the Oxford City parasuicide data, and Allan House made available details of comparable data from Leeds. Stephen Platt has been generous with advice and help at a number of stages, and Breda McLeavey made available details of her studies of the treatment of suicidal behaviour in Ireland. Glyn Lewis of Cardiff gave helpful comments on the primary prevention chapter, Paul Gilbert advised on the 'Cry of Pain' chapter, Phil Cowen of Oxford gave helpful comments on the sections on the psychopharmacology of suicide and Neil Cheshire advised on psychodynamic aspects. A number of colleagues read other parts in draft: Michaela Swales, Isabel Hargreaves, Patrick Vesey, Miriam Shieldhouse, Debbie Lovell, Jean Lyon, Caroline Creasey, Bethan Jones, Mair Edwards and David Nightingale; I am very grateful for their help.

I am grateful to HMSO for permission to reproduce tables and figures from Crown Copyright material (*Population Trends*, 1992), to Routledge for permission to use parts of a previous chapter I had written on cognitive therapy for suicidal patients (in J. Scott, J. M. G. Williams and A. T. Beck (eds.), *Cognitive Therapy in Clinical Practice*, 1989), and to Carfax Publishing for permission to use parts of my paper with Leslie Pollock ('Factors Mediating Suicide Behaviour') that appeared in the *Journal of Mental Health* (1993). Brenda Ellis and Sharon Fraser have helped in the production of the text, and I am specially grateful to Caroline Creasey, who has borne the brunt of transforming my scribbles into readable drawings and figures, and to Peter Ford, for his excellent copy-editing and advice on the form of the final text.

Finally, thanks are owed to close friends and family. Jeff Williams-Jones, Nona Ephraim and Lloyd and Carolynn Evans have shared in many ups and downs during the writing of this book, and to them I am deeply grateful. The project could not have been completed without the help and support of my family. Robert has read parts of the text and commented freely and helpfully upon it. Phyllis, Annie and Jennie have always been prepared to discuss any of the ideas covered in the book. All have allowed me to concentrate on writing when they had every right to expect that I should stop and attend to their needs. For this love and support I am forever in their debt.

MARK WILLIAMS
April 1996

INTRODUCTION

There is much about suicide that presents a real and often tragic puzzle to be solved by family and friends, by physicians and other professionals involved with someone who has committed or attempted suicide. At the level of the individual event the questions are most often: 'Why did they do it?' 'Why did they not see there was help available?' At the larger level, the questions remain whether a biological, sociological or psychological explanation will provide the best clue to suicidal behaviour. Each level of explanation, seen in isolation, has its drawbacks. For example, although the brain is bound to be involved in all behaviour, it seems to many an inappropriate level of analysis for many situations.

The large growth in interest during recent years in the subject of suicide and suicidal behaviour may be partly because of the rapid increase since the mid 1970s in suicides by young people (particularly young men). Although the same period has seen a decrease in the numbers of older people committing suicide (the traditionally most vulnerable group), the change in rates has meant that many more suicide victims have taken their lives 'at the prime of life', challenging society's view of itself as successful.

Secondly, there has been an increased wish within the World Health Organization to challenge health care systems to meet targets to improve the health of their populations. Suicide rates are seen as a visible and quantifiable aspect of the mental health of a nation.

Thirdly, interest in suicide has been fuelled by a renewed fascination, especially in the United States, with euthanasia, medically assisted suicide, and rational suicide (self-deliverance). When Derek Humphry's book *Final Exit* was published in 1991, with its matter-of-fact, detailed discussion of the best way of ending life, it sold more than 500,000 copies in its first year. These are issues and debates in which both public and professionals are interested.

In the main, two types of book are written in response to this increased interest. The first type is written for the mental health professionals. The second type is written for suicidal people, their families, or for suicide 'survivors'.[1] Of all the books which have attempted to be useful to both the professional and lay communities, Erwin Stengel's *Suicide and Attempted Suicide*[2] became a classic. It was written originally in the early 1960s, and reprinted several times. It gave the main facts and figures together with sufficient interpretation to help the reader understand something of the mind of those who feel suicidal. The book kept apart suicide and attempted suicide, but in its revision, Stengel included an extra discussion about the 'appeal function' of attempted suicide, which he believed had been misunderstood, and more on the separation of completed from non-fatal suicide attempts, which was controversial in its day.

There have been many developments in the field since Stengel's death. These include changes in the socio-demographic pattern of suicide deaths; knowledge about which social factors are most likely to produce changes in rates of suicide; a greater awareness of the strategies to prevent suicide (and their limits); more focus on the impact of the media on suicidal behaviour; and an understanding of the way in which depression and hopelessness may act as 'final common pathways' to suicidal behaviour. The present book aims to deal with these issues in such a way that a lay audience may come to know what are the main facts and theories, but also so that health and mental health professionals may have a digest of a subject which will be constantly in the background in their practice.

For this reason, the book's title reflects not the puzzle about suicidal behaviour, but instead summarizes one possible answer. Suicidal behaviour is most often a 'cry of pain'. This perspective is intended to capture the way in which behaviour can have a communication outcome without communication being the main motive. It is analogous to the animal caught in a trap, which cries with pain. The cry is brought about by the pain, but may nevertheless communicate distress in a way which will affect the behaviour of other members of the species. Suicidal behaviour may be overtly communicative in a minority of cases, but mainly it is 'elicited' by the pain of a situation with which the person cannot cope – a cry of pain first, and only then a cry for help.

The distinction thus drawn with earlier ideas about the 'cry for help' is quite deliberate. Stengel acknowledged that suicidal behaviour might have an 'appeal function'. However, having raised the concept in the early editions, Stengel felt he had to try to counteract a fundamental misunderstanding. He had been taken to mean that suicide attempts were only appeals, only manipulative. He had meant to imply that such behaviour had an appeal function in the same way that physical illness has an appeal function – i.e. people will change their behaviour to try and help the person. In this sense, he says, 'the appeal effect of a suicidal act may be the greater the less it was intended'.[3]

However, the scene was set for many years of a misunderstanding which still remains. Even now, many suicidal acts are dismissed as 'mere' cries for help, as if a communication motive was incompatible with a serious attempt to end life, and as if the self-damaging act did not represent a mental health problem which needs to be taken seriously. So the 'cry for help' idea, though originally intended to be a neutral theory about suicidal behaviour, has outlived its usefulness. First, it has become limited to non-fatal suicide attempts (parasuicide) and thus contributed to a widening of the gap between fatal suicide and parasuicide. Secondly, it is almost always used pejoratively, or at least to imply that a certain suicidal act was not so serious, but 'merely' a cry for help. Those who work closely with people who feel suicidal and sometimes act on such feelings know that such behaviour is never 'merely' anything.

Although there are some grounds for maintaining the separation between completed suicide and attempted suicide,[4] it is now widely acknowledged that differences may have been overplayed. There remain many differences between these groups, including age and sex ratio, but not only do the populations overlap, the motivation for both completed and attempted suicide is complex and crosses the boundary between them. For example, anger and communication motives can be found in both, and even relatively low-risk 'suicidal ideation' (which often does not lead to suicidal behaviour) may be dominated by the theme of escape and death rather than communication.

Suicide is usually the most individual of acts, and I realize how difficult it is to try and draw conclusions that are general across a number of situations. Many readers whose professional or personal lives have been touched by suicide or suicidal behaviour will, at many points, be able to think of exceptions to much of what is written here. Yet if we are to understand and help people in the future, there will need to be a dialogue between the general rule and the individual circumstance. This book is offered as a contribution to that dialogue. I shall start with history.

Chapter 1

HISTORICAL PERSPECTIVE

A psychiatrist was talking about suicide risk in her patients. 'I can understand why some of my patients should want to kill themselves. If they really want to do it, there is nothing I can do,' she said. 'Even if I was able to stop them, would it be right to try? Many of them have enough insight to know how their illness has ruined their lives.' Contrast her attitude with that expressed by Professor Gethin Morgan in a UK Health Advisory Service publication in the same year (1993):

Those at risk of suicide come to us in our professional capacity to get help. They have already talked with relatives and friends and we may well be the last port of call. They watch us intently for our response. They are usually ambivalent about suicide and we have a responsibility to encourage the wish to live ... Anyone who has extensive experience in suicide prevention will know that things can improve in a most unexpected way even in the case of individuals facing what may seem enormous adverse odds. It is for us to assume that change for the better is always possible.[1]

This represents a disagreement about whether suicide is preventable, and also a disagreement about whether, even if it could be prevented, such prevention would be morally justified. If suicide were sometimes a rational response to an unbearable situation, what business do psychiatrists and other mental health professionals have in intervening?

These are not the only conflicts in attitudes to suicide. In fact, Western society's attitude to suicide throughout the ages has been at best confused, swinging between punitive severity and tolerant advocacy.[2] Walking along the High Street in Bangor some time ago, someone wearing a sandwich-board thrust a leaflet into my hands. It was concerned with sin, mostly, but included a warning against the danger of a person 'becoming so discouraged to the extent of yielding to the horrible sin of taking his own life . . . Through suicide the opportunity to repent is cut off and soul and body will be destroyed in hell.' To many, this will seem an extreme view from another age, yet it was only in the early 1960s that attempting to take one's own life ceased to be a criminal offence and became the province of the health service rather than the courts. By the last decade of the twentieth century, several research studies seemed to have shown beyond doubt that around 90 per cent of people who commit suicide are suffering some form of mental illness. Yet, if so, why is there such little evidence that psychiatric or medical intervention can affect the probability of suicidal behaviour? If medicine is not the answer, it would be better if we were clear about it, and stopped expecting medical practitioners to work miracles on society's behalf.

Attitudes in classical and medieval times

It is often thought that in Greek and Roman times there was a tolerance for suicide. However, many philosophers condemned self-destruction. Pythagoras, for example, compared suicides with soldiers who deserted their posts. Aristotle said a person should not commit suicide since such an act cancelled unilaterally his or her obligations to the state, the contract between a person and society. On the other hand, Stoic and Epicurean philosophers believed that suicide could be the right course of action in some circumstances, e.g. where there was terminal illness or unremitting pain. They also allowed that in certain circumstances it might be an act of nobility where it was an expression of political rights or values.

In the fifth and sixth centuries, attitudes to suicide shifted gradually away from more permissive Roman philosophical ideals and became more punitive. St Augustine thought the philosophical support of suicide abhorrent. However, the Christian Church has always had to contend with the difficulty that suicide is nowhere explicitly condemned in the Bible. Christian thinkers and philosophers have always had to resort to the commandment, 'Thou shalt not kill.' Appealing to this commandment has difficulties of its own, since most Christian thinkers have wished to make an exception for people who kill as part of a just war. Clearly the commandment, 'Thou shalt not kill,' if taken as absolute in every circumstance, would prevent this sort of killing too. If killing could be excused in times of war, why were there no other circumstances in which the commandment could be set aside? Could not some of these circumstances be precisely those envisaged by the Stoic and Epicurean philosophers?

Since the Bible did not condemn suicide explicitly, Christian thinkers had to find other arguments. St Thomas Aquinas argued that suicide was against the natural law. Since God was expressed in natural laws, suicide was a sin. Adding weight to the Christian thinkers' rejection of suicide was the popular belief in the demonic origin of self-killing. In the Middle Ages the view was encouraged that supernatural activity in the natural world was a relatively frequent occurrence. People who committed suicide therefore showed evidence that they had been possessed by devils. The diabolical causes of suicide found many expressions in literature. One phrase repeated and elaborated throughout the Middle Ages was that of Egbert, an eighth-century writer, who blamed 'self-murder' on 'the instigation of the Devil'.

In England, 'self-murder' became thought of as an offence against God, against the King and against nature. Those who committed suicide were tried posthumously by a coroner's jury. If they were convicted as having murdered themselves, all their goods, including all household items and money and debts owed to them, were forfeit to the Crown or the Crown's Agent. The result was that the family of someone who committed suicide, especially if it was the head of the household, would be reduced to abject poverty.

In addition to these consequences, 'self-murderers' were denied Christian burial. Instead their bodies were buried 'profanely'. The macabre ceremony surrounding such burials seems to have its origins in pre-Christian times. But the belief that suicide was a supernaturally evil act encouraged the desecration of the body of the person who had killed themselves. The individual was buried, often at a cross-roads, naked and with a wooden stake through the body. The hole was filled in, sometimes with the stake showing above the earth so that passers-by might be reminded of the awfulness of the circumstances of this death. The clergy did not attend the ceremony. It was carried out by officials of the parish, including the church wardens and their assistants.

As part of the posthumous trial for self-murder, the coroner's court had to decide whether it was really murder or not. The only mitigating circumstance was if it was found the person was insane. If someone killed themselves when mad or mentally incompetent in some way, they were not convicted. Instead of returning a verdict of *felo de se* (a felon of himself), the person was deemed to be *non compos mentis* (not of sound mind).

Despite all these popular feelings and the fact that committing suicide was considered a crime, during the Middle Ages very few juries actually brought in verdicts of *felo de se*. It was not that suicide was rare, but that juries, often consisting of local people who had sympathy with the family, were reluctant to see them become paupers. The Crown had little control over these local juries, and although from time to time attempts were made to tighten the enforcement of the law, this was rather sporadic. It was not until Tudor times that this aspect of social and legal life was more rigorously controlled.

The Tudor revolution in attitudes: government and folklore combine

During the early sixteenth century, the government tightened up on a number of aspects of English law, enforcing its will where it had not done so before. The law about suicide was enforced using the Court of Star Chamber. This, the King's Council sitting in judicial session, tried (and succeeded) in many areas to enforce those laws where there was a direct financial benefit to the Crown and government. Since suicides considered *felo de se* meant that goods and households were forfeit, the Court of Star Chamber had a great deal of interest in ensuring that the verdicts were thoroughly carried out and the penalties exacted.

The struggles between local juries and the Court of Star Chamber continued, however. Local officials would often declare that the suicide victim had very little possessions. In one extreme case the total value of a person's possessions was declared to be precisely the value (to the last ha'penny) of the value of the person's debts. In this way, local coroners' juries attempted still to protect their fellow-villagers and townsfolk from the excesses of central government.

The results of all the government reforms were reflected in what appears to be a dramatic increase in suicides, or at least those reported to the King's Bench. The average number of suicide inquisitions in 1500 was 61 (*felo de se*), and 1 *non compos mentis*. By 1600 this number had risen to 873 *felo de se* and 7 *non compos mentis* verdicts.

The Tudor revolution in government was reinforced by the attitude of the churchmen, who continued to emphasize their belief that self-murder was an expression of despair brought about by the devil. Both Calvinists and non-Calvinists were equally vehement in their condemnation. For example, George Abbot, one time Archbishop of Canterbury, declared that suicide was 'a sin so grievous that scant any is more heinous unto the Lord'. He was Calvinist, but the anti-Calvinist Lancelot Andrewes was similarly explicit: 'It is worse than beastly to kill or drown or make away with ourselves; the very swine would not have run into the sea but that they were carried by the Devil' – a reference to the story of the Gadarene swine in the Bible (Mark 5, Luke 8).

In popular stories and in sermons the idea of Satan playing on a man's guilt and luring him to his death by abject despair is prominent. In morality plays, a point is often reached where the devil casts Man into a despair or 'wan-hope'. In John Skelton's *Magnyfycence*, a character is persuaded by Despair that his sins are so bad that God will not forgive them. Despair urges him to suicide with the words 'ryd thy selfe rather than this lyfe for to lede'. The character Mischief appears, offering the instruments of self-murder: 'Lo here is thy knyfe and a halter, and all were go ferther, spare not thyself, but boldly thee murder.' The central character is about to use the knife against himself when Hope suddenly enters and urges him not to kill himself 'against Nature and Kynde'.[3]

In such a culture, suicide meant the struggle had been lost, the devil had won. In Christopher Marlowe's *Dr Faustus*, the devil instigates suicide more explicitly perhaps than in many other allegories. The Good Angel and the Evil Angel try to persuade Faustus to repent on the one hand and to despair on the other. Faustus cries, 'My heart's so harden'd, I cannot repent.' When Mephistophilis offers Faustus a dagger after he has yielded to despair, Faustus cries, 'Damn'd art thou, Faustus, damn'd; despair and die!'

Of course there is little doubt that many of the people who tried to kill themselves or actually succeeded were extremely depressed. The fact that *non compos mentis* verdicts were not brought in for them cannot hide this fact. In many cases the depression was clearly of psychotic proportions. A young Puritan, Nehemiah Wallington, imagined himself 'provoked by the Devil' to suicide and made eleven attempts. According to Nehemiah's own account, Satan showed himself in various manifestations: as a crow, as his sister, as a minister and as a disembodied voice. The disembodied voice immediately suggests auditory hallucinations of the psychotic patient. But the pull to life turned out to be stronger than the pull to death, despite 'the temptation of Satan'.

Then Satan temted me again and I resisted him again. Then he temted me a third time, and I yielded unto him and pulled out my knife and put it neere my throat. Then God of his goodness caused me to consider what would follow if I should do so. With that I felle out a weaping and I flong away my knife.

As in contemporary accounts of 'reasons for living' v. 'reasons for dying', the person who had suicidal thoughts would often stop themselves for these religious reasons or because of family. In the early seventeenth century an account is given of a woman whose husband had died and who was tempted to commit suicide but found her love for her child saved her from doing so.

But few such considerations made any difference in the case of someone psychotically depressed. John Gilpin, an ex-Quaker, reported that he was possessed by Satan. On one occasion his hand was carried to take up a knife which lay on the table. His hand was then carried with it towards his throat and a voice said to him 'open a hole there, and I will give you the words of eternal life' (a reference to St John's Gospel: 'Lord, to whom shall we go; you have the words of eternal life' (6:68)). Such involuntary hand movements, in which the limbs appear to be out of the control of the person, are not un-known in schizophrenic states and certain forms of brain damage.

During the sixteenth century there was little change in the overall attitude to the type of 'mitigating circumstances' that might be allowed by the coroners' courts. One might suppose that, because melancholy was seen, as today, as the final common pathway to suicide, this would constitute enough grounds for a *non compos mentis* verdict. However, the religious thinking of the time, combined with the popular belief that melancholy was a sign that the devil had taken over a person's soul, meant that society found it difficult to shake itself free from the conviction that suicide was the outcome of diabolical possession and not caused by madness. The result was that less than 5 per cent of the men and women who com-mitted suicide between 1485 and 1660 were judged to be *non compos mentis*.

Nevertheless, in the sixteenth century, as in other periods of history, there was a lack of uniformity about attitudes. The elements of more tolerant attitudes, later to become more general beliefs, can be found even where the *zeitgeist* was less tolerant. For example, in Thomas More's *Utopia* people who are ill with incurable diseases were imagined to be able to kill themselves with the permission of their priests. This was considered, at least in pagan terms, to be a 'good and wise act', since the death of the person would put an end to torture rather than to enjoyment. In those terms, then, it was considered a pious and holy act. It is not surprising that the intellectual élite of the country, influenced by the Renaissance emphasis on classical literature, should revisit many aspects of such Epicureanism.

The seventeenth century: gradually changing attitudes

During the seventeenth century an increasing range of motives began to be imputed in the case of suicidal thoughts, feelings and behaviour. With it came an increased secular view of suicide as being caused by economic circumstances or psychological state of mind. After the mid 1600s coroners appeared much more ready to accept an alternative to the *felo de se* verdict. However, characteristically of a period of transition, no one could be certain that, should a suicide occur, there would not be a *felo de se* verdict followed by the requirement to forfeit the person's goods. This is well illustrated in Samuel Pepys's *Diaries*.

A businessman called Anthony Joyce, kinsman to Pepys, tried to commit suicide by throwing himself into a pond. Pepys takes up the story in his diary entry of 21 January 1667:

Comes news from Kate Joyce that, if I would see her husband alive, I must come presently. So I to him, and find his breath rattled in the throat; and they did lay pigeons to his feet, and all despair of him. It seems, on Thursday last, he went, sober and quiet, to Islington, and behind one of the inns, the White Lion, did fling himself into a pond: was spied by a poor woman, and got out by some people, and set on his head and got to life: and so his wife and friends sent for.

Joyce explained to Pepys that he had been led by the devil and that he had 'forgot to serve God as he ought'. However, it is interesting to note that Pepys himself believed the real reason for his suicidal behaviour was that his business had failed after losses sustained in the Great Fire. Here we see evidence of the increased secularization of attitudes. But side by side with it another theme emerges.

Pepys goes on to give a first-hand account of the panic a suicide instilled in the bereaved family: panic that their goods would be forfeit (even though technically Joyce survived the suicide attempt a few days). Pepys even agrees to hide some of the family's goods to prevent their being seized and some of the panic transfers to him. Finally, he uses his contacts in high places to avert the crisis:

The friends that were there, being now in fear that the goods and estate would be seized on, though he lived all this while, because of endeavouring to drown himself, my cosen did endeavour to remove what she could of the plate out of the house, and desired me to take my flagons; which I did, but in great fear all the way of being seized; though there were no reason for it, he not being dead. So, with Sir D. Gauden, to Guild Hall, to advise with the Towne-Clerke about the practice of the City and nation in this case; and he thinks it cannot be found selfe-murder; but if it be, it will fall, all the estate, to the King. So I to my cosen's again; where I no sooner come but find that her husband was departed. So at their entreaty, I presently to White Hall, and there find Sir W. Coventry: and he carried me to the King, the Duke of York being with him, and there told my story which I had told him: and the King, without more ado, granted that, if it was found, the estate should be to the widow and children. I presently to each Secretary's office, and there left *caveats*, and so away back to my cosen's. When I come thither, I find her all in sorrow, but she and the rest mightily pleased with my doing this for them; and which, indeed, was a very great courtesy, for people are looking out for the estate.[4]

Shifts in opinion about suicide during the seventeenth century might not have been so absolute had they not been supported by shifts in the arguments from the intellectual élite of the country similar to those witnessed in More's writing a century before. Once again, the continued interest in classical philosophy, with its under-tone of tolerance and understanding, was responsible. The momen-tum of interest in the humanism of the Renaissance, founded on a reverence for classical literature, philosophy and history, was maintained, involving an increasing influence by classical customs. This, in turn, revived interest in Stoic views which were more tolerant of suicide, and indeed recommended suicide as a right act in certain circumstances.

Yet the ambivalence to suicide continued. Even when a work was written that is celebrated as one of the greatest turning-points in the thinking about suicide in the seventeenth century, *Biathanatos* by John Donne, its author dared not publish for fear of where his own arguments had taken him. This work explored the 'Paradox or Thesis, that Self Homicide is not so naturally Sin as it may never be otherwise'. The importance of this work is that Donne relied on theological analysis, rather than returning to classical literature. In this way he was able to undermine the arguments the Church had used for centuries. His arguments included the fact that, first, self-killing is nowhere forbidden in the Bible and that, secondly, many who have committed suicide in the history of the Church have been excused or seen as martyrs.

Thirdly, the reference to the Sixth Commandment, 'Thou shalt not kill', which St Augustine used, ignored the fact that on many occasions killing is found to be legitimate, e.g. in war, or execution of criminals. Donne criticizes Augustine's arguments that biblical and early Christian suicides were permissible and poured scorn on the view that these acts were carried out by the secret command of God. This, Donne says, is mere supposition and cannot be considered a rational argument. Indeed Donne goes further at one point to argue that one could see the death of Jesus of Nazareth as suicide.

Donne's treatise constituted an extremely rare set of arguments since most defendants of suicide of the time relied on classical literature. Even Thomas More, who had written *Utopia* envisaging that suicide would be permissible for humanists in that society, had not envisaged that suicide would be permissible for Christians.

By contrast, the Stoic view was that death 'unlocked the chains of suffering' and no law could forbid it. As Montaigne put it, 'as I offend not the laws made against thieves when I cut my own purse, so am I nothing tied unto laws made against murderers, if I deprive myself of my own life'.[5] Far from imagining that suicide was against the natural law, writers relying on Stoic arguments argued that no one was obliged to live when his or her death might promote some greater good. In fact, they thought that suicide in certain circumstances was consonant with the natural law.

Yet John Donne was so worried about how *Biathanatos* would be received that he refused to permit it to be published in his own lifetime. In presenting the manuscript to Sir Robert Ker, he commented that it was a book 'written by Jack Donne and not by Dr Donne'. It was finally published in 1647. It appears that Donne himself shied away from his own conclusions – not an uncommon occurrence. It was one thing to use arguments for the justification of suicide to undermine the state's wish to punish severely a person who took their own life, another to use arguments in such a way as to give the impression that suicide was an option implying that life could be ended lightly as an acceptable way of dealing with life's difficulties. Why such reluctance to publish? Donne was a poet, but also, as Dean of St Paul's, a pastor. As a pastor he may have had to deal with people bereaved by suicide, and may well have felt it anathema to take a punitive line. But the complexity of what is said as part of a private pastoral relationship does not transfer well into public pronouncement or public policy.

Madness as illness

By the end of the 1700s, the *felo de se* verdicts were as rare as the *non compos mentis* verdicts had been in the early Tudor period. The prevailing belief had become that suicide was either a product of rational choice or a medical calamity.

Once again a case-by-case leniency exercised by individual courts confirmed the change. The coroner's jury became increasingly reluctant to enforce penalties for self-murder. Two trends drove the change: increasing resistance to a law which seemed too draconian, and increasing willingness to see suicide as the product of an unbalanced mind. Assisting the first trend against property forfeit was the increased belief, expressed by John Locke, that no government should interfere with the cult of private property. Government should not 'take to themselves the whole or any part of the subjects property without their own consent'. Such beliefs had been confirmed and emphasized by the English Revolution of 1688.

Assisting the second trend towards mental illness as an explanation was the rejection of religious enthusiasm, whether Puritan or Catholic. Although it is likely that popular belief in supernatural forces continued, and still continues, the intellectual élite gradually, during the Enlightenment, came to reject almost absolutely the belief in supernatural intervention in the natural world. This gave way, in the case of suicide, to a medical interpretation which greatly influenced the middle-ranking men who served on coroners' juries. Now, evidence of melancholy, previously evidence that the person had given in to the devil, was found sufficient proof that a person's balance of mind was disturbed.

The suicide verdicts reflect the trends. Less than 7 per cent of the suicides reported to the King's Bench were declared to have been *non compos mentis* in the middle of the seventeenth century. By the 1690s, around 30 per cent of suicides were thought to be *non compos mentis*, and this proportion steadily increased over the next few decades into the eighteenth century. Forty per cent of verdicts were *non compos mentis* in 1710, and by the last third of the eighteenth century this had become the usual verdict.

Indeed, in Norwich the figures between 1670 and 1799 show the percent *non compos mentis* at the early part of that period as being quite low, below 30 per cent; but by 1770–1800 100 per cent of the verdicts were *non compos mentis*. The *non compos mentis* verdict itself implicitly rejected the folklore and religious interpretations of suicide as a supernatural intervention by the devil. Instead it substituted a medical explanation which declared explicitly that the suicide was excusable.

The increased tolerance for self-murder can be seen in various writers of the time. William Ramesey in *The Gentlemen's Companion* (1672) suggested that those who killed themselves, because they were frequently the victims of mental illness,

should rather be objects of our greatest pity than condemnation as murderers, damned creatures and the like. For, 'tis possible even for God's elect having their Judgements and Reasons depraved by madness, deep melancholy, or somehow otherwise affected by Diseases of some sorts, to be their own executioners. Wherefore let's be slow to censure in such cases.

One consequence of this change was that no more were *non compos mentis* verdicts used simply as a device for protecting some and not others. During the medieval and Tudor periods a person's social standing, his personality, his relationship with his neighbours, and his survivors' claims on the sympathy of the local community all played a part in determining which verdict was brought in by the coroners' courts (as in the Pepys example). Families of the rich who committed suicide were able to bribe the coroner or the jury, or perhaps more commonly could afford to bring in an expert medical opinion to certify that the person had undoubtedly been unbalanced at the time of death. Gradually, as coroners' juries became more reluctant to find the suicide guilty of *felo de se*, and more likely to bring a *non compos mentis* verdict, these differences and influences became less and less significant.

Despite these changes, the law of self-murder remained on the statute books. It was deemed necessary to discourage people from suicide (it was thought suicide would cause a disintegration of society) and offered a means of condemning men and women who had committed suicide to escape punishment after being found guilty of an offence. In such cases, the rituals associated with self-murder were used as a way of stigmatizing the dead for some offence committed previously. In 1790, *The Times* reported a story of a woman who poisoned sixteen inmates at the Epworth Workhouse for whom she was responsible. Four of them died, and she afterwards overdosed herself fatally with the arsenic she had used. The coroner's jury was shocked by this crime and not only brought in a verdict of *felo de se* but also ordered her body to be buried in the public highway with two stakes driven through it.

But this use of the *felo de se* verdict for extreme cases of the punishment of known criminals emphasizes how much the culture had changed and how difficult and unusual it was becoming to bring in a similar verdict for suicides who had not committed such crimes. Increasingly the suicide itself was not judged to be the crime. The coroners' juries judged the rest of the person's life, not the act of suicide.

The situation in other countries

In the early days of the colonies in America, most colonies adopted the traditional English punishments though not all enforced the laws of forfeiture. Pennsylvania and Delaware explicitly abolished forfeiture in 1701. After the Revolution, Maryland and New Jersey decriminalized suicide as part of their constitutions. Thomas Jefferson attempted to abolish forfeiture and argued against punishing suicide. He also pointed out that juries disapproved of such severity and it was therefore sensible to get rid of the severe rules altogether.

The enforcement of laws on suicide in Germany, Spain and Italy is an unknown quantity. Few records remain. However, there is some evidence from France and parts of Switzerland. French law consisted of a collection of regional customs and codes, and different punishments were stipulated in different regions of the country. In some places penalties were worse than those imposed in England, in others they were mild. The major difference, however, was that throughout France the laws against self-murder were applied very infrequently. In 1670 they were standardized in a law decreeing that every convicted suicide should forfeit his goods and be drawn on a hurdle to a profane grave. But interestingly, after this standardization, the customs and laws were enforced even less often. By the time it took place, the growth in Enlightenment philosophies had begun to undermine the case for such punitive handling of suicide. In 1770 in France, the Rites of Desecration were abolished. Suicide was decriminalized completely twenty-one years later in 1791.

Switzerland, or at least the Swiss city states, Geneva and Zurich, were more rigorous in attempts to enforce regulations against self-murder. Their Calvinist regimes attempted to impose strict religious rules and customs. However, while suicides were often convicted, they seldom gave rise to severe punishment. As in France, by the time the authorities tried to reform the punishment of suicide, opposing trends had already moved towards the secularization of suicide. The last example in Switzerland of dragging the corpse of a suicide victim through the streets occurred in 1732, and although the old law remained in force, as it did in France, until the early 1790s, the city officials in Geneva, for example, declared in 1735 that all suicides were insane and were to be spared punishment. The only exception was made in England, for those who killed themselves after being sentenced to death for another crime.

Ambivalence within the Church

Although the Church had roundly condemned self-murder for most of its history, it did not actively participate in the rituals of desecration. It did not stand in the way either. Many of these rituals may have pre-dated Christianity, and it was sufficient that the Church did not object to them. It did not say prayers for the dead and did not permit a Christian burial in consecrated ground for suicides. Of course, if somebody was found to have committed suicide because the balance of their mind was disturbed, there was nothing to stop Christian ministers from burying in consecrated ground. However, even into the sixteenth and seventeenth centuries many conservative clergymen felt uneasy about such burial even for someone declared 'insane'. In the 1662 Book of Common Prayer, a rubric was added (not there in the 1549 and 1552 versions), saying that a clergyman could not bury in consecrated ground any 'who have laid violent hands upon themselves'. Whoever drafted the rubric failed to insert the word 'feloniously'. The rubric as it stood might exclude all people who killed themselves.

In the light of such confusion, clergymen looked for a compromise which they hoped would meet the private need without making a public statement. They allowed burial to be in churchyards, but buried such people on the north side of the church, alongside executed felons, excommunicates and unbaptized infants. This compromise had one unfortunate consequence. The north side of the church gradually came to be considered by local people as polluted, with the result that by the late eighteenth century, despite some churchyards running out of space to bury bodies, clergymen could not easily persuade families to bury relatives there. Families would rather dig up the bones of ancestors to make space for burial on the south side of the church. The Church was often relatively powerless to argue against popular superstition. But having been partly responsible for fostering such superstitions, it perhaps deserved to become victim to them.

The end of the crime of self-murder

Parliament did not abolish the religious penalties for self-murder until 1823, and did not abolish the secular punishments until 1870. Why it took so long to change these laws remains something of a mystery. The main reason seems to have been the relation between the law on suicide and other criminal laws.

The problem of deterrence was the main issue. It is somewhat bizarre now to recall that divines such as John Wesley called for victims of suicide to be gibbeted and for their corpses to be left to rot. In 1823, however, Parliament acted to repeal the custom of profane burial. Sir James MacIntosh in the House of Commons declared that punishing suicide was 'an act of brutal folly'. Although the Commons defeated MacIntosh's resolution, as soon as it had failed in its passage through the House T. B. Lennard introduced a separate Bill to abolish the ritual penalties for *felo de se* and substitute the milder sanction of night-time burial. He called the Rites of Desecration 'an odious and disgusting ceremony'. Such practices were useless as regards the dead and 'only tortured the living'. The Bill passed with only one amendment to make it clear that this change in the law did not mean that clergymen were required to perform the usual rites over the bodies of suicides. Instead the services they provided were left to their own devising. Some conservative clergymen resisted pressure to read the burial rites, and there is evidence that in the dying years of the nineteenth century the controversy among the Anglican clergy raged as fiercely as ever.

The provisions for the forfeiture of property for self-murder were repealed in 1870 as part of an omnibus Bill that covered felonies of every kind. *Felo de se* is mentioned only once in the Bill itself, and suicide was not discussed in the debates on the Bill, presumably because forfeiture for suicide was such a rare event and no longer a current topic.

One interesting development which arguably allowed the law on suicide to change was the gradual emergence of a common-law crime of attempted suicide. In earlier centuries, suicide had been against the law, but it had not been a crime to try and kill oneself. During the 1700s, people who 'attempted suicide' were sent to madhouses, gaols or workhouses to prevent them killing themselves. However, during the nineteenth century there is evidence that, in London at least, people increasingly began to be arrested for 'attempting suicide'. By 1850 this crime was recognized by the courts, and by the later part of the century the courts all over England were arresting and occasionally trying people for attempted suicide.

In part this trend arose from the increase in police forces throughout the country. Previously there would have been very few officials who could have enforced such a law had it existed. But the rise in prosecutions for attempted suicide was also an answer to those who complained that the law of suicide punished the innocent (the family) and spared the guilty (the one who committed suicide). After about 1850, the law could be used as a measure to punish (and perhaps rehabilitate) these would-be suicides.

The criminal status of suicidal behaviour did not end for the United Kingdom until 1961, when Parliament repealed the common-law felony of self-murder. Coroners and physicians subsequently no longer needed to attest that someone who killed him or herself had done so when 'the balance of the mind was disturbed'.

Concluding remarks

The history of attitudes to suicide could be interpreted as a journey from the darkness of ignorance and belief in the supernatural to the light of a modern and tolerant era. It is immensely more complex, however. While these attitudes have varied throughout the ages, and every age has seen a range of value systems brought to bear for a variety of reasons, we have also seen that some in our own day would argue that suicide is a giving in to sinful despair brought about by the devil, as witnessed by the leaflet alluded to at the start of this chapter. Ambivalent attitudes to suicide and towards people who harm themselves may partly reflect our failure to understand how someone is capable of taking this ultimate step. Part of us may admire their apparent control over when their life should end. Another part abhors it, for fear we might take the same route (rather like stepping back from the platform edge for fear we may be seized by the impulse to throw ourselves under a train).

Why does the diabolical metaphor survive? One obvious reason is that a proportion of society still believes Satan exists and influences human affairs. Additionally, the 'devil' vocabulary may persist because, for those who have been seriously depressed, it can feel as though they have been taken over by something outside themselves. The devil metaphor matches and gives shape to this inner feeling, even for those who would normally reject supernatural explanations of experience. In fact, one of the advantages of the metaphor is that it locates the source of the problem 'outside' the individual. In this respect, modern psychotherapies that emphasize the collaboration between therapist and client against the 'common enemy' of the problem use a secularized version of the devil myth to achieve their ends. It is ironic that such forms of psychotherapy have shown the most promise in helping people to deal with suicidal thoughts and behaviour.

Chapter 2

SUICIDE: THE STATISTICS

Suicide is the most individual of acts, yet it happens too often for us to ignore the possibility that there may be trends within the data when these individual acts are examined together. Some questions can only be answered by taking account of entire populations. Is the number of suicides on the increase or decrease – and in which groups of people? How is the figure related to gender, and to social class? What means do most people use? Are any trends limited to a single country – do suicidal trends respect national, cultural or ethnic boundaries? How is suicide related to socio-economic conditions? And what about unemployment and other such sources of stress – can we say definitively whether they affect the suicide rate, and if not, why not? This chapter aims to address each question as essential background to later chapters which ask for explanations.

Durkheim defines suicide as 'the termination of an individual's life resulting directly from a positive or negative act of the victim himself which he knows will produce this fatal result'.[1] But are such definitions useful in the real world of the inquest? Interpreting suicide statistics is often said to be difficult because they are inherently unreliable. 'Suicide' is a legal definition, so official statistics inevitably underestimate the number of suicides. The authorities have to be certain beyond reasonable doubt that death was caused by self-inflicted injury and that the deceased intended to kill him or herself. One result, for example, is that passive methods of dying are less likely to be called suicide than active methods. Thus drowning is called suicide in 54 per cent of cases whereas hanging is called suicide in 98 per cent. Another result of definition problems is that a verdict of suicide may be less likely when a young person is involved. A further limitation of statistics is that many countries do not report suicide rates. The World Health Organization collates this data, but as its 1992 report shows, of the 166 member states of the United

Nations only 36 countries had returned data reporting suicide rates. If these countries' suicide rates merely reflect different criteria used to bring in a verdict of suicide, surely the data, even where available, are almost uninterpretable.

Such a conclusion would be too pessimistic, however. Where there is insufficient evidence to justify the conclusion that a sudden death was suicide, the alternative is most likely to be an open verdict ('undetermined'). When these verdicts are examined, the sex, age, and social-class profile of the deceased resembles closely the profile for people known to have committed suicide. Some researchers have therefore included such open verdicts in their statistics when trying to estimate the total number of people who kill themselves. However, research has shown that such trends are affected very little whether the open verdicts are included or excluded.[2] Further evidence for the reliability of suicide figures from country to country is that statistics largely agree on which sub-populations are most at risk for suicide.[3]

The scope of the problem – UK statistics

In males in the United Kingdom, suicide is the second most common cause of death in 15- to 34-year-olds (after motor-vehicle accidents).[4] For example, in 1990, among 15- to 24-year-old males, 14 per cent of all deaths (1 in 6 male deaths and 1 in 8 female deaths) were by suicide. Between the ages of 25 and 34, 17 per cent of all deaths among males were by suicide. Overall, suicide and undetermined deaths (referring mostly to open verdicts which parallel suicide statistics very closely) account for 8.5 per cent (males) and 3.8 per cent (females) of years of life lost before the age of 65. These figures are similar in most Western countries (see page 26). Given these statistics, it is not surprising that governments should be turning attention to trying to reduce the suicide rate. Their concern is not only the untold suffering the statistics represent, but also the huge economic cost of such loss of life. It has been calculated that each suicide of a young person in the United States (aged 15–24) represents $432,000 of lost economic productivity.[5] In total, therefore, suicides in this age group alone represent 276,000 years of life lost, and $2.26 billion loss of economic productivity. Over 645,000 years of productive life are lost each year in the United States as a result of deaths by suicide. Figures for Europe are likely to be at least three times these amounts.

Figure 1 shows the number of suicides in England and Wales since 1911 for men and women separately. The data, taken from the Office of Population Census and Surveys (OPCS),[6] has been smoothed by averaging each three-year period. In these data one can see the effect of the First and Second World Wars (where there was a reduction in suicides) and the rise in suicides in the Depression between the wars (which peaked, as in the United States, in 1932). After 1945 the suicide rate rose steadily to a peak for both men and women in 1963 (though the increase up to 1963 was more evident for women).

Since that time a number of quite dramatic changes have taken place. Firstly, the suicide rate in women has fallen continuously. Secondly, the suicide rate for men fell until the early 1970s, then started to rise. This is the first time in the century that suicide rates for males and females have moved in opposite directions. Towards the end of the data in Figure 1, we see the effect of adding to the suicide rate the number of people where the verdict was 'open/ undetermined'. The undetermined deaths add a constant factor to the suicide rate. The rate of undetermined deaths does not appear to fluctuate with the suicide rate, but simply adds a constant number of deaths.

In Figure 2, we see the England and Wales data for five-year age groups for men and women, making use of the five-year average death-rates. For women, the suicide rates for all age groups started to fall after 1953, apart from the youngest (15–24), which were very low then and have remained low since. Older women are now less likely to commit suicide. The result of the convergence towards lower rates in older women is that for women over 45 there is little evidence of an age-related increase in risk.

Figure 2 confirms that since the early 1980s suicide rates for men aged 45 and over have fallen. However, the rate for men under 45 has risen considerably, and for the 35–44 age group it now exceeds

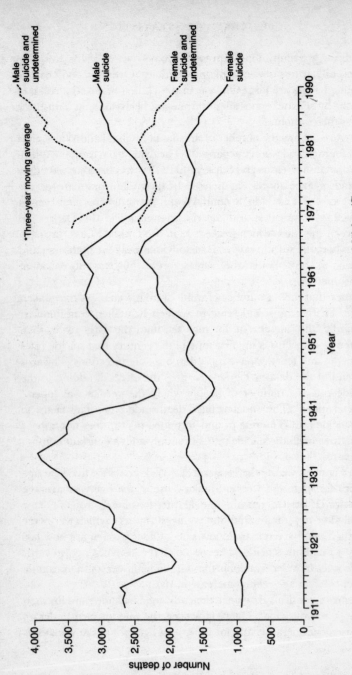

Figure 1. Number of suicide deaths* by sex, 1911–90, England and Wales. (Crown Copyright, reproduced by permission of HMSO.)

the rate for all but the oldest men (those over 75). There has been a particularly dramatic rise (75 per cent) in suicide rates among males aged 15–24 since 1982. Although the rate in this age group is still lower than that of the older age group, in general the younger and older adult rates for suicides have been converging over the past thirty or forty years. Currently over 40 per cent of all suicides occur in males between the ages of 15 and 44, and this differs from previous times when the rates were much higher for older people, giving rise to the widely held belief that the greater suicide risk in the older male was a general truth. In fact, the situation in 1990 was that for men between 25 and 75 there was little difference in age-related suicide risk.

Why this steep increase in young male suicides? One clue lies in the changing pattern of marriage and divorce. Figure 3 shows suicide rates in relation to marital status. These show that divorced and widowed men have the highest rates. Widowed men have higher suicide rates than divorced men in every age group. In general, apart from the 15- to 24-year-olds, single, widowed and divorced men have suicide rates about three times greater than married men.

International suicide rates

Figure 4 shows the rate per 100,000 population of the countries in Europe and the United States from 1970 to 1991. Notice how, in each case, the suicide rate is much lower for women than for men. In many of the countries the rate for women has remained flat or decreased while the rate for men has increased, most markedly in Ireland, Spain, Netherlands, Norway, Belgium, France, Luxembourg, Denmark, Finland and Northern Ireland. In the United Kingdom and the United States it is clear that the figures for men and women are actually moving in opposite directions. A notable exception to international trends is in West Germany, where there has been a substantial decline in both male and female suicide.

Are the trends within the suicide statistics from North America similar to European trends in general and UK trends in particular?[7] The US data since the early 1900s are shown in Figure 5. During the past century, the rate in the United States has averaged a rate

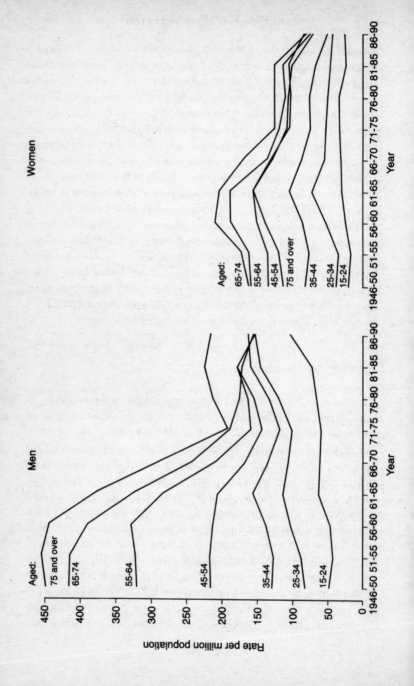

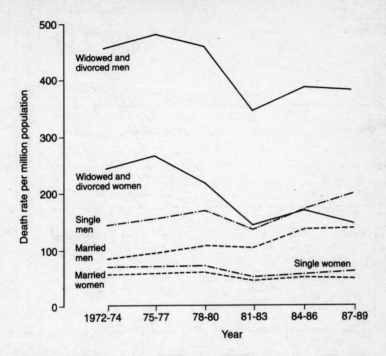

Figure 3. Suicide rate per million population by sex and marital status for people aged 15–44, 1972–89, England and Wales. (Crown Copyright, reproduced by permission of HMSO.)

rather similar to that in the United Kingdom: 12.5/100,000. A high rate of 17.4 was observed during the Depression in 1932 and a low point of 9.8 in 1957. This rose again steadily to a peak of 13.3 in 1977, then dipped to a rate of 12.7 in 1987. These rates are also very similar to those of Canada, where the 1992 rate was 13 per 100,000 (20.7 per 100,000 in men and 5.5 per 100,000 in women).

Figure 2 (opposite). Recorded suicide deaths: rate per million population by sex and age, 1946–50 to 1986–90, England and Wales. (Crown Copyright, reproduced by permission of HMSO.)

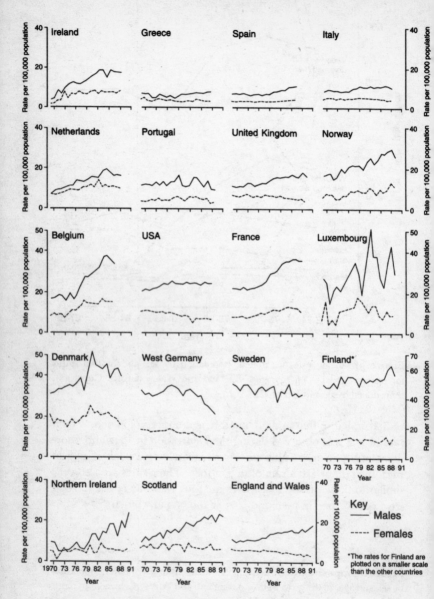

Figure 4. International comparisons of recorded suicide rates for men and women aged 25–44, 1969–91. (Crown Copyright, reproduced by permission of HMSO.)

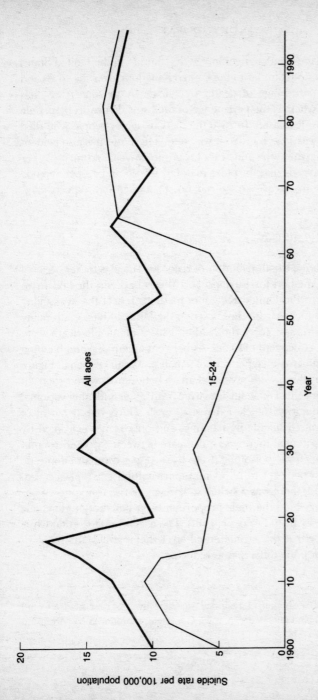

Figure 5. Comparison of suicide rates for the general population and for persons aged 15–24 in the United States, 1900–1992. (Data are from the National Center for Health Statistics, Vital Statistics of the United States.)

There have been changes in age distribution in the United States over this period. Similar to the United Kingdom, over the 1970s and 1980s the percentage of deaths by suicide by persons 15−25 has increased, whereas the percentage of total suicide deaths by people over 44 has decreased. In 1970 the median age of people who died by suicide was 47.2; by 1980 it was 39.9. This pattern is also evident in Canada, where the 1992 rate for 20- to 29-year-old men (29 per 100,000) exceeds that for older men (25, 26, 20 and 28 per 100,000 for the age groups 40−49, 50−59, 60−69 and 70−79 respectively).

Methods of suicide

Figure 6 shows the distribution of recorded suicides by sex, year of death and method for England and Wales between the late 1940s and 1990. In the United Kingdom methods reflect the availability of different means from those used in the United States, with many fewer firearms. In 1970, the leading causes of suicide death were poisoning (31 per cent of males, 65 per cent of females) and hanging (23 per cent of males, 9 per cent of females). As can be seen in Figure 6, however, there were several changes between 1970 and 1990. In 1990, 35 per cent of male suicides were from 'gases and other vapours' (the vast majority vehicle exhaust deaths). Thirty-one per cent of men committed suicide by hanging, and only 14 per cent died by poison. In women, there was a decrease between 1970 and 1990 in the numbers using poisoning (from 65 to 44 per cent) and domestic gas (from 9 per cent to nil as non-toxic natural gas replaced coal gas). Instead, there was a switch to hanging (a rise from 9 to 23 per cent, approaching the male proportion of 31 per cent) and vehicle exhaust (a rise from 1 to 13 per cent). These trends suggest that while it used to be true that women used less lethal methods than men in their suicides, the difference is reducing.

Figure 6. Distribution of recorded suicides* by sex, year of death and method, England and Wales. (Crown Copyright, reproduced by permission of HMSO.)

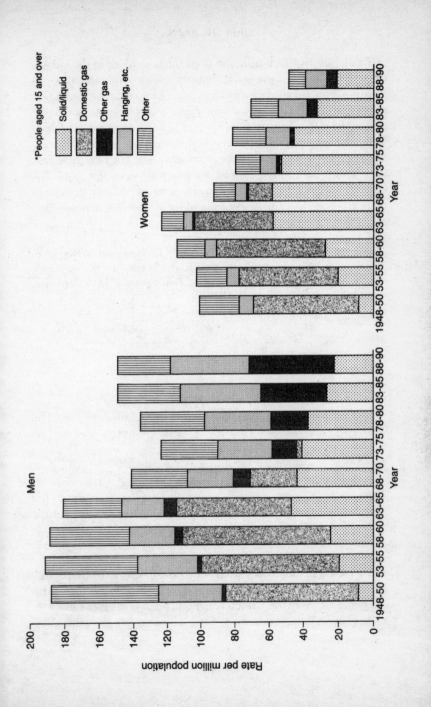

*People aged 15 and over

Legend:
- Solid/liquid
- Domestic gas
- Other gas
- Hanging, etc.
- Other

Men

Women

Rate per million population

Year

1948-50 53-55 58-60 63-65 68-70 73-75 78-80 83-85 88-90

Table 1 shows the distribution of methods included in the 'other' category. As can be seen, the largest proportion of other methods is firearms (27 per cent, representing 5.7 per cent of the total number of suicides) for men and drowning (33 per cent, representing 6.6 per cent of the total number of suicides) for women. However, jumping from a height remains a relatively high category of 'other methods'. Some trends are visible over the past forty years. For men there has been a reduction in the proportion drowning since the 1940s. By contrast, there has been a slight increase in use of firearms. In women there has been a dramatic decrease in the proportion of drowning, and a slight increase in jumping from high places.

Table 1. Distribution of 'other methods', England and Wales (from Charlton, Kelly, Dunnell, Evans, Jenkins and Wallis, 'Trends in Suicide Deaths in England and Wales', *Population Trends*, 1992). (Crown Copyright, reproduced by permission of HMSO.)

Method	1948–50	1988–90
Men		
Drowning	35	14
Firearms	21	27
Cutting	20	10
Jumping	9	16
Other	15	33
Women		
Drowning	60	33
Firearms	3	5
Cutting	10	9
Jumping	15	23
Other	13	30

When methods of suicide are examined for the US population, there are clear differences from the United Kingdom. Males still choose more violent means than females, but use many more firearms (64 per cent). As in the United Kingdom, females are more likely to choose non-violent means, e.g. drug overdose (26 per cent). (See Figure 7.)

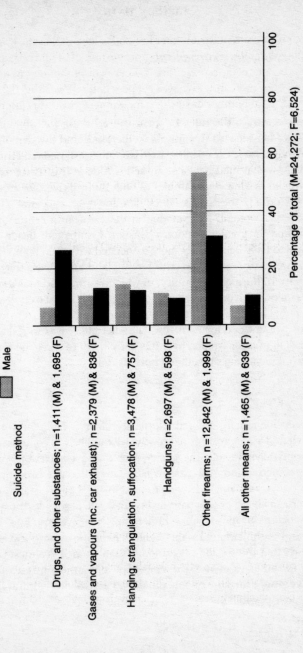

Figure 7. Number and percentages of suicide method by gender, US rates 1987. (Data are from the National Center for Health Statistics, Vital Statistics of the United States.)

Female

Male

Suicide method

Drugs, and other substances; n=1,411 (M) & 1,695 (F)

Gases and vapours (inc. car exhaust); n=2,379 (M) & 836 (F)

Hanging, strangulation, suffocation; n=3,478 (M) & 757 (F)

Handguns; n=2,697 (M) & 598 (F)

Other firearms; n=12,842 (M) & 1,999 (F)

All other means; n=1,465 (M) & 639 (F)

Percentage of total (M=24,272; F=6,524)

Factors affecting suicide rate

Gender

In all countries, the rates for men exceed those for women by a factor of between 2:1 (Denmark, Netherlands and Sweden) and 5:1 (Finland). This sex ratio has existed from the earliest days. Historical data show that men have committed suicide at least twice as often as women in almost all samples of data that survive. For example, the sex ratio in the King's Bench data for 1485–1714[8] was 1.8 men for every 1 woman; for Norwich in the eighteenth century it was 2.3:1; and for greater London it was 2:1. Completed suicide seems always to have been an act more associated with men than women.

As we have seen in the data for England and Wales (Figure 1), the pattern during this century, in which women and men's suicide rates follow each other fairly closely (albeit at different overall levels), has now changed. The rates for women fell during the 1970s and 1980s, while those for men rose. The net effect was to reduce the overall figures for women over this period, but to leave the rates for men (taking all ages together) rising steadily.

Ethnic group

The suicide rate for different ethnic groupings is different: whites in the United States are approximately twice as likely to commit suicide as non-whites. In 1987 the suicide rate among Caucasians was 13.7 per 100,000, in non-Caucasians 6.9. This difference is particularly pronounced for the older age group. In the United States, native American young people have a very high rate of suicide, the highest rate being in those tribes undergoing the greatest and fastest cultural assimilation. In the United Kingdom, there have been reports that the suicide rate among Asian women is almost double that for other women of the same age, and although research has not yet established the reason, difficulties in resolving cultural clashes is a clear possibility.

Sexual orientation

A 1989 report from the US Department of Health and Human Services, *The Secretary's Task Force on Youth Suicide*, suggested that gay youth were two or three times more likely to complete suicide than other young people.[9] It suggested that lesbian and gay young people may comprise up to 30 per cent of youth suicides annually. However, this part of the report was not backed by any evidence. Elsewhere it admitted that this was a neglected area, with virtually no research on youth suicide having taken sexual orientation into account. The two studies that have been published (both US surveys) suggest much more conservative figures: that between 2.5 and 5 per cent of suicides are gay, and that these figures are not significantly different from the proportions one would expect by chance. One study[10] surveyed 283 adolescent and adult suicides, finding that 5 per cent were gay. Another study, using psychological autopsy techniques, studied 120 consecutive suicides under the age of 20, and 147 community age-, sex- and ethnic-matched controls living in the Greater New York City area.[11] Three (3.5 per cent) of the 95 teenage suicides in this sample (2.5 per cent of the total sample of 120) were reported to have had a homosexual experience. Both studies concluded that psychiatric disturbance and/or substance abuse were critical predisposing factors regardless of sexual orientation.[12]

Religious affiliation

Rates vary according to religious affiliations. A number of studies have found that Protestants are more likely to commit suicide than Catholics or Jews. The Catholic countries of Spain, Italy, Portugal, Greece, Ireland and Poland have fairly low suicide rates. Yet there are other Catholic parts of Europe, such as France, where the suicide rate is relatively high, though the increased secularization of France, and reduced churchgoing, may be responsible. In one study in New York, rates for Protestants per 100,000 was 31.4, those for Catholics 10.9 and those for Jews 15.5. However, many studies have also found that churchgoing in general is associated with lower suicide risk,

presumably because of the social network and sense of meaning in
times of suffering it can sometimes provide.

Social class

Table 2 shows the proportional mortality rates calculated for different
social classes in England and Wales. Social class I is defined as
professional; II as intermediate (lower professional and executive);
III as skilled (manual and non-manual); IV as partly skilled; V as
unskilled. The proportional mortality ratio (PMR) is a ratio which
enables the impact of a disease upon an exposed population to be
examined. The PMR is calculated in the following way:

$$\frac{\text{Observed deaths from suicide}}{\text{Expected deaths from suicide}} \times 100$$

Table 2 shows that the risk of suicide is greater in social class I
and social class V, with the highest risk of all carried by those with
no occupation at the time of the census.

Table 2. Deaths from suicide among men (aged 16–64) in different social
classes, England and Wales, 1979–90.

Social Class	PMR	Observed deaths
I	116	1,319
II	99	5,202
IIIN	102	3,083
IIIM	87	9,004
IV	100	5,649
V	111	3,582
'Unoccupied'	126	3,885

The pattern whereby people of higher socio-economic status show
as high a suicide rate as those of low status may be a feature of the
United Kingdom not found elsewhere. Studies in the United States
and Canada have found a strong association between differences in

socio-economic status between communities (e.g. in proportion of substandard housing) and the suicide rate in that community. The poorer the housing, the higher the rate. The exception to this trend is the poor areas occupied by a high proportion of African Americans, who have a lower suicide rate, most usually attributed to the strong social bonds within and between families.

Unemployment

Economic conditions have been studied many times, with some conflicting results. Studies on unemployment in suicide have found that men who are unemployed and seeking work are at two or three times greater risk of suicide death than the average. Suicide is thought by many investigators to be one of the possible consequences of unemployment, and yet, in the United Kingdom at least, there seems little relationship between change in unemployment levels and the suicide rate over time.

National unemployment rates in the United Kingdom increased substantially at the end of the 1970s, stayed high until the mid 1980s, started to decline until the late 1980s and then began to rise again. In the 1981–90 period male suicide rates were at their highest at the time when unemployment rates were lowest. However, the relationship is a complicated one. Most unemployment is short term (under six months) and unemployment totals are net figures taken at a fixed point in time. This means that unemployment rates never give the whole picture of the distress caused by unemployment. Stephen Platt has pointed out that the impact of unemployment depends on whether an entire firm has been made unemployed in a community (in which case there may be some increase in social support – an ameliorating factor in suicide risks). By contrast, if an individual is made unemployed, independent of other people becoming unemployed, then this may be more of a stress factor.

In fact, other studies have found that the United Kingdom is an exception in not finding a connection between unemployment and suicide. Boor (in 1980)[13] compared the unemployment rates with the suicide rates in the following eight countries: United States, Canada, Sweden, France, Great Britain, Germany, Italy and Japan. The suicide and unemployment rate correlated positively in all but two countries, Italy and Great Britain. Boor also found that the relationship between unemployment and suicide held for both men and women. The rate of unemployment among suicide victims is 50 per cent across a number of studies.

Rural areas

Geographical region also plays a part in different suicide rates across countries. As in Great Britain, where rural areas have the highest rates, so in the United States the mountain regions have the highest overall rate, Nevada ranking highest at 17.6 per 100,000. In a study with my colleagues Leslie Pollock, John Hollis and Patrick Vesey, we examined the suicide rates in Powys, Wales, one of the least densely populated areas of Europe. We found a suicide rate greatly in excess of the UK average (around 20 per 100,000). Looking closely at the data for a three-year period, we found that farmers or farm labourers accounted for 22 per cent of this figure, though they only represented 11 per cent of the population. We also examined whether it was the lack of access to primary care services in rural areas that determined the high rates, but could find no evidence that these individuals had visited their doctor any less frequently than happens in more urban areas. Rather, it appeared to be the greater availability of lethal weapons that accounted for the high rates, with firearms used more commonly than the national average.

Imprisonment

The number of prison suicides a year has risen considerably since the early 1960s. In 1961 there were fifteen suicides a year in the United Kingdom, and this figure had increased to 40 per year in 1988/90 (see Figure 8). Most of these are in the 15–44 age group of men. This increase represents 4 per cent of the increase in the young male suicide rate over this period. The increase has given cause for concern, especially since most of the suicides of the under-45 group are male prisoners on remand, not yet found guilty of any crime. Dooley has examined 300 prison deaths between 1972 and 1987[14]

36

and analysed the reasons for each suicide. Forty per cent of suicides could be attributable to the prison environment (overcrowding, etc.). Fifteen per cent were attributable to outside pressures, 12 per cent to guilt feelings for the offence, and 22 per cent to already diagnosed mental illness.

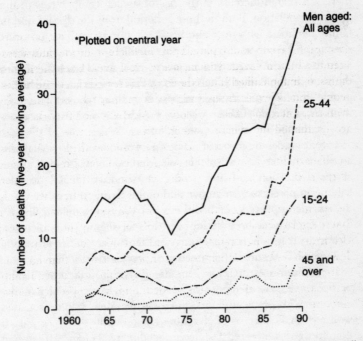

Figure 8. Prison suicides: number of male deaths (five-year moving average*), 1960–90, England and Wales. (Crown Copyright, reproduced by permission of HMSO.)

Medical illness

There are several medical conditions that increase the risk of suicide. For example, the risk of suicide among those with epilepsy is four times that of normal controls, and for temporal-lobe epilepsy it is twenty-five times greater than controls. Cancer has been associated with increased risk of suicide, the risk highest immediately following diagnosis, and in those receiving chemotherapy. (Those with a severe and morbid fear of cancer are also at increased risk.) People with peptic ulceration have a high risk, probably because of the prevalence of alcoholism as a cause of ulceration. With Huntington's chorea there is a sixfold increase in the risk of suicide compared with the general population, both in those suffering from the disease and in family members who may also be at risk but as yet have no overt symptoms. People undergoing renal dialysis have been said to have a ten to a hundred times greater incidence of suicide compared with the general population. There is also an increased rate of suicide in people who have spinal-cord injuries and in those who have multiple sclerosis. The risk of those who have Aids is some thirty-six times greater than in the general population.

In many cases the co-occurrence of depression with physical illness combines to increase the suicide risk. Medical illness can precipitate severe depression and also produce an organic mental disorder leading to perceptual, cognitive and mood changes. In other cases, the suicide appears to be a rational act where the person decides that the prospect of suffering and loss of dignity is intolerable. However, research evidence suggests that suicide in the physically ill very rarely occurs in the absence of psychiatric disorder.

It is important, therefore, for the physician and other health professionals not to ignore associated psychiatric problems that co-occur with physical illness. For example, depression associated with terminal cancer is often ignored or thought to be 'normal'. It therefore goes untreated despite the fact that psychological treatment is often very helpful in alleviating the depression. Depression in such patients goes beyond sadness and includes a sense of worthlessness and failure which is not justified on the basis of the person's experience.[15]

Life-span issues

In all countries, suicide is extremely rare in children under 12, but it becomes steadily more common after puberty, and the risk then increases with age. For older people to be more at risk of suicide appears to be the predominant pattern across all countries and cultures, though there is some variation in whether the increase is linear, or has peaks and dips across the life-span. The highest rates are found for elderly men (over 75) in almost all countries, but in many (especially for Scandinavian countries) the peak for women comes earlier. Is suicide the same phenomenon in young adults as in older adults?

One factor explaining life-span differences would be the increase in *substance abuse* which has occurred to a much greater extent in younger members of the population and in young males in particular. Furthermore, there is some evidence that the most vulnerable young men are those from working-class backgrounds who have fewest employment opportunities. These are just the groups that have suffered the greatest rise in suicide rate over the past twenty or thirty years.

Different rates of *medical illness* across the life-span might also contribute to differences between different ages. Illness is associated with 50 per cent of adult completed suicides, contributing more prominently for older adults. Medical illness in older adults contributes to suicidal risk in a number of possible ways. Depression may be worsened by the fact that the physical illness puts an increased burden on the fewer social supports that exist. There are also cognitive impairments often associated with ageing in general and with physical illness in the aged in particular. Finally, the use of certain medications to alleviate the physical illness sometimes lowers mood and impairs judgement.

Do different *psychiatric disorders* increase the risk of suicide at different stages in life? We shall see in the next chapter that the individuals most at risk are those suffering from depression and schizophrenia. Right across the life-span, if these conditions co-occur with particular personality traits such as impulsivity and aggression, and with alcohol and substance abuse, the risk is increased. However, there are changes over the life-span in the particular combinations of these disorders. Adolescents who commit suicide tend to show a combination of depression and conduct disorders, though the depression is often only recognized after the event.[16]

It is possible that it is psychiatric disorder *per se* which is the important issue. Different psychiatric disorders may appear to raise the suicide risk at different points in the life-span simply because they are more prevalent at that point. Some have argued that it is changes in the action of the major neurotransmitters over the life-span which are implicated. For example, brain serotonin metabolism is believed to change during the adult life-span. This remains speculative.

Alcohol and substance abuse

Alcohol and substance abuse has been on the increase since the 1970s. One indication of the increase is the number of people each year who die from alcohol- or drug-related deaths (other than suicide). The data suggest that, since 1968, there has been a sixfold increase in drug-related deaths among men aged 15–24, and a fivefold increase for males aged 25–44. There are similar trends among women, but the rates are generally much lower. The data for alcohol show a similar pattern, with men aged 25–44 showing the largest increase in rates (more than fourfold between 1968 and 1990) followed by men aged 15–24. Once again, rates for younger women rose as well, but the levels were very low compared with those for men.

Alcohol and substance abuse represent major risk factors for suicide right across the life-span. The prevalence of alcohol and drug abuse increases steadily from 15 until about 45, then declines. The number of years somebody who completes suicide has typically been abusing alcohol is between twenty and twenty-five, possibly because, as alcoholism progresses, it destroys those factors known to protect against suicide. First, it destroys social supports because of the alcoholism-related guilt and anger. Secondly, it destroys intellectual function through brain damage and brings about reduced health and increased incidence of medical complications. Thirdly, chronic alcoholism reduces personal control and increases helplessness. Since, however, 60 to 70 per cent of patients with a diagnosis of alcohol problems have additional psychiatric diagnoses, it is possible that the substance abuse exacerbates the course of any psychiatric illness.

However, alcohol and substance abuse raises the risk of suicide as soon as the abuse starts. Substance abuse has been diagnosed in over one third of young people committing suicide.[17]

The rise in young male suicide

In the 1990s the United States found itself with one of the highest suicide rates for young men in the world, even exceeding Japan and Sweden. The question of why there had been such an increase in youth suicide became very pressing indeed. It appeared to parallel the increase in risk factors associated with suicide in young people: depression, conduct disorders and substance misuse. In addition there are population effects such as that the proportion of youth in society is high, implying increased competition for opportunities (jobs and education). This is consistent with the finding that there was also a high youth suicide rate at the beginning of the twentieth century when young people also comprised a higher proportion of the population. Other factors blamed have been the increased divorce rate, increased geographical mobility (with its consequent loss of important attachments figures), changes in family structure, and decreased religious affiliation. However, some of the evidence for these remains patchy. The rise in the number of younger males committing suicide in the last few years has been almost universal.

There are two classes of explanation. The first type sees the rise as part of an unexplained change in rates within a group of people born within a few years of each other, a *cohort* effect. The second type lays the blame at the door of prevailing social conditions, employment opportunities, drug and alcohol abuse, disempowerment. That is, it sees the change in rates as a *period* effect. Clearly there can be interactions between cohort and period effects, as where a certain cohort is exposed to increase in availability of some substance (e.g. illicit drugs). There is evidence of higher rates of depression, bipolar mood disorders and substance abuse for the generation born just after the war (the 'baby boom' generation), which may explain some of the changes in the suicide rate.

41

A cohort effect?

Studies by Murphy and Wetzel for the United States, by Solomon and Hellon in Alberta, Canada, and by Goldney and Katsikitis for Australia followed through the suicide rates for people born within a few years of each other – each 'cohort's' suicide rate could then be compared with cohorts born at other times.[18] Each study found that if a cohort had a high suicide rate at a young age, then the increased rate continued throughout the life of that cohort. Is this also true of England and Wales?

Cohort data were published by the Office of Population Census and Surveys in 1992,[19] and are shown in Figure 9. These confirm the existence of a cohort effect for both men and women for the suicide rate in England and Wales. For men, more recent cohorts have higher age-for-age mortality than earlier ones (people born between 1962 and 1971 have a higher risk of suicide than those born between 1952 and 1961, who in turn have a higher risk of suicide than those born between 1942 and 1951). The rates for the more recent cohorts may not yet have peaked, in which case we may expect a continued rise in suicide rates by younger men for some years to come (as the high-risk cohorts move through the different age ranges). The graph also shows that the single point for the cohort born around 1971 is even higher still.

For women over 45, successive cohorts show lower age-for-age suicide risk, people born in the 1910s, 1920s, 1930s and 1940s showing gradually reducing rates. If this trend continues, we may expect that rates for women will remain low.

But how could a cohort effect come about? Some studies have pointed to the size of a birth cohort. Where there is a large number of babies born during the same period, there is increased competition for resources (as occurred at the turn of the century). This results in higher unemployment and decreased access to educational opportunities for that cohort.

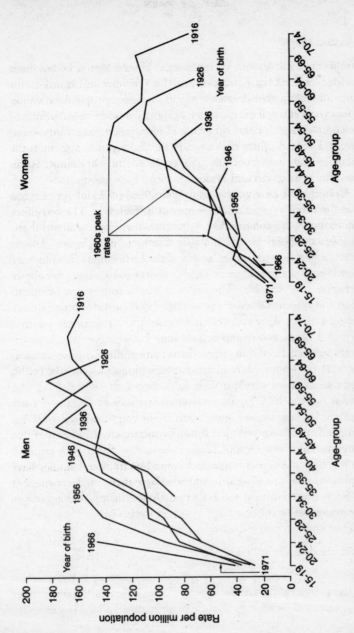

Figure 9. Recorded suicide deaths: rates per million population by sex, age and birth cohort, England and Wales. (Crown Copyright, reproduced by permission of HMSO.)

A period effect?

It is also possible that the recent trend for increases in young male suicides does not represent a cohort effect (i.e. people born recently may not have a greater disposition to suicide), but might rather be a period effect (something in current society is pushing up the rates). Taking the data for the 1936 cohort for women, when they were 25–29 (Figure 9), their curve was rising sharply at this time, but it turned out to result from the 1960s period effect. On that occasion, the same period effect was evident for older age groups too.

Although the recent increase in young male suicides appears not to be reflected in older males, it may nevertheless be a period effect combining with a cohort effect. Whatever current stress factors there may be, they may be differentially affecting young males. This is increasingly likely the larger the size of the birth cohort. Throughout their lives, more people in the larger cohort will be chasing whatever resources are available. The effect of the cohort size will depend upon the amount of resources. A large birth cohort will not always have this effect, if, by chance, there are sufficient resources to sustain members of the cohort throughout their lives.

However, if the number of jobs in a country falls during a recession, then the effects are likely to fall disproportionately on those in the population who are members of the large cohort, whatever age the cohort has reached. Suddenly too many people of about the same age will be chasing too few resources. This is consistent with the suggestion that the reduced status of men caused by changes in employment prospects and family cohesion, together with reduced anticipation of long-term roles as husband and parent, has produced a rise of alcohol and drug abuse in this subpopulation that contributes to the increased suicide rate. Is there evidence to support this particular causal pathway?

Decreased family cohesion

Charlton *et al.* estimate that about half the increase in the number of men committing suicide is likely to be caused by the increase in the number of young men who are single or divorced.[20] They estimate this by comparing the suicide rate for men aged 15–44 in 1972–4 (11.5 per 100,000) with the rate prevailing by the end of the 1980s (18.6 per 100,000). Using the marital status distribution in suicide rates, they calculated what the suicide rate in the late 1980s would have been if there had been no change in the proportions of men in different marital groups. They calculate that it would have been 14.9 per 100,000; hence their conclusion that about half the increase in rates of suicide in young men may be attributed to the smaller proportion who are married. This means we must seek additional reasons for the increase. A major piece of evidence about exactly which young people are becoming most vulnerable emerges from data of Norman Kreitman and his colleagues at Edinburgh, who found that the increase in young male suicides was explained by an increase in the more working-class populations.[21] These are the populations which have been most exposed to reduced employment opportunities and increased misuse of alcohol and other drugs.

Changes in rates of depression

Part of the rise in young male suicide may also reflect changes in age-related depression over the twentieth century. Figure 10 gives the 1992 data from the Cross National Collaborative Group.[22] These show that people born more recently (since 1955) have the highest rates of depression across several countries. People are becoming depressed at younger ages. Further analyses of these data suggest this change is especially true of males. The cause of the change is unknown, but researchers into depression have come to similar conclusions as those investigating suicidal behaviour: that social and demographic changes such as the changing structure of families, social mobility and increased isolation, disengagement from the community, and limited access to resources combine to explain the pattern of change. Both changes in rates of depression, and changes in rates of suicide, have occurred in parallel with important economic changes and changes in family structure over the past twenty or thirty years.

Figure 10. Birth cohort changes in rates of depression, Paris, Florence, Puerto Rico, Edmonton (Alberta) and United States (five sites).

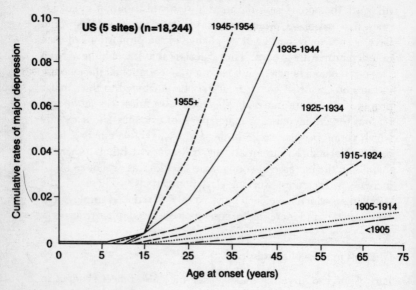

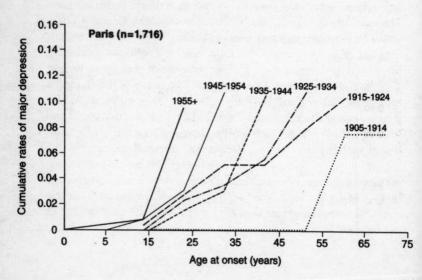

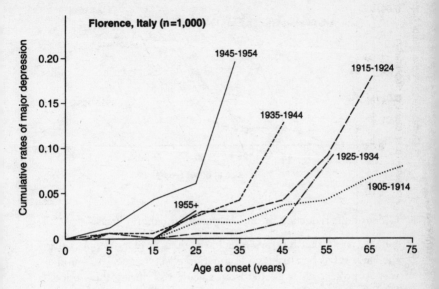

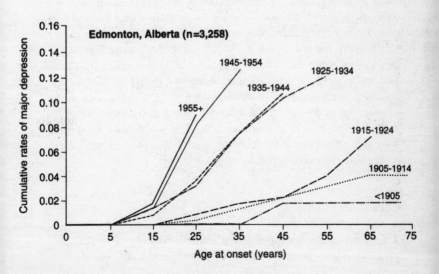

47

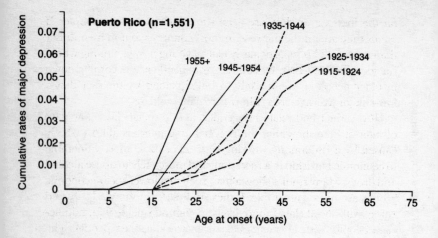

Older adults reduction in suicide: period or cohort effect?

Finally, could the trend towards lower rates in older people since the early 1960s be attributed to a period effect: has society found a way to protect older people from suicide risk during this period? Such a claim is open to considerable doubt. The current rates for older people of both sexes are no lower than those for younger people: they are simply lower than the very high rates seen earlier this century for older people. So the currently 'reduced' rates are largely attributable to the fact that the cohorts born since 1910 have had more 'average' suicide rates throughout their lives (despite the cohort peaks) compared to the very high rates of those born in the period 1870–1900 (i.e. those who contribute to the older age data in the suicide figures of 1946 onwards). It is not that we have done something to reduce the suicide rates for old people, but that we are seeing low-risk cohorts reaching old age.

Concluding remarks

To return to the questions posed at the beginning of this chapter and summarize what the statistics tell us: is the number of suicides on the increase or decrease – and in which groups of people? It seems they are on the increase in most countries, but in men rather than women. This is particularly true of younger men, among whom suicide rates are rising. By contrast, the suicide rate is coming down in older people, a trend likely to be explained by the fact that a low-risk (or average-risk) cohort is reaching old age.

How is the trend related to gender, and to social class? The data of interest here show that the rise in young males is almost wholly caused by a rise among working-class men, those most vulnerable to economic hardship in a recession, and most likely to abuse alcohol and drugs. Many studies show a bias, such that lower socio-economic groups are more vulnerable. Other studies (UK) show a U-shaped curve, with social class I more likely to commit suicide than middle-class people, with an increased risk in working-class people. The increase in young male suicides, however, is due to working-class men committing suicide more frequently, apparently a combination of cohort and period effects.

What methods do most people use? We have seen that men use more lethal methods than women, though the difference is reducing. Do suicidal trends respect national, cultural or ethnic boundaries? While the methods used from country to country may vary (firearms being much more common in the United States, for example), the trends across virtually all Western nations are remarkably similar. Within each country, however, there are ethnic differences to be taken into account. African Americans are much less likely to commit suicide than Anglo-Americans, but native Americans have a higher rate than either.

Finally, do unemployment and other such stress factors affect the suicide rate. Studies across a number of countries show the United Kingdom to be an exception to the general rule that changes in unemployment rate are associated with changes in suicide rate. Even in the United Kingdom, however, those who commit suicide are very much more likely to have been unemployed at the time than a person matched for age.

Chapter 3

PSYCHIATRIC AND SOCIAL FACTORS IN SUICIDE

'Suicide has been so closely associated with insanity only by arbitrarily restricting the meaning of the words.' So wrote Émile Durkheim in rejecting a psychiatric interpretation in his study of social causes of suicide in 1897.[1] Some hundred years later Susan Blumenthal, Chief of the Behavioral Medicine Program at the US National Institute of Mental Health, said: 'Over 90 per cent of patients committing suicide have a psychiatric disorder.' These authors appear to contradict each other completely about the significance of psychiatric disorders in suicide. Is the difference explained by the different eras in which they wrote? Do we have more data now that shows Durkheim's analysis to have been wrong? That is possible, though it is worth bearing in mind that many prior to Durkheim concluded that 'insanity' was the most probable cause. At the end of the seventeenth century, to say someone committed suicide because they were 'insane' was one of the few ways of being non-censorious, of showing gentleness to the memory of the victim and care for the family.

Durkheim found an alternative way of being non-censorious. Suicide should be seen as a feature of society, not of the individual. He accepted that 'insanity' was sometimes involved as a cause of suicide, but rejected the argument that understanding psychiatric disturbance was the key to understanding suicide. Instead, he pointed to a number of social facts about the incidence of suicide and its correlation with social integration and disintegration. Most famously, he pointed to anomie – the state associated with detachment from society – as a central feature of many suicides.

Many studies looking for a link between suicide and psychiatric disturbance have been done since Durkheim wrote his treatise, and I shall examine them and conclude that Blumenthal's proposition is correct, though this does not entail that Durkheim was wrong. Even if it proved to be that psychiatric disturbance precedes suicide in over 90 per cent of cases, its causal status would remain unclear. Mental illness may precede suicide because some circumstances drive people both to psychiatric breakdown and to suicide.

Evidence for psychiatric illness as a cause of suicide

Researchers have come to the conclusion that suicide is closely associated with psychiatric illness by using two methods. In the first, the researcher follows up people who have been psychiatrically disturbed in the past, to see what proportion eventually die by suicide. Since the risk of suicide in the population as a whole is between 1 and 2 per cent, it can then be calculated how much greater risk this particular group carry. The second method is known as *psychological autopsy*. This involves careful interviewing of relatives and friends following a suicide, and asking questions about the mood and behaviour of the deceased in the period leading up to the death. The results from this method have been used to support the conclusion that the majority of suicides were suffering psychiatric problems beforehand.

Research by Brian Barraclough in the United Kingdom has shown that 70 per cent of suicides would have been diagnosed as suffering from major depression, 15 per cent from alcoholism, and 4 per cent from schizophrenia or schizoaffective disorder (though other studies have found that a much greater proportion of suicide victims, up to 30 per cent, have suffered from schizophrenia in the past).[2] The total proportion of his sample of a hundred who would have attracted a psychiatric diagnosis was 93 per cent. He also showed that those who complete suicide are ten times more likely to have attempted suicide than other depressed patients.

Taking these two methods of assessment, Table 3 represents the current best available evidence on the likelihood of completed suicide in groups having different psychiatric diagnoses. The results agree with Barraclough's findings that the three diagnoses carrying the highest risk are depression, alcoholism and schizophrenia.

Table 3. Suicide vulnerability and psychiatric status.

Diagnosis	Long-term risks	Notes
Major depressions	10–15%	1. No difference between endogenous and non-endogenous sub-types 2. Psychological autopsy post-suicide reveals 70% suffered from depression 3. Insomnia, self-neglect and impaired memory are key predictive symptoms 4. Hopelessness, loss of pleasure and mood cycling in index episode predict suicide
Bipolar affective disorder	10–30%	Suicide risk is associated with depressed rather than manic symptomatology, although at times it is related to apparent improvement
Schizophrenia	around 10%	1. First admission schizophrenia annual rate of 500–750/100,000 2. Psychological autopsy post-suicide reveals 30% suffered from schizophrenia 3. Mean age of suicide = 33 years (younger than normal suicide) 4. No correlation between suicidal thoughts or behaviour and hallucination 5. History of depressive features (including past history of ECT or antidepressant treatment) increases vulnerability to suicide 6. Male patients most vulnerable to suicide after 4.8 years of disorder. Females after 9.8 years. Period after discharge most vulnerable.
Alcoholism	187/100,000	Alcoholism present in 15–25% of suicides Mean length of excessive drinking prior to suicide = 20 years
Neuroses	119/100,000	
Personality disorder	130/100,000	

Depression as a normal mood state is a common experience. In minor depressive states, the person ruminates on negative themes. He or she feels resentful, irritable or angry much of the time, feeling sorry for themselves and constantly needing reassurance from those around them. Often they have a variety of physical complaints that do not seem to be caused by any physical illness.

As depression deepens, more symptoms become apparent. These include further emotional changes (feelings of extreme sadness and hopelessness); changes in the content or process of thinking (low self-esteem, guilt, memory and concentration difficulties); changes in behaviour and motivation (feeling agitated or slowed down, reduced interest in social or recreational activities); and bodily changes (sleep, eating and sexual problems, loss of energy). If the depression is intense enough to include five or more of these symptoms for more than a two-week period, it is called 'major' or sometimes 'clinical' depression. Twelve per cent of men, and 20 per cent of women will experience an episode of such major depression at some time in their lives. At any one time, around 5 per cent of the population is suffering depression of this severity. Twenty-five per cent of these episodes of depression last less than a month; a further 50 per cent recover in less than three months. However, the depression can develop into a longer-term problem, with around a quarter being seriously depressed one year after symptom onset and one fifth remaining depressed two years later. The lifetime risk of suicide in depression is 15 per cent, with the greatest risk associated with those episodes of depression that last longer.

Alcoholism: Alcohol intake is not evenly spread through a population. In the United States, 50 per cent of alcohol is consumed by 10 per cent of the population. Studies in the 1980s found that 13 per cent of the US population suffer alcohol dependency at some point in their lives, with the ratio of male to female being between 2:1 and 5:1. Such dependency can show itself in one of three ways: by regular excessive intake of alcohol on a daily basis; by regular excessive intake limited to weekends; and by periods of abstinence interspersed with extremely heavy drinking binges lasting weeks or months. The lifetime risk of suicide in alcoholics is similar to that of depressed patients, 15 per cent, with male alcoholics six times more likely than women alcoholics to commit suicide. The mean age for suicide in alcoholic patients is 47, following an average twenty-year drinking history.

Schizophrenia, which up to 1 per cent of the population suffer at any one time, involves a range of symptoms. These include delusions, a disorder in the content of thought (e.g. the belief that one's thoughts are being broadcast from one's head, or being controlled by a dead person), ideas of reference (e.g. that events or people have a special and unusual significance, such as the change in a traffic signal, or the expression on the face of a television newscaster meaning one has been chosen for a special mission). A second set of symptoms includes disorder in the form of thought. These may include the loosening of associations, in which ideas flow from one to the other without any apparent connection, sometimes to such an extent that speech is incomprehensible. A third set of symptoms involves disorders of perception, especially auditory hallucinations, in which (most commonly) the person hears voices speaking to him or her, and perhaps commenting on his/her behaviour. Sometimes, and very dangerously, the voices command the person to carry out certain acts, including suicide. Fourthly, there is often a change in mood, with normal expression of emotion being disturbed in one of two ways. Either the mood is 'flat', with little sign of emotion, the voice and face remaining expressionless. Or the person seems to have moods inappropriate to the situation, laughing or smiling at events or descriptions that would normally evoke sadness or pity. Finally, and unsurprisingly in the light of these other symptoms, the person may experience a disturbance in their sense of 'who they are'. There may be a disruption of the will, with a person finding it almost impossible to initiate any activity at all. In consequence, there is often major disturbance in a person's relationships with other people. The person withdraws, and becomes detached, though may sometimes cling to or get too close to others.

Schizophrenia may take many forms, so that some have suggested the term itself is meaningless, or we should talk of 'the schizophrenias'. Others have maintained that as long as we realize the complexity of the disturbances, and that giving something a name does not really explain it, then continued use of the term is permissible.

Several studies point to the fact that up to 15 per cent of patients with a diagnosis of schizophrenia (especially males) will end their lives by suicide.

Other psychiatric disorders found to have a higher than average risk of suicide include *anxiety disorders* in general, and *panic disorder* in particular, but to date there have been too few studies to establish the exact risk in these groups.

Personality disorder (especially borderline and antisocial personality disorder), carries an increased risk of suicide. 'Borderline' patients were originally so called because it was believed they lived at the edge between psychosis and neurosis. They have affective instability, a history of self-damaging acts and damaging relationships, chronic feelings of emptiness and boredom, intolerance of being alone, and brief dissociative episodes, often associated with flashbacks of sexual abuse. Recent evidence suggests that between 4 and 10 per cent will eventually kill themselves. In antisocial personality disorder, although 46 per cent have some form of suicidal behaviour, the risk of completed suicide appears to be around 5 per cent.

Gender and age effects not explained by psychiatric illness

Despite these apparently strong relationships between psychiatric diagnosis and suicide, there are several reasons to look for causes other than psychiatric illness. One such is the gender difference. Women are more likely to become clinically depressed, but men are more vulnerable to suicide (see Chapter 2). Neither can psychiatric illness explain the way such gender differences change with age. Whereas female vulnerability tends to rise linearly but very slightly with increasing age, the male vulnerability rises markedly from ages 15–24 to 25–54. It falls again between 55 and 74, then rises again for the over-75s. This increase in the elderly is very likely caused by the helplessness following loss of loved ones suffered by men in this age group. Indeed, men over 65 who are married have a suicide rate of only 13 per 100,000, whereas those who are widowed have a suicide rate of 51 per 100,000. Men of *all* ages, however, are vulnerable to loss of their wife by death. Young men whose wives die have the highest rates of all. Women widowed young are at an increased risk, but this is not so marked as the effect of bereavement on men.

The vast majority of older people, even those who are depressed, who have been bereaved, who are suffering from a medical illness, or even those who are terminally ill, do not end their lives by suicide, however. This raises the question of what are the important risk factors in the older age group. The following have been identified: a history of poor adaptation to life's stress, vulnerability to loss and disruptions, loss of mastery and control, cognitive impairment caused by organic mental disorder. Once again, we need to look further than simply the presence or absence of psychiatric problems to understand the data.

Durkheim's view of psychiatric causation

Before Durkheim the connection between suicide and psychiatric disturbance had been made many times. Some arguments had been relatively weak. Some had suggested that, even where no other symptoms of mental illness were present, the fact of suicide itself justified a psychiatric diagnosis. Suicide had been thought by some to be a disease in itself, *sui generis*, a specific form of insanity. In such a 'monomania' (a sick person whose mentality is perfectly healthy in all respects but one), suicide was argued to be the sort of behaviour 'not to be found in sane persons'. Émile Durkheim easily showed how this was a circular argument. To establish that suicide is caused by mental illness, we need to be able to say more than that suicide itself constitutes such a diagnosis.

Instead, Durkheim considered three types of psychiatric suicide. The first was *maniacal suicide* (caused by hallucinations or delirious perceptions), in which the person acts to escape an imaginary danger, or obey a mysterious order from on high. Today, such experiences would be associated with a diagnosis of schizophrenia. The second type was *melancholy suicide*, associated with extreme depression and exaggerated sadness. Such a state 'causes the person no longer to realize the bonds which connect him with people and things about him'. The third type was *obsessive suicide*, in which suicide was thought to be caused by no other motive, but only by a fixed idea of death. The person was tormented by the idea, since they were also aware that there was no reason to kill themselves. Trying to resist the idea seemed hopeless, and the person, it was thought, sometimes simply gave up the struggle. Additionally, Durkheim pointed to the possibility of *impulsive or automatic suicide*, as unmotivated as obsessive suicide, but differing in that the idea comes suddenly with full force 'not preceded by any intellectual antecedent', little apparent warning for themselves or others. The person sees a knife, or walks near a cliff-edge, and the idea of suicide comes suddenly into mind. If the patient survives, they may say afterwards that they were not aware of or cannot remember any reason for their action.

In summarizing the psychiatric suicides, Durkheim notes that all such suicides are either 'devoid of any motive' (obsessive and impulsive suicides), or are determined by 'purely imaginary motives' (maniacal and melancholy suicides). Where psychiatric disturbance itself explains the motivation, it does so by indicating how the illness acts to produce the behaviour either in the absence of motive, or through the way it distorts the way the person views their world. Durkheim points out that 'many voluntary deaths fall into neither category; the majority have motives, and motives not unfounded in reality. Not every suicide can therefore be considered insane, without doing violence to language.'

The alternative – the importance of social facts

Durkheim's main argument was that social facts have to be taken into account as realities external to the individual. Social institutions (families, churches, non-religious groups) were extra-personal forces, definite realities whose influence needed to be subject to scientific analysis, an argument that gave most impetus to the evolving science which would be called 'sociology'. (Durkheim was not translated into English until 1951.) The incidence of suicide was one such element – a reality explicable only by looking for links to other social facts about society. Each society was thought to have a 'collective inclination to suicide'. This inclination was found in the suicide rate within the society or sub-group, and would not change while the character of the society or sub-group did not change. Thus a certain number of suicides was to be expected in every society, and it would be problems in the structure of society that led to an increase in suicide rates. It followed that the more strongly any individual was integrated into a social group (e.g. close-knit families or religious groups), the less was the likelihood of suicide. Any changes in society that caused greater disintegration would increase the suicide rate.

The three types of suicide delineated by Durkheim reflected the three categories of breakdown that might occur in the relationship between an individual and the society. In *egoistic suicide*, a person comes to have no concern for the community, and no interest in being involved with it. This category includes people with physical or mental illness, together with those who suffer deprivation and bereavement. The result was a reduction in society's control, and weakened immunity against society's natural collective inclination towards suicide.

By contrast, in *altruistic suicide*, society has too strict a hold, and a person has too little individualism. Self-destruction is motivated by altruism, inspiring respect and admiration among other members of the group. The suicide bomber would be counted among those who commit altruistic suicide, as would religious 'martyrs', – Japanese samurai warriors who committed hara-kiri rather than fall into the hands of their enemies, and kamikaze pilots of the Second World War. More controversially, those people who kill themselves because they are old or terminally ill, and do not wish to be a burden to family, friends or society, may be said to have committed altruistic suicide. However, it is often difficult to determine how much their sense of being a burden, or that 'everyone would be better off if I were not here', arises from their depression rather than from a clearly thought out and tested set of reasons (see Chapter 6).

In *anomic suicide*, society has failed in its regulation and integration of its members. Changes in family structure, reduced employment opportunities, declining religious beliefs and practices, changes in marital codes – all were manifestations of anomie, resulting in disturbances of collective organization. The result was a reduction in individuals' immunity against suicidal tendencies. In strict societies and subcultures, suicide would remain low because such integration of the individual with his or her social group would remain (e.g. suicide has traditionally been low in Catholic countries, but has increased as these countries have gradually become more secularized).

Evidence to support the social theory

Much of the data on suicide within and between populations is broadly consistent with the notion of anomie and societal disintegration as a major factor in explaining differences in proneness to suicide. A study of twenty-four localities in the Bristol area in the United Kingdom found the occurrence of non-fatal suicidal behaviour was highly correlated with deprivation (assessed by a number of factors, such as the proportion of people that own houses or cars, how many households are overcrowded, levels of unemployment). Furthermore, the list of factors that increase the risk of suicide in those who have made a previous attempt makes the importance of social factors obvious:

Older age;
gravity of previous attempt;
living alone;
psychosis;
left a suicide note;
unemployed or retired;
from a broken home;
men more than women;
multiple attempts;
not married;
poor physical health;
lethal method used before; and
infrequent use of health agencies.

The picture that emerges is one of poor circumstances with few resources to sustain the individual. Most significantly, there is an obvious lack of other people to support the person. This is consistent with Durkheim's hypotheses.

In many countries, suicide is more common among those members of society most affected by economic downturns: semi-skilled and unskilled manual workers. It is more common in rural communities, where there is a special vulnerability to economic downturn (because of the possible loss of farms that generations of a family might have built up), combined with a mechanization of farming that has seen decreased employment opportunities for many and increased social isolation of those few left.

Unemployment, whether in a rural or urban setting, appears to make suicide more likely. Even after controlling for social class, men aged 15–64 who are unemployed have a standard mortality rate greatly in excess of that of men in work. However, the relation between unemployment and suicide is complicated by two factors: first, the possibility that some may be vulnerable *both* to becoming unemployed and to suicide;[3] secondly, the fact that, in some cases of sudden unemployment in whole communities following closure of factories, people may (at least for a while) feel more integrated with their community as they fight the 'common enemy'. However, such fellow-feeling may not offset the effects of economic hardship for long. Within individual families, increased depression in the former wage-earner reduces energy levels. This can then be the cause of family friction as one partner accuses the other of 'not trying' to find employment. It is not uncommon to find single mothers talking frankly of how their unemployed (and now estranged) partner was only a drain on their family's resources, especially if he had been spending money on alcohol or gambling.

Studies of how sociodemographic factors contribute to changing rates of suicide over time also confirm the main thrust of Durkheim's theory of anomie. Suicide rates in eighteen countries across Europe between 1960 and 1980[4] showed that *increases* were associated with (a) reduction in the population aged 15 and under, taken to be an indicator of the extent to which people are not living in family groups; (b) an increase in the percentage of the population aged 65 and over, i.e. the age group with the relatively highest rate in European countries; and (c) an increase in women's tertiary education

– taken to reflect changes in the family structure. Changes in suicide rate over the same time interval among 15- to 29-year-olds found some factors which overlapped with those of the earlier report, and some new factors (see Table 4).

Table 4. Factors associated with suicide rates among 15- to 29-year-olds in Europe, 1960–80.

% unemployed (+)
% of population under 15 (–)
% women employed (+)
divorce rate (+)
homicide rate (+)
change in alcohol use (+)
change in church affiliation (+)

+ = increase in factor associated with increased suicide rate
– = decrease in factor associated with increased suicide rate

The correlation between suicide and the divorce rate emerges from several studies. What is more questionable is whether this correlation will continue, as divorce becomes more common and society develops more ways of dealing with and normalizing single-parent families. For example, in the Netherlands the suicide rates among divorced people are tending to stabilize or decline.

Social facts and the individual

Durkheim has been criticized from various quarters. First, some have pointed out that he needed a better and more operational definition of social integration. Later sociologists have come up with clearer definitions of terms, e.g. of 'status' (a category of people with clearly defined roles). Thus a person may have a variety of statuses and roles: within society (male, white), within the family (father, husband), within work (teacher, counsellor). In this way it is possible to calculate the frequency with which any person's combination of statuses conforms to the combinations most common in the society in which they live. In similar vein, sociologists have much better definitions of 'social support' than those proposed by Durkheim.[5]

Secondly, he based his conclusions on studies of a Western society, and there is evidence that in other societies risk factors are different. For example, although the association between divorce rates and suicide holds for Western nations (the correlation for the United States has been found to be 0.78 for the forty-eight continental states), it does not hold for Taiwan. The correlation between the divorce rate and suicide rate among the sixteen counties of Taiwan is an insignificant 0.05.

Thirdly, Durkheim too readily separated melancholic from other depressive suicides. He allowed that many normal persons who kill themselves may also be depressed and dejected, but maintained that they did not fall thereby into the category of melancholic mental illness. The difference, he suggested, is that in melancholy the person's depression was unrelated to their external circumstances, whereas in those he wished to call 'normal' the state of depression and the act of suicide had an objective cause. In this respect, Durkheim's analysis was wrong. There is no clear-cut difference between different types of depression, based on some having been preceded by negative life events and others coming 'out of the blue'.

Whereas it used to be thought that some depressions were 'reactive', caused by life circumstances, and others were 'endogenous', caused by biological factors ('endogenous' means 'originating from the inside'), research has shown that negative events and circumstances precede all types of depression equally often, and all types of depression have some biologically driven features. Even in depressions which follow directly after major loss or disappointment, there is evidence to show that, as the depression deepens, so certain neurochemical pathways in the brain undergo a change, affecting a person's eating and sleeping patterns, energy levels, and capacity to enjoy previously enjoyed hobbies, interests and social contacts. Such changes sometimes self-correct in time, and where they do not, antidepressant medication or types of psychotherapy that provide a structure within which the person can regain control over their moods have been found to help.

Nevertheless, the central thrust of Durkheim's argument remains true: we need to look for factors other than mental illness to explain why risks of suicide differ between individuals and between societies. The importance of social support cannot be over-estimated in moderating the impact of other stresses. Not only is it important at times of stress, but people who have social support tend to adhere to the treatment suggested, and it is therefore no surprise that they respond better. With social support, people are more likely to take the opportunities given to begin to solve the problems in their life, with or without the help of mental-health professionals.

However, understanding the social facts needs to be combined with understanding the individual circumstances in causing particular suicidal acts. If this were not so, suicidal behaviour would be much more common than it is.

The causal significance of psychiatric illness and social facts

It certainly seems that suicide is closely associated with psychiatric disturbance. What, then, are we to make of Durkheim's scepticism about psychiatric illness, and how can we make sense of the equally compelling data linking suicide to factors external to the individual?

Although psychiatric disturbance precedes suicide in many cases, it remains unclear whether its presence explains very much. Certainly we can readily see that, although up to 15 per cent of depressed patients commit suicide, the majority do not. We therefore have to understand what is different about those who do commit suicide. Secondly, even within the 15 per cent who do commit suicide, why did they choose that particular moment, when the disorder from which they suffered had been with them a long time? Finally, there remains a proportion of people who commit suicide either as a catastrophic response to a negative event (usually a loss, or perceived loss), or as a matter of honour, or because they feel on rational grounds it is time to die.

These cases are linked in the feelings of uncontrollability they involve. Such feelings arising from inside a person are particularly damaging, yet are often ignored. Why? Perhaps because psychiatrists and psychologists often take account only of negative life events (such as bereavement, loss of job, marital breakdown) in explaining the onset of a psychiatric illness. Once the psychiatric illness has been diagnosed, however, the search for causes often stops. The illness has been explained. But this does not explain how the disturbance is maintained, why it sometimes lasts a long rather than a short time, or gets worse rather than better. Occasionally there are further negative external events that explain such prolongation. But we need also to take account of the negative effects of experiencing unpleasant psychiatric symptoms themselves: e.g. hearing voices that cannot be switched off, in schizophrenia; feeling constantly tired but unable to sleep, in depression; feeling at the mercy of craving, in alcoholism. Such uncontrollable stresses that arise from within are as likely to produce a state of helplessness as uncontrollable stresses that arise from outside. It is these that explain why psychiatric illness so often precedes suicide, and why most people who become psychiatrically ill do not commit suicide.

I suggest that the presence of mental illness does add significantly to the explanation of suicide in many cases, but, when it does, does so to the extent that the symptoms of the condition engender hopelessness. To state the hypothesis more strongly: psychiatric illnesses carry an increased risk for suicide only to the extent that the person feels they cannot escape their symptoms. For example, it may not be the frequency of 'bizarre' symptoms that predict suicidality in schizophrenia, but how the person feels about having such symptoms: the extent to which the person feels entrapped by such symptoms. The hypothesis also predicts that it will be the longest and most persistent depression that is associated with suicide, and that other predictors of suicide will all be elements that decrease a person's sense of control over external and internal events.

The evidence is quite compelling. In depression, it is the people who have been depressed longest, and who are therefore most likely to feel hopeless about recovering a normal state of mind, who carry most risk of suicide. Furthermore, retrospective analysis of suicidal behaviour in people who have been depressed in-patients, and of suicide in those who have previously attempted suicide, has found that the greatest risk was for those who showed severest depressed mood, alcohol problems, long-term use of sleeping pills, and long-term physical illness.[6] Finally, whereas attributing suicidal behaviour to the diagnosis of depression does not explain why the period immediately after discharge is the most vulnerable time, especially for men, such increased risk is more easily explained by the exacerbation in a sense of hopelessness brought about by the change in circumstances.

Similarly in schizophrenia, the suicide risk is particularly strong for those who feel hopeless, have suicidal ideation, fear mental disintegration, have made previous suicidal attempts, do not adhere to treatment and experience many relapses in symptoms. Indeed, it is a history of *depressive* features (past use of ECT or antidepressants in treatment) which is an important predictor, not the extent of the schizophrenic symptoms (e.g. voices). This supports the view that it is not the voices themselves which increase the risk of suicide, but how the person feels about them. The external stresses with which schizophrenic patients have to cope are well known: decreased job prospects, family disintegration, poor network of relationships. Entrapment theory would suggest that such events have most impact upon those who can compare current reality with what might have been. Studies have found that most schizophrenic suicides are young males, functioning at a high level prior to the onset of the schizophrenia but now unemployed. Those who previously had the most promising careers are at greatest risk; the contrast is for them the most stark. As in depression, any event that increases a sense of helplessness can increase the suicide risk, and change in circumstances is particularly likely to do so. This may include changing wards when an in-patient, or discharge from hospital. Each finding points away from the particular psychiatric diagnosis of schizophrenia *per se* as the element that increases suicide risk and towards the increased helplessness and hopelessness such a disorder shares with other serious mental problems.

The link between suicide and helplessness in the face of feelings of entrapment in alcoholics is striking. Once again, discharge is a vulnerable time, often made worse by the fact that family contacts have broken down. Such people often have vulnerable or fragile personalities, and social problems that may have precipitated their drinking but are then exacerbated by the drinking itself. Connected to this is the fact that alcoholic individuals who commit suicide are very likely to be either unmarried or divorced. Life events (especially loss events) are most closely connected to suicide in alcoholics, with 50 per cent having suffered loss of an important relationship in the year preceding the suicide (the figure for depressed patients is 20 per cent). Indeed, one third of alcoholic suicides have suffered such a loss within six weeks of the suicide.

These patterns in the suicide data both confirm the significance of psychiatric illness and show how they combine with a psychosocial perspective in explaining suicide risk. Psychiatric diagnoses, especially depression, schizophrenia and alcoholism, act as a marker of increased suicide risk. But suicide is not unique to any particular diagnosis. It arises from a secondary aspect of mental illness. In such mental states, the person experiences symptoms that can give rise to an inner turmoil that seems inescapable and uncontrollable. It is the combination of uncontrollable stress factors arising from sources external and internal to the individual that increases hopelessness. The most potent preventative factor when such uncontrollable stress threatens to overwhelm the individual is the availability of social support from friends and family. When the suicidal feelings are too strong, however, even support of the highest quality will be ignored by the suicidal individual; the hopelessness they experience includes extreme pessimism about whether anyone can help them.

Chapter 4

ATTEMPTED SUICIDE: THE STATISTICS

'I have to admit that I am a failed suicide. It is a dismal confession to make, since nothing, really, would seem easier than to take your own life.' So wrote Al Alvarez in his book *Savage God*.[1] Alvarez knew first hand what it was like to experience suicidal despair, and be driven to take the final step. The crisis took place ten years before, on Christmas Eve. After a 'final, terrible quarrel' with his wife, she left to stay elsewhere for the night. Alvarez went upstairs to the bathroom and swallowed forty-five sleeping pills. Impulsive? In some senses, yes, but the act had been prepared for some time. His account illustrates, among other things, the premeditation of suicidal behaviour (he had been hoarding sleeping pills), the precipitation of the act by some 'final straw', and the unwillingness of the police to intervene in the late 1950s.

I had been collecting the things for months obsessionally, like Green Stamps, from doctors on both sides of the Atlantic . . . hoarding them in preparation for the time I knew was coming. When it finally arrived, a box was waiting stuffed with pills of all colors . . . I gobbled the lot.

My wife got back at noon, took one look and called the ambulance. When they got me to the hospital I was, the report says, 'deeply unconscious, slightly cyanosed, vomit in mouth, pulse rapid, poor volume'.

I was still unconscious the next day and most of the day after that . . . During the afternoon of the third day, December 28, I came to . . . In a fog I saw my wife smiling hesitantly, and in tears. It was all very vague. I slept . . .

At some point the police came, since in those days suicide was still a criminal offence. They sat heavily but rather sympathetically by my bed and asked me questions they clearly didn't want me to answer. When I tried to explain, they shushed me quietly. 'It was an accident, wasn't it, sir?' Dimly, I agreed. They went away.

Alvarez's experience raises many of the questions that need to be answered in relation to attempted suicide. First, what proportion of people who think about harming themselves actually go on to do it, and what proportion of those who do, go on at some time in the future to kill themselves? Secondly, if ending one's life is not the only motive for such self-harm, what are the other motives? Thirdly, how can one distinguish a failed suicide attempt (where the full intention was to end life) from self-harm intended to change some aspect of oneself or others?

Definitions

To answer these questions, we need a clear definition of what we mean by 'attempted suicide'. Is all and any self-harm to be deemed an attempt at suicide, even self-cutting, or burning with cigarette ends? And what of the elderly woman who takes four sleeping pills, and telephones the physician in great distress. In this case the physician would be well advised not to ignore the behaviour, even though it represents no risk to life. Such a person may be used to taking half a sleeping pill to help her get to sleep at nights, and therefore believe four such tablets (eight times her normal dose) will kill her. Turning a blind eye may be to miss someone who is extremely suicidal.

On the other hand, a young person who takes a hundred paracetamol may be at considerable risk of dying without medical intervention as a result of liver failure (especially if they have taken alcohol with the paracetamol), yet may at no point have thought of killing him or herself. Indeed, the availability of large quantities of such lethal substances over the counter (not possible in France) may give a completely false impression of safety. Such a person can hardly be said to have been attempting suicide, though their risk of dying may have been greater than that of the elderly person, who was at no significant risk.[2]

To overcome the confusion about the term 'attempted suicide', clinicians and researchers have, over the past twenty years, adopted the term 'parasuicide' or 'deliberate self-harm'. *Parasuicide*, perhaps now the most widely used word for all such self-harm (whatever the explicit or implicit intention), is defined as follows:

An act with non-fatal outcome, in which an individual deliberately initiates a non-habitual behaviour that, without intervention from others, will cause self-harm, or deliberately ingests a substance in excess of the prescribed or generally recognized therapeutic dosage, and which is aimed at realizing changes which the subject desired via the actual or expected physical consequences.

Defining parasuicide is one thing, collecting data about it another. Most hospitals do not officially record attendance at accident and emergency in these terms. For example, in the United Kingdom 'parasuicide' does not exist in the classification system used by the Department of Health! The closest approximation, 'adverse effects of medical agents', is used for statistical purposes instead. For a complete picture of parasuicide rates and trends, we must rely on data from those centres that have made special efforts to collect information over the years. Fortunately, these have presented a remarkably consistent picture.

Parasuicide statistics

In 1961, when it ceased to be a criminal offence to attempt suicide, there were some 20,000 parasuicides in the United Kingdom each year. During the 1960s and 1970s there was a steep rise in numbers of people harming themselves, reaching a peak around 1977 of some 100,000. Numbers then levelled off, and even began to fall. But during the 1980s the rates turned upwards again. Current estimates are that there are at least 100,000 episodes of parasuicide known to the hospital service per year in the United Kingdom (17,000 of whom are teenagers). There are perhaps a further 30,000 (of all ages) who never reach hospital, either telling no one about their self-harm, or seeing their family doctor, who may not refer them to the hospital. Another slight fall at the end of the 1980s has been followed by a rise at the beginning of the 1990s. In the United Kingdom this represents a rate of 264 per 100,000 for men, and 368 per 100,000 for women.[3] (This ratio of female:male of 1.4:1 has declined from a ratio of 2.1:1 in 1976, and 1.9:1 in 1984. Most recently the ratio has declined again, so that men have caught up with women in parasuicide numbers.)

Throughout the 1980s our understanding of the problem of parasuicide was based on these statistics. Overall numbers were rising, but the general characteristics of the data remained relatively stable. Whereas suicide appeared more a problem of older men, parasuicide was more a problem of younger women. Two thirds of parasuicide cases were women, and two thirds were under 35. Around 90 per cent of such cases harmed themselves by taking an overdose, with younger people more likely to take analgesics such as aspirin or paracetamol, and older people more likely to take sleeping pills or antidepressants. (This pattern of age-related overdose by different substances reflects the fact that all ages take whatever is available to them. Younger people are less likely to have sleeping pills and antidepressants prescribed, so take whatever else comes to hand. If they do take psychotropic medication, it is often because they have taken the medication prescribed for someone else in the family.)

How far is this pattern of data still true? To answer this, we need to examine data in more detail.

Oxford data in detail

The city of Oxford contains a mix of population, with a large university population combining with areas of great social deprivation. When the pattern of data from the city has been compared with other UK centres, the trends are remarkably similar both for total numbers, balance between the sexes, socio-economic status data, and methods used. The picture of parasuicidal behaviour begins in the mid 1970s, at a point where the rates (increased fourfold in the ten years to 1973) began to decline (see Figure 11). The decline was more marked in women than men, corresponding to the earlier greater increase in women. The household composition of parasuicide cases is shown in Figure 12. High numbers were still living with parents (around a quarter of both men and women). This comes from the often reported trend for young people to be at most risk of parasuicide, which has not changed over the years. The data for 1989–92 are shown in Figure 13, where it can be seen that the peak age for women remains between 15 and 19 (the rates for this age group being 760 per 100,000), whereas the peak age for men lies between 25 and 29 (420 per 100,000).

The data for marital and employment status help fill out the picture. Most parasuicides are single or divorced (see Figure 14) and one third of the males are unemployed (see Figure 15). However, despite the population of parasuicides being heavily weighted towards the single or divorced, a majority live with parents or a partner (67 per cent of those who said they were single were living with a partner, and 52 per cent of those who were divorced were living with a partner). Only 22 per cent of the total number who parasuicided between 1989 and 1992 lived alone. This is consistent with research that shows most parasuicidal behaviour occurs in the context of problems in relationships.

The data also reveal that the majority are from lower socio-economic status backgrounds. The rate for social classes I and II is around 50 per 100,000 for women and 20 per 100,000 for men. This rate goes up over eight times for women and over twelve times for men in social classes III–V.

What proportion will harm themselves again? Estimates over the years and from various centres have varied between 10 and 25 per cent, but settled down to around 15 per cent. This is reflected in the Oxford data, where 15.5 per cent of men and 12.8 per cent of women repeated the attempt within the first year. Some go on to make further repeat attempts, so that in any sample of cases coming to hospital, around 44 per cent of both men and women have a previous parasuicide episode.

In terms of methods used in self-harm, although 9.5 per cent cut themselves, the vast majority use self-poisoning (86 per cent medicines, and 3 per cent other chemical substances), a pattern unchanged over the years. However, the pattern of substances used has changed (see Figure 16). Tranquillizers and sedatives used to be the most common method, but their use has declined from around

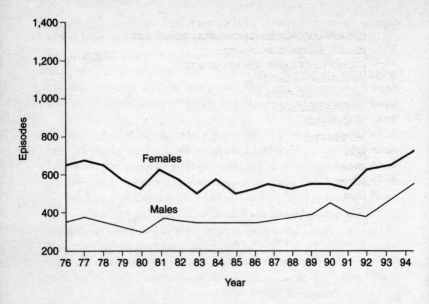

Figure 11. Episodes of attempted suicide referred to the John Radcliffe Hospital, Oxford, 1976–94.

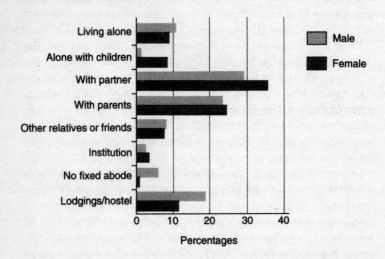

Figure 12. Suicide attempts (persons) by household composition and gender, Oxford data, 1989–92.

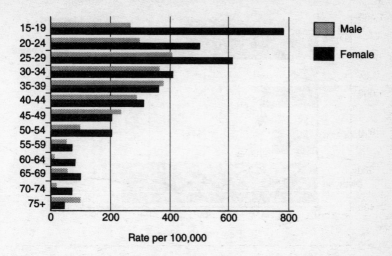

Figure 13. Oxford City parasuicide rates, 1989–92, by age and gender.

40 per cent of all overdoses to around 16 per cent, most likely because of the marked decline in prescribing these drugs over the period. Their place has been taken by an increase in paracetamol (from around 14 to 42 per cent). Often the tablets are either taken with alcohol (32 per cent of men and 20 per cent of women) or within a few hours of consumption of alcohol (56 per cent of men have taken alcohol in the previous six hours, as have 37 per cent of women).

Parasuicide: international trends

How do these data differ from those of other countries? Figure 17 shows the Oxford data (which can be taken as representative of the United Kingdom) alongside data from other European centres from the WHO/EURO Multicentre Study of Parasuicide in Europe. The most salient conclusion to emerge is that the United Kingdom has one of the highest rates of parasuicide in Europe. The parasuicide rates for 1989–92 vary from 48 per 100,000 for men in Padua, Italy, to 345 per 100,000 for men in Helsinki, Finland. Oxford's rate over

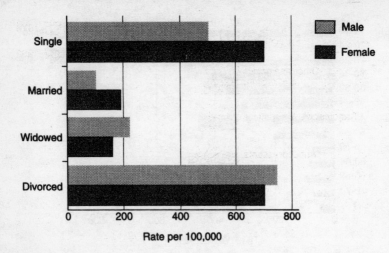

Figure 14. Mean annual attempted suicide rates (persons aged 16+) for Oxford City, by marital status and gender.

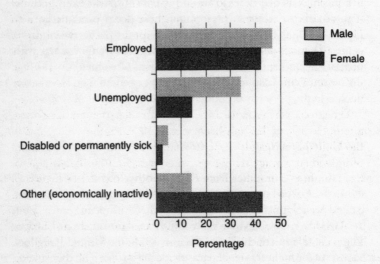

Figure 15. Suicide attempts (persons) by employment status and gender, Oxford data, 1989–92.

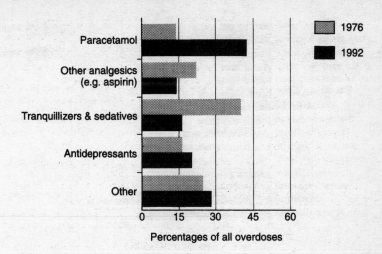

Figure 16. Methods of self-poisoning, Oxford: changes between 1976 and 1992.

this period was 264 per 100,000 for men (second highest) and 368 per 100,000 for women (the highest). In a direct comparison with Utrecht in Holland as part of another study, Keith Hawton and colleagues have found that the higher UK rates arise from the larger number of teenage females in the UK sample. However, this will not account for all the difference, and the exact reasons remain unclear.

Data from North America are more difficult to obtain. In Canada, attempted suicide has not been reportable since the 1960s, and in the United States study of parasuicide is limited by the protection of individual privacy. However, where research has been done, it has found rates of parasuicide comparable with the higher end of the European spectrum, with annual rates in Canada being estimated as 304 per 100,000.[4]

The most comprehensive survey of parasuicide rates in the United States comes from the National Institute of Mental Health's Epidemiologic Catchment Area study (1980–85). As part of this survey, over 18,000 people answered questions about suicide ideation and previous suicidal behaviour. The results showed that 2.9 per cent

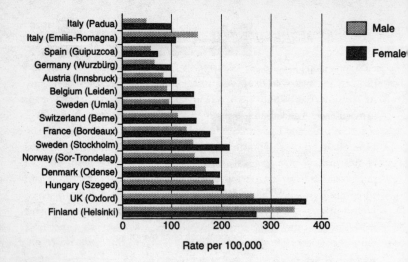

Figure 17. Rates of parasuicide (per 100,000), 1989–92, across European centres.

had made a suicide attempt at some point. The ratio of men to women was 1:1.4; 59 per cent of those saying they had ever attempted suicide were women.[5] This survey also found that the prevalence was significantly higher for persons aged between 25 and 44 than for those over 44. With regard to marital status, the highest rates were found among the separated or divorced, and the lowest among the married and widowed. There was an increase in the rate of parasuicide with decreasing socio-economic status, but the most powerful risk factor was a lifetime diagnosis of psychiatric disorder. Many aspects of these US data coincide with conclusions reached from the European studies, but because they were collected in the early 1980s they cannot inform us about recent changes. There is some evidence that a major shift is taking place in the gender distribution of parasuicide.

The reversal of the female:male ratio

Across Europe for the period up to the 1990s, the number of women parasuicide cases has exceeded those of men in most countries. Only in Helsinki is the pattern reversed. However, recent reports from around the United Kingdom suggest the gap is closing. In Oxford, whereas the male to female ratio had been 2:1 in the mid 1970s, the ratio changed rapidly in the 1990s and in 1994 stood at 1.35:1. This comes on top of a general upward trend for the total number of parasuicides over the period 1992–4. The rise between 1993 and 1994 alone was 21.8 per cent, the increase occurring in both sexes. Despite these changes, the age ratio has not changed, with 71 per cent of attempters in Oxford in 1994 being under 35, and the most vulnerable age for women remaining at 15–19, and for men, 20–24. Keith Hawton's preliminary observations for Oxford in 1995 suggest that men may well have overtaken women in the total number when the official figures are published. This would be consistent with figures from other parts of the United Kingdom which show a number of disturbing trends. For example, in Leeds, according to data from the Leeds General Infirmary, the overall number of parasuicide episodes has increased by 18 per cent between 1992/93 and 1994/95. Secondly, there has been a change in the sex ratio that is not the result of a fall in the number of women harming themselves; their numbers have also risen, but the risen in males has been steeper. The male–female ratio in Leeds is now 1:1. This finding parallels a report for the same period from the Samaritans, when the number of calls from men exceeded those from women. There appears to be, for the first time since records were kept, a reversal of the usual female/male bias in parasuicide.

Suicidal ideas and suicidal behaviour

What proportion of people have thoughts about suicide at some point in their lives? Studies vary in their estimate, from very low (3.5 per cent) for those that merely ask about 'recent' thoughts, through

19 per cent (if the question is asked about the past year), to 53 per cent (if people are asked if they have ever thought of suicide).[6] Perhaps we should not be surprised that over half the population have had suicidal thoughts at some time in their lives, but that one in five have had such thoughts in the past year is quite alarming. Of these, only 1 to 2 per cent go on to harm themselves in some way, but when someone has harmed themselves once, how can we assess whether the person is at future risk of harming themselves again?

There is no one single predictor, but the most commonly found factors that predict repetition of parasuicide are:

1. Problems in use of alcohol.
2. Previous diagnosis of 'sociopathy' or other personality disorder.
3. Previous in-patient psychiatric treatment.
4. Previous out-patient psychiatric treatment.
5. Not living with relatives.
6. Previous parasuicide.

In one of the earliest studies of prediction of self-harm, it was found that with 0 or only 1 of these factors involved, the risk of repetition in the following year was 5 per cent; with 5 or 6 of them, the risk was 48 per cent.[7]

A more recent study by Norman Kreitman in 1991[8] re-examined these and other factors in people admitted to hospital following parasuicide. The following were found to be predictive:

1. Previous parasuicide.
2. Clinical diagnosis of personality disorder.
3. Alcohol consumption (more than 21 units per week in males; more than 14 units per week in females).
4. Previous psychiatric treatment.
5. Unemployment.
6. Social class (V).
7. Drug abuse.
8. Criminal record.
9. Violence (given or received in the past five years).

10. Aged between 25 and 54.
11. Single/widowed or divorced.

Those patients who scored 3 or less had a repetition rate averaging 4.9 per cent (5.1 per cent for females, 4.6 per cent for males). Those with a score between 4 and 7 had a repetition rate of 20.5 per cent (18 per cent for females, 22.9 per cent for males). Those with a score of 8+ had a repetition rate of 41.5 per cent (36.9 per cent for females, 46 per cent for males). So that almost 60 per cent of those with a score of 8+ did *not* repeat parasuicide.

Motivation for self-harm

If death is not the intended outcome of a 'suicide attempt', then what is? The person's own report is one important consideration. A study by John Bancroft and colleagues found that over half of those who had recently taken an overdose said they did not want to die at any stage, and of those who did say they wanted to die, a proportion said there were other reasons, such as 'showing how much I loved someone'.[9] The most common reasons given for taking an overdose are listed in Table 5.

Note that the most commonly endorsed reason is, 'The situation was so unbearable, I had to do something and I didn't know what else to do.' This gives an important clue to what is going on in the mind of the person who is desperate – up against a 'brick wall' and come to the end of coping. This fits with the often reported feeling that they didn't care whether they lived or died. They will, as it were, let the Fates decide. It is more like Russian roulette than a considered act.

Suicidal intent

How can we tell if someone really intended to kill themselves? In the past, a number of terms have been coined to refer to people who, it is assumed, did not mean to kill themselves, such as 'gesture',

Table 5. Proportions of people endorsing various 'reasons for overdose' (from Williams, 'Differences in reasons for taking overdoses in high and low hopelessness groups', *British Journal of Medical Psychology*, 1986). (Each person was allowed to endorse as many items as they felt fitted their case, so the numbers do not add up to 100.)

	% endorsement
The situation was so unbearable that I had to do something and didn't know what else to do.	67
I wanted to die.	61
I wanted to escape for a while from an impossible situation.	58
I wanted to get relief from a terrible state of mind.	52
I wanted to make people understand how desperate I was feeling.	39
I wanted to make things easier for others.	36
I wanted to get help from someone.	33
I wanted to show how much I loved someone.	30
I wanted to try and get someone to change their mind.	15
I wanted to try and find out whether someone really loved me or not.	12
I wanted to make people sorry for the way they have treated me.	9
I wanted to frighten someone.	3
I wanted to get my own back on someone.	3

'manipulative' and 'cry for help'. These too easily assume that different motivations for parasuicide are mutually exclusive, being either an attempt to communicate (gesture), to influence others (manipulation) or to die (suicide attempt).

Instead, it is important to build up a picture which includes a range of information, including details of the circumstances surrounding the episode (if necessary, obtained from relatives or friends) as well as the patient's own report. The following issues need to be taken into account:[10]

(a) *External circumstances*
1. *How isolated was the person at the time?* The greater the intention, the more likely it is the person will choose to harm themselves in a place away from people.
2. *Was the act timed so that intervention was likely or unlikely?* The highly suicidal person will calculate what time to harm themselves so the likelihood of interruption is minimal.
3. *Were there precautions taken against discovery?* Some people will lock doors, write notes saying they have gone away, travel to remote locations without telling of their whereabouts, or book into hotels under other names, all to avoid discovery.
4. *Did the patient do anything to gain help during or after the attempt?* It sometimes happens that someone will have second thoughts, either just before or during a suicidal act, and telephone or tell someone what they are about to do or have just done. The highly suicidal person is less likely to do this.
5. *Did the patient make any final acts anticipating they would die?* Those with greater suicidal intent write wills, cancel regular orders, clear their desks, and do other things in the expectation they will die.
6. *Did they write a suicide note?* Although only 30 per cent of people who commit suicide leave a suicide note, it usually denotes a high degree of suicidal intent.

(b) *Self-report*
1. *Did they believe what they did would kill them?* People vary in how much they know about the lethality of suicidal acts, particularly overdoses. The amount of drugs taken has been found to correlate

with suicide intent if a large enough sample is taken,[11] although other studies have not found this to be the case.[12] Medical lethality is useful for judging seriousness of intent where it is known the person who has taken the overdose is aware of the relative lethality of drugs. Otherwise, the person's own report about what they *thought* the outcome would be is the most important factor.

2. *Do they say they wanted to die?* Many studies show that over half of people who parasuicide say they did not want to die. High suicide intent is associated with a clear indication that death was the intended outcome.

3. *How premeditated was the act?* Two thirds of patients have not thought about it for more than an hour beforehand. The longer the idea of suicide had been in the mind, the greater the suicidal intent.

4. *Is the patient glad (or sorry) to have recovered?* Clinicians are always concerned about the person who has harmed themselves, and afterwards says they are sorry to be still alive.

Research has found that high suicidality, defined in this way, predicts future suicidal behaviour and future suicide.[13] One study found that 21 per cent of patients with high suicide intent later committed suicide.[14] Another study, by Aaron Beck and colleagues,[15] compared the Suicide Intent Scale scores of 194 patients who eventually completed suicide against data from 231 other suicide attempters. They found that the completers had higher scores on the 'Objective Circumstances' items of the Suicide Intent Scale. Further, those attempters who had another parasuicide within a year of discharge (n = 19) had a higher total intent score for this last episode. Further studies from the same research group[16] have found that the 'Precautions against Intervention' factor of the Suicide Intent Scale predicted eventual suicide among suicide attempters and that intent was higher just before completion of suicide.

Of particular interest is how suicide intent relates to age, and whether intent is related to the use of alcohol, either in general, or specifically around the time of the parasuicide. Results have shown that people who harm themselves with high suicide intent are more likely to have had previous episodes of self-harm, are more likely to be single or divorced and to live alone. However, they are no more

likely to be depressed or personality disordered, no more likely to have
had psychiatric treatment in the past, and show no difference in the
type of drug used in overdose or in whether alcohol was taken. By far
the largest predictor is a chronic problem with alcohol abuse. Since
chronic alcohol abuse itself puts a person at high risk of suicide, the
joint influence of abusing alcohol and harming oneself with high suicide intent should be taken as a very serious indicator that a person is
vulnerable to suicide.

Alvarez revisited

On the basis of the above descriptions, was Alvarez's parasuicide a
serious attempt on his life? He very nearly died, so nearly became
another suicide statistic. Barbiturate sleeping pills were very unforgiv-
ing, unlike more modern equivalents. But taking account of the
external circumstances, the episode would have to be judged as of
low suicidal intent. He took the pills in his own house on Christmas
Eve, after a row with his wife, not making any attempt to isolate
himself. The timing was more ambiguous in that she had just left to
sleep at their flat for the night, but there is little indication that he
believed she would not return the next morning. In any event, there
was a house guest, who brought him a cup of tea in the morning,
and his wife returned at noon. The house guest was able to bring
the tea into his bedroom, so he had taken no precautions against
discovery, such as locking the door. He did not act to gain help
before or during the attempt, which might indicate high suicide
intent, but he had tried to contact his psychotherapist earlier on
Christmas Eve. When an immediate appointment was difficult to
arrange, nothing was done. He made no final acts in anticipation of
death, and did not leave a suicide note.

Alvarez's internal feelings about what was going on indicate more
suicidality than the external circumstances. He seemed to think the
pills would kill him, seems to have wanted to die, and had been
hoarding pills for some time (indicating premeditation). Whether he
was sorry he had not died is less clear. He does express disappointment, but not so much at being alive as from a sense of being cheated

by death. 'Death had let me down,' he says. There had been no moment of cathartic truth when the meaning of his life was revealed. 'All I got was oblivion.' 'As for suicide . . . it is not for me. Perhaps I am no longer optimistic enough. I assume now that death, when it finally comes, will probably be nastier than suicide, and certainly a great deal less convenient.'

Chapter 5

THE CAUSES OF ATTEMPTED
SUICIDE

What causes people to harm themselves? I begin this chapter by taking a temporal perspective, looking briefly at the three aspects (or phases) in the build-up to a parasuicide episode: long-term vulnerability factors; short-term vulnerability factors; and precipitating factors.

Long-term vulnerability factors

The *long-term vulnerability factors* could be taken to include all those factors in the person's past or current relationships and living conditions which act as background to the shorter-term crises. Ronald Maris, for example, found that 83 per cent of attempters, as compared with 31 per cent of a control group, had experienced either early loss by death or separation (from fathers more often than mothers) or other major traumas within the families, such as alcohol or drug abuse, mental illness, criminality, or a sibling in a foster home.[1]

Other long-term vulnerability factors for parasuicide are to be found in the living conditions of the patients. In a study of attempted suicide in 13- to 18-year-olds by Keith Hawton at Oxford,[2] 12 per cent had been in care at some time in their lives, over half had problems with school-work and relationships with teachers, and three quarters had difficulty with one or both parents. Indeed, 36 per cent were living with only one parent, and 12 per cent with neither parent. Social isolation was a fairly common background factor.

Parenting

Although there is an association between loss of parents (through death or divorce) and parasuicide, this does not imply that all parasuicide cases have this in their background. Nevertheless, several studies suggest that poor parenting occurs unusually frequently. A study by Robert Goldney[3] in Adelaide examined the type of care that young (18–30) female overdose patients reported having received as children. They used the Parental Bonding Instrument,[4] a questionnaire that measures how much people perceive their parents cared for them versus being indifferent or rejecting. It also assesses how much parents were overprotective versus encouraging independence. Several research studies have established the reliability and validity of this instrument.

Results showed that suicidal patients reported their parents as having been more rejecting *and* more overprotective. It seems that these young women, through their experience of deficient parenting, perceived themselves as less deserving of care. They had poor self-esteem and placed a lower value on their own life. The curious combination of a more rejecting style and overprotection is significant. Overprotection undermines the growing child's sense of autonomy and sense of being in control of events in its own life.

Sexual abuse

Several authors have suggested that a high proportion of suicide attempters have an even more acute disruption in early social relationships: they suffer sexual abuse. Only recently has this been studied systematically. A 1993 study by Marjan Van Egmond and colleagues[5] from the Department of Clinical and Health Psychology, University of Leiden, Netherlands, examined the extent of sexual abuse in a sample of 158 female suicide attempters aged 20 or older. The degree of sexual abuse was established by asking two questions: 'Have you ever in your life been forced by anyone to have sexual intercourse?' and, 'Has anyone ever forced you to perform or allow sexual contacts other than sexual intercourse?' Around 50 per cent of subjects (79) reported having been sexually abused at some time in the past. The sexually abused women made their first suicide attempt earlier than the non-abused women: when they were 27 years old, on average, compared to an average age of 36. The abused women also had almost double the number of previous suicide attempts.

The 79 women had often been abused many times; 57 by an unknown man or boy, 30 by a friend or acquaintance, 27 by relatives other than a stepfather or father and 12 by a father or stepfather. Four had been abused by a professional care giver. Only 20 per cent of these women had been abused once. The vast majority had been abused repeatedly by the same abuser or by multiple abusers. For 75 of the 79, the first suicide attempt took place after sexual abuse.

As other research has found, once a person has been abused they often find themselves being victimized again by other men in later childhood or adulthood. One woman had been raped and physically abused by six boys at the age of 17. A year later she was raped and abused by two unknown men. She made her first suicide attempt when 21, but found herself hardly able to talk about the rapes, except to say that on the second occasion her body was mutilated by the men using cigarettes. The suicide attempt was precipitated by an innocent remark by another member of her family about an article of their clothing being destroyed by burning cigarettes. The memories came rushing back and shortly afterwards she gathered all the medicines she could find at home and swallowed them.

Particularly worrying in van Egmond's study is the finding that women who have been abused have a much greater probability of multiple suicide attempts later. They followed up the women for a year, and found that significantly more sexually abused women (48 per cent) had made further suicide attempts during this period than women with no history of sexual abuse (29 per cent). They found no difference within the group of sexually abused women between those who had been the victims of child sexual abuse (below 16) and those first abused when 16 or older. Similarly, and somewhat surprisingly, there was no difference in the pattern of suicidal behaviour between those who had one sexual abuse experience and those who had suffered multiple experiences. Neither did the history of sexual abuse affect the characteristics of the suicide attempt: for example, the method used, or the reasons to explain the suicide attempt, or even the suicidal intent.

This is an important finding. It undermines the argument that a suicide attempt by a woman with a history of such sexual abuse is a cry for help – the view that people with a history of such experiences come to believe that only an extraordinary measure such as a suicide attempt will gain attention. They did find that women who had been sexually abused had, as others had found, poor relationships with people around them, problems with achieving a sense of fulfilment from their lives and more problems in integrating with others. The difficulties with self-fulfilment suggest a reduction in ability to see meaning in their lives.

The fact that these women also predict (accurately) that they will be suicidal in the future is worrying for those interested in reducing suicidal behaviour. The pattern they show is consistent with the pattern of learned helplessness, where a person believes there will be nothing they can do to achieve fulfilment in their life in the future, or to stop nasty things happening to them. Even if small unpleasant events happen in their daily lives, they are likely to explain these in terms of *stable* factors (something that won't go away) and *global* factors (something that affects all areas of life). For example, if they get into an argument with a friend, they are likely to believe it was caused by their long-term difficulty in making a relationship with that person, and this same problem in making relationships will also affect their relationship with everyone else, including future boyfriends and girlfriends, future employers, and so on. In future stressful situations this pattern of attribution is likely to produce an overwhelming sense of helplessness and hopelessness, even when there might have been something the person could have done.

This is consistent with the results of a study that Raymond Jack and I conducted in which we found that women who attempted suicide were much more likely to attribute negative events in their lives in this stable and global way. They were followed up a few weeks later after most of the upset mood had subsided. Although the women had become less depressed, angry, anxious and confused, there had been little or no change in the pattern with which they explained negative events in their lives.

Short-term vulnerability factors

The *short-term vulnerability factors* could be taken to include all those factors in the current situation which, against the background of the long-term factors, put an additional burden on, or actively reduce, the person's coping ability in the month prior to an attempt. Whereas both parasuicide and depressed patients have increased incidence of life events compared with controls, the parasuicide group suffer a steep increase. Additionally, there is an increased incidence of physical illness (especially in women). Given the preponderance of sources of physical and emotional stress, it is not surprising that 57 per cent of attempters, including 82 per cent of adolescent attempters,[6] contact some helping agency (most of them the GP) during this crucial month.

Investigators have also found an increase in disturbance in relationships and work during this phase. Both male and female attempters report equivalent levels of relationship difficulties, though more males than females report significant work difficulties.

Employment status

A large study in Edinburgh, conducted by Stephen Platt,[7] examined a two-year cohort of male parasuicide cases, comparing the employed (n = 158) with the unemployed (n = 199). The unemployed men were less likely to be married, and less likely to live with their family; they were more likely to be of a lower social class, to have been given a diagnosis of abnormal personality, to misuse drugs, to be in trouble with the police and to have a criminal record. This conclusion has important implications for studies that have found a relationship between unemployment and parasuicide. Unemployment is undoubtedly an important additional stress on people, but we must be careful to be sure that the relationship is not caused by other factors (e.g. drug abuse) that predict both unemployment and parasuicide.

Substance abuse

Keith Hawton, in studying how many of the parasuicide cases his team see in Oxford City are abusing alcohol or drugs,[8] found that 41 per cent of men and 21 per cent of women were abusing alcohol. Sixteen per cent of men, and 6 per cent of women were habitually abusing drugs. In an earlier study of predictors of suicide in 15- to 24-year-olds, substance abuse emerged as a key predictor of suicide following an earlier parasuicide. Habitual abuse of alcohol and drugs provide the person with a readily available means of overdosing; it also decreases the sense of risk in doing so. Finally, the abuse can affect judgement so that normal ability to solve problems (which may already be suspect in this group) becomes even more impaired.

Precipitating factors

Precipitating factors are those events which occur in the few days prior to the attempt. Disharmony with 'key other' people in the person's life is the most common event; disharmony with relatives, anxiety about work/employment, financial difficulties and physical pain or illness are other reasons. One study[9] found that almost half their female patients had had a quarrel with their spouse or boyfriend in the week (mostly forty-eight hours) prior to the attempts. Some clinicians say that, for those who harm themselves repeatedly, different types of events precede self-harm of differing levels of lethality. This suggestion warrants further research.

Special dates

Days in the calendar that are special for some are likely to be the most difficult for others. When everyone else appears to be enjoying themselves, those who are depressed and hopeless are at their most vulnerable. We have already seen how parasuicide is sensitive to interpersonal disruption: boyfriend/girlfriend disputes are one of the major precipitating factors. Putting these facts together, one might predict that a date such as St Valentine's Day, 14 February, will be a time of particular vulnerability. To examine this, data was collected for parasuicide cases in Birmingham, England, for 1983–8.[10] The numbers on 14 February for the six years were 11, 11, 10, 10, 11 and 16 (a total of 69). Comparative figures for 7 February in each of the same years were 3, 6, 3, 7, 5 and 5 (a total of 29). St Valentine's Day doubled the number of parasuicides! Furthermore, the proportion of cases that were adolescents/young adults (aged 12–20) was 45 per cent on 14 February, but only 17 per cent (the national norm) on 7 February.

Why do events have such a catastrophic effect?

Events involving a key person, such as arguments with spouse or partner, are very common immediately preceding a parasuicide. Such events are particularly associated with parasuicide in the context of an ongoing difficulty, like a poor relationship. Relative to others, parasuicidal individuals have weak social support systems. When asked, they report interpersonal situations as their chief problems in living. The family background may be disturbed and current living conditions fraught with difficulties. Yet, when such people come for help, they often blame themselves. It sometimes seems as though the very act of seeking help confirms to them that everything is their fault. Why else, they think, would they be needing help?

Someone who has undergone long-term stress may suffer from a number of psychological difficulties. Not all who have suffered such stress will experience these, and there may be some who have these difficulties without their having been brought about by a difficult past. But the association between such difficulties and suicidal behaviour is well-established.[11]

Interpersonal problem-solving

Difficulty in solving problems involving relationships is an obvious effect of past interpersonal problems, and also the cause of further problems. To investigate deficits in problem-solving, the most commonly used measure is the Means–Ends Problem Solving Test (MEPS).[12] The MEPS includes a number of different social scenarios. For each scenario, people are given some initial circumstances in which a problem has to be solved (e.g. argument with boy/ girlfriend) and a positive outcome projected (the friend likes him/ her again). The task is to complete the middle part of the story, providing different ways in which the initial problem can be solved. The MEPS is scored for the numbers and quality of 'relevant means' (problem-solving steps).

Using this test with psychiatric in-patients who had expressed suicidal ideas and a group of equally depressed but non-suicidal in-patients, one study[13] found that suicidal patients were able to provide fewer than half as many ways of solving problems as the non-suicidal. This result might have come about because the MEPS items did not fit these people's experience, so the investigators also devised a modified test based on patients' personal situations. Patients were asked to provide a personal problem which had led to their being in hospital. Here, too, suicidal patients were more ineffective, their suggested ways of solving a problem often being irrelevant to its solution. Interestingly, they judged their proposed solutions as effective, but were realistic enough to note associated drawbacks.

Even when suicidal people come up with solutions, these differ from the type of solutions given by others.[14] People who have made a suicide attempt are more passive (relying on others for solutions) and less active in their problem-solving than either people who have had unenacted suicidal thoughts or non-suicidal psychiatric in-patients. This is one of the few studies to show differences between those with suicide ideation and those who go on to parasuicide. Others have found that parasuicide patients' solutions differ on a range of other qualitative aspects, including showing more avoidance, being less versatile and being less relevant.[15]

Given the increased number of stressful events known to precede a suicidal episode, the reduced ability to solve personal problems is especially problematic. An increase in such stresses, combined with a reduced ability to think of steps to solve the problems generated, increases the likelihood of suicidal behaviour. As we saw in the previous chapter, the person feels they have no further ideas about what to do over the problems in his or her life.

In suicidal adolescents, anger and the severity of initial suicidal behaviour predict repetition. Studies have shown where this anger may arise: repeated suicide attempts by adolescents are more likely if the young person has suffered loss of a parent and is living outside the parental home. Stress seems to be cumulative, building from early loss, through family disruption to interpersonal disputes occurring closer to the time of self-harm. Whether or not all such family backgrounds are this disrupted, it remains true that suicidal adolescents view their family as disengaged and inflexible. However, it is difficult to determine to what extent this view arises from the depression, anger and hopelessness of the adolescent who is suicidal for other reasons. Adolescents often judge their own internal and external problems in ways that differ from the judgement of either their parent or a health professional.

Nevertheless there is sufficient evidence of a link with objectively identified loss in the background to raise concern. Studies that extend the age range from 16 to 30 show that the greater stress experienced by younger people combines with a greater exposure to others that have self-harmed. One such study in Texas[16] found that 40 per cent of the suicide attempters had a family member who had made a suicide attempt (as opposed to 8 per cent of the control group). The parasuicide group was also more likely to have been arrested at some time, and more likely to have had a recent break-up with a girlfriend or boyfriend (38 per cent v. 10 per cent for both comparisons).

What is the basis for poorer problem-solving by suicidal individuals? A possible clue comes from research on problems such people have in their memories of events from their past (the main topic of Chapter 10, but relevant to mention here briefly). Patients who have recently taken overdoses tend to remember their past in a summarized, over-general way. For example, in response to a cue word such as 'happy', an overdose patient might say, 'When I'm out with friends'; that is, their memory response does not single out a particular event. In contrast, non-suicidal people retrieve specific, datable events, such as 'Last Friday when I went out for a meal with friends.' Parasuicide patients prefer to recall a general description of a class of events. They stop short of retrieving a specific memory contained within that general description, though after further prompting often recall such an event. As we will see in Chapter 10, getting 'stuck' at the stage of recalling a general category of events has implications for problem-solving.

Future-directed thinking and hopelessness

Suicidal individuals differ in the way they think about the future. When they talk about the future, they use less elaborate descriptions. Furthermore, they seem to think less far into the future, and psychological testing reveals that they use fewer future-tense verbs when asked to finish incomplete sentences. Roy Baumeister calls this disengagement from the future 'cognitive deconstruction', and attributes it to an attempt to avoid contemplating a painful future. In fact, Andrew MacLeod, Gillian Rose and I have found that suicidal individuals do not seem to spend time thinking of negative things that might happen in the future.[17] Instead, their thinking has a marked absence of any positive events they are looking forward to. The 'painful future' is not the anticipation of negative events, but rather a sense of hopelessness arising from the prospect of few positive events.

This hopelessness about the future plays a central role in suicidal behaviour. Many British and American studies report that hopelessness is more closely related than depression to suicidal behaviour. People seem able to bear depression so long as they are able to think the future might improve, but if they begin to feel hopeless, the risk of suicidal behaviour rises. If a person harms themselves on one occasion, the chance they will repeat the behaviour within the next six months is higher if they are more hopeless at the time of the first attempt. Even more worryingly, such highly hopeless individuals are at greater risk of completing suicide over the following ten years.[18]

Most studies on hopelessness have relied on Aaron Beck's Hopelessness Scale,[19] a self-report questionnaire which measures global attitudes towards the future, such as, 'My future seems dark to me.' But what is hopelessness? Our study examining the relative importance of positive and negative anticipation in hopelessness showed that parasuicide patients were less able to think of future positive events, but showed no difference from controls in being able to think of future negative events. Importantly, we also found that this problem with thinking of positive things to happen in the future was just as true for the immediate future (the next day and week) as for the long-term future (a year and ten years). The fact that highly hopeless people lack short-term routines, as well as long-term plans and goals, is important for therapy.

Reasons for living

Some years ago Marsha Linehan and her colleagues developed a Reasons for Living Inventory.[20] Compared to both the general population and psychiatric controls, parasuicide patients endorse fewer important reasons for living. Some of the main items from her scale can be seen in Table 6. The importance of knowing about such reasons for living is that individuals may be very motivated to commit suicide or parasuicide, yet not do so because they have reasons for staying alive. Reasons for dying may vary independently from reasons for living, and both need to be taken into account. There is particular danger when someone who has long been suicidal suddenly finds he or she has lost their reasons for living (e.g. their children, partner, religious faith).

Why do suicidal people have problems thinking about positive things that might happen in the future, which might give them a reason for living? An obvious answer is that poorer circumstances and reduced opportunities mean they actually have less to look forward to. Poorer upbringing, stressful events, marital and family disputes, poverty and unemployment all feature in the lives of many such people. A poorer outlook for the future may be realistic in many cases.

But our research has found that hopelessness adds significantly to the burden. Not everyone who has had such stress in their lives is suicidal. People differ widely in the extent to which their mind translates specific stress events into the general feeling that nothing

Table 6. Sample of items from Marsha Linehan's Reasons for Living Inventory.

Survival and coping beliefs
I still have many things left to do.
I want to experience all that life has to offer and there are many
    experiences I haven't had yet which I want to have.
I believe I can find a purpose in life, a reason to live.
No matter how badly I feel, I know that it will not last.
I am curious about what will happen in the future.
I believe killing myself would not really accomplish or solve anything.

Responsibility to family
It would hurt my family too much and I would not want them to suffer.
I have a responsibility and commitment to my family.

Child-related concerns
It would not be fair to leave the children for others to take care of.
I want to watch my children as they grow.

Fear of suicide
I am afraid of the actual 'act' of killing myself (the pain, blood, violence).
I am afraid of the unknown.

Fear of social disapproval
Other people would think I am weak and selfish.
I am concerned about what others would think of me.

Moral objections
My religious beliefs forbid it.
I am afraid of going to hell.

can be done, a sense of helplessness that goes much wider than the original situation. It is the over-generalization from one situation (that may indeed have been impossible to do anything about) to other situations (that might be solvable) which is at the root of hopelessness. If a person is hopeless that anything can be done about the second situation, they either do nothing or they give up too early. There is then a self-fulfilling prophecy ('I said nothing would help, and nothing has') which serves only to increase the sense of helplessness about any new situations.

The result is that such people may disengage from thinking about the future. This is adaptive in some ways. It may reduce how upset they feel right now, but at a cost. They are less likely to become aware of any future possibilities for happiness or to make plans which could bring about positive events. So whereas negative events appear to play a major role in the onset of suicidal feelings and hopelessness, whether people are able to anticipate positive events is important in determining how quickly they can recover from hopelessness.

Emotional experience

There is a strong, convincing relationship between emotional experience and suicidal behaviour. Interestingly, the emotions typical of individuals who parasuicide may be different from those of individuals who commit suicide. While both parasuicide and completed suicide are related to depression, parasuicidal behaviour appears to be related to anger whereas suicide may be more related to apathy or an absence of strong emotions. Parasuicide patients are more angry, hostile and irritable, compared to non-suicidal psychiatric patients and the general population, both before the parasuicide and after. Often the relationship with close family, friends and partners has deteriorated into hostility, demandingness and conflict. In contrast, persons who commit suicide seem to have been less angry, appearing apathetic and/or indifferent. Suicidal individuals appear unable to regulate their own emotional responses or experiences of emotional pain.

This does not mean that parasuicidal behaviour is merely an expression of hostility or manipulation intended to harm or get back at others. For many, the very experience of intense anger, especially if it is ongoing and they cannot seem to control it, is painful and intolerable. In some cases, most notably in self-cutting (see below), parasuicidal behaviour is itself used by the individual for emotion regulation. The regulating mechanisms here may be several, e.g. sleep (following an overdose), distraction from emotional stimuli or some sort of direct biological effect on the emotion system (e.g. by cutting or ingesting drugs).

Emotion regulation and self-cutting

Self-cutting as a form of self-harm needs to be dealt with separately, since people who harm themselves in this way appear to be a special group. They are in the minority, accounting for about 10 per cent of parasuicide episodes. Even so, this means that in the United Kingdom 10,000 episodes of self-cutting come to the attention of accident and emergency departments of hospitals each year.

Although the cutting may not be serious, repeated attempts to self-harm in this way may be associated with other personality problems: impulsivity, instability both in emotion (especially anger) and in interpersonal relationships (experienced as very intense). Such individuals are extremely sensitive to stress, especially that arising from interpersonal problems. They are particularly prone to look for any signs that others are abandoning them, and react to the situation as if the abandonment were already complete.

If such unstable emotion and unstable relationships dominate the person's life, they may be said to have a 'borderline personality'. The 'borderline' category refers to those who show impulsive self-damaging behaviour, unstable and intense interpersonal relationships, inappropriate and intense anger, problems with the experience of self (frequent crises of self-identity), extremely unstable emotions, chronic feelings of emptiness or boredom, and intolerance of being alone. They are desperate to have company, but may treat their companions with so much intensity (clinging behaviour alternating with anger) that they are left alone again very soon. Their physically self-damaging acts often occur after dissociative states (e.g. out-of-body experiences, experienced very negatively).

In the most extreme cases, all sense of self (of being a voluntary agent, having personal memories and body) disintegrates. In the resulting 'out-of-body' experience, the scene is viewed from another angle as observer rather than as participant. Experiences of alien control, and of hallucinations, may also occur following extreme or long-lasting stress associated with such a failure to control emotion that it simply escalates catastrophically. Such experiences occur spontaneously for the first time under extreme stress (such as sexual abuse, often found in the background of the most severe cases). Once such a dissociative experience has occurred, the threshold for the reappearance of such a phenomenon is lowered: it can be reactivated under conditions of future (and often lesser) stress.

People who cut themselves often report that the cutting is the only way they know that stops the intense feelings they are experiencing. One adolescent girl said it felt as if her head would explode unless she did something to stop it. She knew that cutting would stop it and put her back in touch with herself and her body. What explains the catastrophic escalation of emotion that often precedes self-cutting? To understand this we need to understand that negative emotion often results from breaking the rules one has set for oneself.

Consider the situation in which a person has been punished in the past for the expression of emotion. In relatively mild cases, this occurs every time a parent tells a child to 'pull yourself together'. The child may learn the lesson, 'It is shameful to display your emotions.' Or, in the most extreme case, a similar thing may happen in sexual abuse by an adult, where a child has been threatened with punishment if he or she becomes upset. In both the mild and the severe case, there is conflict between the expression of emotion and the suppression of emotion to avoid future punishment.

In later life, when the person feels emotional, the very fact of feeling emotion is breaking one of their rules. But breaking the rules causes more emotion, which then leads to attempts to suppress it. The result is a rapid escalation of negative emotion arising from such a positive feedback loop: the expression of emotion itself violates a goal ('do not feel or show emotion'), but the consequences of violating any goal is increased emotion. This leads to patients *feeling* upset but telling themselves they *should not feel upset* (one of the 'invalidation strategies' that maintains the very emotion it is designed to abolish, identified by Marsha Linehan in her treatment for people who suffer from 'borderline' symptoms). Linehan has also developed a number of specific strategies for dealing, in a non-harmful way, with the escalation of emotion. As part of her therapy, she may advise a patient to hold an ice cube in each hand until it melts. The pain of the cold ice is often sufficient substitute for self-cutting, but without the physical damage.

Concluding remarks

Several areas of psychological functioning contribute to increased risk of parasuicide, often by adding to the burden of already stressful lives. Suicidal behaviour is associated with poor problem-solving ability, especially active problem-solving; and with difficulty in recollecting events from the past in sufficient detail to help solve current interpersonal crises. It is also associated with hopelessness, the inability to imagine future positive occurrences (even for the next day, never mind the following weeks, months or years). Finally, suicidal people have difficulty regulating their emotion, a feature particularly strong in those with 'borderline' features, who may deliberately harm themselves many times.

Chapter 6

RATIONAL SUICIDE, EUTHANASIA AND MARTYRDOM

In the last few days of 1994, the State of Oregon was blocked in its bid to change the law to allow assisted suicide. From 8 December 1994, the terminally ill were to be allowed to ask their doctors to prescribe a lethal dose of medication. The move, which followed a state referendum held just over a year before, was always likely to cause controversy. Up to the last moment, it looked as if Oregon's decision in favour of assisted suicide would stand. However, reports said that many doctors were unprepared for the changes.

Agreeing with the move towards such a change, a 47-year-old man suffering from Aids said, 'Whose life is it anyway? It should be between me, my God and my doctor.' Elsewhere, a woman who two years previously had been told she would not live, argued against the measure. She was now well again, but said that at the time she was so depressed she would have asked a doctor to end her life.

The Catholic Church in the state vigorously opposed the change in the law, and continue to campaign against it. They argued that it would put the weak and the vulnerable at risk. At least six other states were considering similar legislation and were looking carefully at what happened in Oregon.

In Britain it remains illegal for anyone to aid someone to take their own life under any circumstances, but the courts are sometimes lenient. In December 1994, the courts decided not to prosecute a man who had administered a lethal dose of morphine to his terminally ill wife. In this case the Voluntary Euthanasia Society (Exit) were careful to distance themselves from supporting the man. They pointed out that there was no evidence that the wife had agreed to her life being ended in this way.

Developments in this area are occurring at some speed. Euthanasia was legalized in the Northern Territories of Australia in 1996. Assisted suicide was legalized in New York in April 1996 when two federal appeals courts lifted the ban on doctors helping their patients to die. Esther Fein of *The New York Times* posed a stark question: 'Will the right to die become the duty to die?' Let us look more closely at the arguments for and against.

The word *euthanasia* (from the Greek words *eu* and *thanatos*) literally means 'easy' or 'gentle death'. It was declared unethical by the World Medical Association in 1950, and to understand why we have to see its background. Two forms of euthanasia are normally distinguished. The first is *compulsory euthanasia*, or 'mercy killing', done without the consent of the person concerned, and mostly applied to grossly deformed children. For example, a Dutch gynaecologist in 1994 admitted killing a three-day-old girl at her parents' request. Her brain was only partly developed, she had spina bifida and partial paralysis, her limbs were malformed, and the doctor judged she faced a life of constant pain.

The usually cited problem with this is that it constitutes a 'slippery slope'; and that it violates the fundamental right to life, this being backed up by religious people's belief in life as God-given. However, a distinction is often made between an analgesic and lethal dosage of pain relief. An *analgesic dose* may have the unintended effect of shortening life, but a *lethal dose* has the direct intention of shortening life (the ethical doctrine of 'double effect' allows the first but not the second).

The second form of euthanasia is *voluntary euthanasia*. Here, individuals in sound mind ask that their life should be ended in the event of their becoming victims of irreversible illness. Advocates (e.g. the Hemlock Society in the United States or members of Exit) maintain that, with safeguards, the law should permit it and people should be supplied with the means to take their own life or a doctor should be authorized to end their life provided the request is made before witnesses.

The difficulty here is the assumption that we have the right to decide over our own life or death absolutely. The argument from these groups suggests that we 'own' our own lives. This argument has a long history.

Historical background

Charles Gilden in 1695, searching to justify the death of his friend Charles Blount, attempted to put Blount's death in the context of Stoic philosophy and dealt head-on with some of the classical arguments against suicide. Whereas Aristotle had argued that self-killing injured the state and was illegal even when no decree specifically forbade it, Gilden denied that society had the right to stop a man killing himself any more than it could rightfully prevent him emigrating. 'Now if I can leave any one particular Body Politick I have the same right to leave another and so on through all those of the World, and then by consequence I offend not, if by my Death I take myself away from all.'

Pythagoras' view was that men were put on earth like soldiers at their post. It was therefore 'desertion' to end one's own life. Gilden points out that, first, a simile is not an argument. Secondly, the simile is inexact since soldiers enlist willingly in the army in which they serve. Human beings do not choose to be born.

In the Middle Ages, Aquinas (1225–74) argued that God had instilled in humans an instinctual desire to preserve their own lives. Thus suicide violated natural law. Gilden replied this was not so. Rather, suicide was consistent with 'the precepts of Nature and Reason'. Human nature cannot desire the continuance of pain and suffering, so a life of such pain should be allowed to be ended. To end one's life in such circumstances is thus a greater good than self-preservation. It cannot therefore be contrary to natural law.

The arguments against suicide eventually lost their power to stop the inexorable march of change towards the secularization and medicalization of suicide. The arguments of the philosopher David Hume in his essay 'On Suicide', written in the early 1750s, were particularly telling. The essay was suppressed and Hume was forced to withdraw it from a print run of the *Five Dissertations* in which it was to appear. Nevertheless it did circulate and proved to be a robust statement of the secular view.

Hume argued (a) that in as much as one believed in the providence of a Deity, this 'providence appears not immediately in any operation, but governs everything by those general and immutable laws that have been established from the beginning of time'. (b) Human life and death do not depend on God, but rather on 'the general laws of matter and motion'. (c) It is not valid to argue that men and women are 'owned' by God, since people come into being through natural processes of reproduction. God no more owns us than do our parents. (d) People who commit suicide cannot break the laws of nature since all our powers (including those that empower us to take our own lives) are natural faculties. So, even employing them to kill oneself, one cannot 'encroach upon the plan of his providence or disorder the Universe'.

Finally Hume conceded that humans display a 'natural horror of death', but this does not thereby imply that such horror represents a 'general law of matter and motion'. Although such a horror might explain why suicide is not more common, it does not have the authority that natural-law theorists such as Aquinas implied.

Hume was consistent with other thinkers of the eighteenth century who wished to base their ethics on social rather than religious grounds. In this respect he needed to meet head-on the argument that somebody who commits suicide commits a wrong act because they let down society. Hume argued that 'a man who retires from life does no harm to society; he only ceases to do good; which, if it is an injury, is of the lowest kind'. The important calculation is to balance the good to society against the harm the suffering person sustains by continuing to live. Where the suffering person has grown so infirm as to become a burden to society, Hume concludes that suicide is a service which has benefits: 'resignation of life must not only be innocent, but laudable'.

What would Hume, as an empiricist, have made of the evidence which has now emerged about the aftermath of suicide? In many instances suicide appears to have such a devastating effect on the survivors that, if it were only the balance of suffering one were examining, one could conclude that the suicide was not ethically justifiable. By confining the argument to people under unbearable suffering, one may to some extent clarify the issue about the ethical dilemma, but this may not thereby be taken to imply that it covers all instances of suicide.

Anxiety about assisted suicide also has a long history. Indeed, we might say that the field of medicine was founded on the need to separate life-enhancing treatments from more superstitious beliefs that would allow the person to die in some circumstances. The Hippocratic oath arose from a situation in which Hippocrates and his disciples were not clearly distinguished as physicians from magicians and witch-doctors. Their oath that they would use treatment to help the sick according to ability and judgement, that they would never use it to injure people or wrong them, was devised at a time when the blurred distinction between physician and magician meant that these people could and did kill with impunity.

Physicians are taught to cure and to relieve suffering; psychologists are taught to help people find their way through the intolerable burdens of living. But we have no ultimate power over our patients and clients. In most cases the law will not require people to accept medical or psychological treatment against their wills. Provided a sufferer has received information from a physician and can make an informed consent, there is no legal obligation on a person to accept medical treatment.

Recent exponents of Hume's position

In our own day, there are many people who, standing in the tradition of David Hume, take a more liberal view than the original Hippocratic oath envisaged. Jack Kevorkian is such a person. He began to assist terminally ill people with suicide in the United States in 1990. The court's reaction at first was to prosecute for murder, but the jury refused to return such a verdict. The Michigan state senate then passed a temporary Bill making it illegal to help anyone commit suicide. Subsequently, three local judges and a Michigan Appeals Court panel declared the ban unconstitutional. In November 1994 Kevorkian assisted with his twenty-first suicide hours after the temporary law lapsed. By March 1996, he had assisted in twenty-seven suicides. The state senate has not been prevented, however, from voting overwhelmingly to introduce a new Bill to outlaw the practice of assisting suicide.

Another who stands in the Hume tradition is Derek Humphry, author of *Final Exit* and executive director of the Hemlock Society in America since 1980. The Hemlock Society, which believes in voluntary euthanasia, has 40,000 members in the United States. Derek Humphry reasonably points out that it is no good for psychologists and psychiatrists to say that all 40,000 members are mentally ill or depressed.

Hemlock members believe it is a basic civil liberty to be able to end their lives at the point they choose. They are offended by the thought of having to make their exit in a secretive and ultimately violent manner.[1] (However, this is expressed as a choice of euthanasia versus suicide rather than of euthanasia versus another form of living.)

Derek Humphry suggests that euthanasia may actually extend the life of someone who, on hearing a bad diagnosis, gets depressed and commits suicide prematurely. With the option of lawful medical euthanasia, they would realize that they need not end up a vegetable and might hang on longer. He claims that in the Netherlands an estimated 4 per cent die from euthanasia and the family are involved and consulted. Many have found it hard to disagree with Humphry's conclusions in many individual cases. He goes further and says that, if the law continues to forbid assisted suicide, it is putting an intolerable burden on the family.

Institutional support for assisted suicide: the Netherlands

The Netherlands is one country where doctors are given greater freedom to decide. In 1995, television audiences throughout the world were able to watch a Dutch doctor featured in a television documentary, *Death on Request*. Dr Wilfred van Oyjen carries out this 'good death' three or four times a year. The film featured a man who had developed Lou Gehrig's disease, which brings about incurable degenerative wasting of the muscles. His feet and legs became paralysed first, then his right shoulder and arm, then his face. He and his family realized that, unless some decisive action was taken, he faced death by suffocation, as the weakening muscles of his chest finally collapsed.

His requests for euthanasia were repeated as the guidelines in Holland prescribe (a voluntary, well-considered and lasting request to die). Dr van Oyjen is one of those who feels it would be letting his patient down to refuse his request. The guidelines also prescribe that there must be no other solution acceptable to the patient; that the time and manner of the death must not cause unnecessary suffering to others (such as next of kin), and the doctor must prescribe and administer the right drugs.

This contrasts with the situation in the United Kingdom, where it is accepted that doctors often use the 'doctrine of double effect' to deal with situations of unbearable suffering. This permits doctors to use drugs in sufficient quantities to relieve suffering, even if that hastens death, so long as they do not intend to kill. According to the Voluntary Euthanasia Society (Exit), one survey of British doctors showed that 50 per cent had been asked by a patient for help to die. Of these, one third of the doctors said they had complied.

This is not ethical, according to Dr van Oyjen. Such surreptitious euthanasia can take several weeks, and is dishonest. It also means that the patient can die in delirium brought about by huge doses of morphine. 'I am giving people the possibility to make choices. What kind of quality of life, and death, do they want? Death is not always awful. With a good doctor, death can be faithful, like a good friend.' Perhaps most importantly, the doctor can choose the right moment, when he judges that the person and his family are most at peace with the ending of life. Wilfred van Oyjen will take hours, days if necessary, waiting for the right moment after the decision has been taken. He feels it essential to get close to the family if a 'good death' is to be brought about.

When the arguments are expressed in this way, they seem very compelling. Yet many have continued to maintain that assisted suicide is either intrinsically wrong or socially undesirable.

Arguments against euthanasia

Consent

One argument against euthanasia is that a terminally ill patient may not be in a state, at the point near death, to be able to withdraw consent. Suppose someone was to agree, before witnesses, family and doctor that, in the event of breakdown of bodily function, active steps should be taken to end their life. Once they have deteriorated, how could they ever withdraw that consent should they change their mind? The right (at any time) to withdraw consent from or change one's mind about a medical procedure is seen by many to be paramount. Yet, with the very frail, this right may be denied because of their frailty.

On the other hand, this raises the question of the prolongation of life, and with it a number of imprecise issues. Should we withhold or continue efforts to prolong life, for example by using modern life-support equipment? Under these circumstances, ethical theories usually refer to the *ordinary/extraordinary principles*. That is, there is an obligation to use ordinary means but no strict obligation to use extraordinary means to prolong life. Extraordinary means refer to those means which do not offer a reasonable hope of cure or remission or those which require excessive hardship to obtain. So most ethical theories assume there are limits to preserving life, but that there is a presumption of a duty to preserve life in most circumstances. Ethical principles need to be brought to bear.

The first principle cited is usually that of autonomy and individual conscience. The patient's attitude is primary, but if the patient cannot be consulted, there is a secondary role for others on the grounds of principles of beneficence and social justice. Proxy decisions are therefore possible, indeed necessary in the case of life-support machines. In these cases there is a rank order of people to be consulted, the family, the physicians, a designated committee, and the courts (in that order). These make the decisions based on 'substitutive judgement' standards, which involve asking what the patients themselves would have decided, based if at all possible on the patients' own expressed wishes.

Slippery slope arguments

The World Medical Association's decision in 1950 to declare euthanasia unethical was made on the grounds that it would undermine trust between patient and doctor, and between patient and family just when they are at their most vulnerable. For every time a doctor assists someone to die to ease their burden, or that of their families, there arises the possibility that someone, somewhere will seek the death of someone for the wrong reasons. This is the slippery slope argument, which asserts that a small change to allow assisted suicide would have wider and undesirable consequences. The first of the two most often cited undesirable consequences is where old and infirm people are seen as a burden on their families, even more urgent at a time when there is much in the news about old people being a burden on society because of increased life expectancy.

It is not possible to speak of general policies of euthanasia without this being raised as a specific issue in many individual households. Talk of euthanasia in a household where there is an older relative could fuel talk about them being a burden. In his article on euthanasia,[2] Humphry quotes the ex-governor Richard Lamm of Colorado, who made a speech about the rationing of healthcare costs, suggesting the elderly took more than their fair share. Humphry quotes Lamm to show that economics will force this on the public agenda sooner rather than later. But many would consider that where economic considerations are brought in is when the euthanasia argument is at its weakest.

The second most often cited undesirable consequence is that people who are depressed will make what appears to be a rational request to end their life. In a controversial case in 1994 in the Netherlands, a doctor assisted a woman to die who appeared, on all accounts, to have been depressed. This raised an important issue. People may consider it is never justified to assist the suicide of someone who has a condition, a symptom of which is itself a wish to die.

Are such slippery slopes likely to occur? Those who argue against euthanasia say the 'slippery slope' is already taking place in the Netherlands. Guidelines issued for doctors are being overstepped, they claim, second opinions are regularly abandoned, and when a euthanasia death is reported, there is rarely an investigation. Indeed, those who oppose euthanasia allege that many euthanasia deaths are not recorded even on the death certificate; all evidence in these matters falling under the control of the physician. This, it is suggested, does not provide satisfactory safeguards against abuse.

No man is an island

Another argument against 'rational suicide', assisted or not, is the 'no man is an island' argument (it is ironic that the quote comes from a meditation by John Donne, who believed that suicide was justifiable, and argued so strongly in *Biathanatos*).

One version of this argument is that by ending our life we deny our family and society the opportunity to fulfil their duty of care to us. Another version is more simple: those who would justify committing suicide on the grounds that their life is their own property, are failing to take into account that each of our lives is shared by parents, brothers and sisters, partners, children, neighbours and friends, colleagues at work and so on. Not to take account of their reaction to our death, or worse, to make assumptions (e.g. that they would be relieved of a burden) without checking, is hardly to take a 'rational' decision.

In what way does suicide affect others? Research shows how suicide affects family, friends and community. It can be the worst of all deaths in its impact on survivors. It causes grief they may never resolve, guilt in a way no other death does, even raising the risk of suicide in others. A truly rational approach to self-killing or assisted suicide must take account of all these things. If a rational person says, 'But no one would mind if I ended my life,' then it will be inappropriate to call it rational unless they have sought evidence. It is irrational to make a 'mind-reading error', to presume opinions without checking.

Perhaps, though, in the case of assisted suicide, especially of people who belong to societies such as Hemlock, the family are fully involved so the death has less impact. However, Humphry himself cites an 85-year-old woman, a member of Hemlock, whose husband had died the previous year. When she took an overdose and died, a neighbour phoned him in distress, and Humphry felt he was able to reassure him. However, two years later, when he was giving a talk in Hawaii, a young man asked his views on suicide in the elderly and turned out to be a grandson of the woman. At a meeting later in Dallas, a woman asked a similar question and turned out to be a daughter. Both said they had come to the Hemlock meetings to find out more about the organization to which their relative had belonged. Humphrey claims they found it cathartic to share their experience, since 'they were still coming to terms with the manner of the death'.[3]

This story supports the idea that such a death never occurs in isolation but always has knock-on consequences. It is, as one physically handicapped campaigner against euthanasia put it, like a delicate game of pick-up-sticks. You carefully pick up another stick, hoping not to disturb the intricate web, but just when you think you've succeeded, your independent action ends up jiggling the fragile balance and everything falls apart.

Rational versus depressive suicide: Arthur Koestler

Perhaps the most difficult dilemma is to distinguish between those who ask for suicide because they are depressed, and those who ask for it when 'of sound mind'. Take one often cited example of someone who decided rationally to kill himself: Arthur Koestler, who died by suicide with his wife Cynthia in 1983. Because he was vice-president of the Voluntary Euthanasia Society (Exit) and wrote a preface to its publication, *Guide to Self-deliverance*, he is commonly said to be the paradigm case of rational suicide.

Yet in his own prolific writings he shows that he suffered much from depression, punctuated by bouts of mania. His uncle had committed suicide, and in his autobiographical book, *Arrow in the Blue*, he tells of his own troubled life.[4] He was an only child, born when his mother was 35. She was very possessive, yet capricious in her moods. There were often abrupt changes from effusive tenderness to violent temper. He talks about being tossed from 'the emotional climate of the Tropics to the Arctic and back again'. Plagued by guilt and often feeling he deserved to be punished, he felt bewildered and rejected, and suffered suicidal depressions and recurrent suicidal fantasies. He attempted suicide twice, once at 29 by coal gas, the second time in prison in Lisbon by an overdose.

At the end, suffering from leukaemia and Parkinson's disease, he killed himself and his wife did likewise. However, one week before the suicide, Cynthia had told a friend that Arthur was having hallucinations. Cynthia herself had a family history of suicide, her father having committed suicide when she was 10. It is also clear from her writings that she had seriously contemplated suicide before. Professor Robert Goldney of Adelaide University, in a seminal paper in 1986,[5] points out the irony that, had Koestler owned a copy of the *Guide to Self-deliverance* in the 1930s, the world would have been denied the vast majority of his writings.

Rational and irrational: can a distinction be made?

Joseph Richman, Professor Emeritus at the Albert Einstein College of Medicine, New York, argues that to drive a wedge between rational suicide and other forms of suicide is illusory.[6] All suicides have features in common. There is usually evidence of a crisis and often the confrontation of loss and separation; there is the role of others. To make a dichotomy between the sick and the healthy obscures the issue. When there is a crisis around illness, loss and death, all unresolved problems and conflicts of the ill person come to the fore and can be seen as overwhelming.

Many believe that being terminally ill is itself sufficient reason to want to die. The terminally ill find that their depression is often seen as natural and therefore goes untreated. Yet deep sadness is natural, while depression is more than sadness. It brings with it a sense of guilt, of being a burden, of worthlessness, and a feeling of failure. Further the person often believes that no one will want to see them in their condition, so there is no point in contacting anybody. They may feel guilty about things they have done, or about situations or relationships that remain unresolved, and the depression will ensure it is not worth trying to resolve them.

Is there a role for therapy here? The evidence suggests there is. People can, in fact, overcome their depression even within the context of a terminal illness, evidence the hospice movement has been citing for some years.[7] Do people seeking assisted suicide need a psychotherapist? Proponents of rational suicide discourage people from seeking help on the grounds they are not mentally ill. This is probably right, but you don't have to be crazy to see a therapist any more than you have to be stupid to go to school.[8]

All wishes to die represent in some degree a problem perceived as insoluble except through death. In that situation one needs to respect a person's autonomy. But personal autonomy should not be confused with isolation and loss of social cohesion. How can we judge whether or not someone is in control of their own actions? Depression leaves little room for argument. We know it affects chemical pathways in the brain and results in lack of energy, lack of pleasure and lack of interest in social activities and social contacts. It also results in recurrent thoughts of death or suicide. Compounding this is the sense of hopelessness that occurs in many depressions: a foreshortening of the future and an inability to see anything to look forward to. Depression therefore leaves little choice. It pushes the person, impels them to certain actions. It is not open to reasonable argument.

Proponents of rational suicide say that people have chosen this option and are not depressed. In that case they must expect to be able to discuss rationally the pros and cons of their actions. They must also expect that their reasons will be questioned. The major presupposition, that each of us has an overall right to decide on our own life, can be questioned, and only where the full social and family context is taken into account can it ever be justified deliberately to shorten a life.

Martyrdom

The definition of martyrdom is closely tied to the group that shares the belief of the one who dies. A suicide-bombing by an Islamic fundamentalist may be called martyrdom by his or her own group, but is to the non-Muslim merely terrorism. Each group, religious or political, has its martyrs. They differ in a number of respects from the types of suicide so far considered.

Most people who commit suicide are depressed when they do so; they see death as the end to their suffering. One of two feelings usually predominates in the mind of the person who is suicidal in this depressive sense, both stemming from hopelessness. The first is that they have been abandoned by everyone; the second that they are a burden to everyone, especially to those they love. Contrast this with the martyr. They see hope, and believe in a cause. Although there are many different contexts for martyrdom, all martyrs believe that by their death they are bringing about some combination of the following gains: (a) advancing a cause by inspiring members of their own group; (b) harming the enemy; (c) delivering others from suffering (but not suffering that has been caused by them, as in depressive suicide); and (d) gaining entrance to an afterlife.

In this sense, martyrdom is a paradigm of Durkheim's altruistic suicide. These people kill themselves because they are totally submerged in their groups. Death for them is a duty. They are seen as making heroic sacrifices for the group or its leadership. In altruistic suicide, the individual's life is not their own property. His or her own goals of behaviour emanate from the external source, the group.

Is there a distinction between the suicide bomber and others who put their lives at risk for what they believe in? There seems to be a continuum between altruistic suicide and other forms of altruism in which a person risks his or her life for their group and is prepared to accept death as the unavoidable consequence of performing some act of bravery, charity, justice, mercy, or piety. The difference is that, in these cases, the person does not will their own death. If there were any other way, they would take it.

Are suicide bombers, 'martyrs' to their own cause, psychiatrically disturbed – or is it simply belief in a cause that drives them on? Altruistic suicide is not performed through madness – the person, as far as we know, is in full possession of his or her faculties. Indeed, it would not have the impact it clearly does on the group if it were suspected that the person was mentally ill.

Is martyrdom always associated with religious faith? Belief in God is clearly an important component of some acts of martyrdom in that it provides a moral context. Most martyrs moreover have a belief in an afterlife, even when the belief in a god is not conventional. Those who took part in the mass suicide in Jonestown, Guyana, in November 1978, led by Jim Jones, believed in reincarnation. But they also believed that the revolutionary principles they stood for would achieve immortality through their deaths. Jones said, 'We are not committing suicide; we are committing a revolutionary act.' The followers of David Koresh had also planned a mass suicide, with hand grenades, if he died during the battle with law-enforcement officers at Waco, Texas. One witness at the inquest said that following Koresh's death, 'We were all to be translated . . . come out of our bodies and go to heaven.'

But not all the deaths that occurred or were planned in these contexts were suicide. Some people in Jonestown were murdered. Other suicides there appear to have been not so much altruistic as fatalistic. Many were malnourished after a poor diet, and their emotional disturbance was heightened because the community thought it was under attack. In a chilling parallel, a witness from Waco said that if any follower had been afraid of killing themselves, another could do it with a shotgun.

The kamikaze

Learning about the mind of the martyr seems impossible since they are not here to study. However, there are some 'wartime martyrs' who, though they volunteered to die, escaped death: Japanese kamikaze (literally 'divine tempest') pilots who survived when their planes were shot down on their way to a target in the Pacific and were awaiting recall to another suicide mission when the war ended.

By the last year of the war, the US Navy thought itself invincible in the Pacific, but the kamikaze shook its confidence. So keen were the young Japanese pilots to participate in this 'spirit of the Samurai' that some signed their papers in their own blood to try and increase chances of selection. By the end of 1944, over 500 kamikaze missions had been flown against the US Fleet, but Japan was still losing. A new élite, 'The Thunder Gods', was formed to pilot aircraft equipped with large missiles. These turned out to be too cumbersome and the pilots were shot down before they could reach their targets. The Thunder Gods were therefore asked to undertake a different sort of mission: to take ordinary planes and crash them into the fleet.

On 1 April 1945 the United States invaded Okinawa, and on the 6th, after an ominous silence, the US Fleet was attacked by up to 350 planes at a time. By the end of June, after about 2,000 kamikaze missions, thirty-six Allied ships had been sunk, ten times as many damaged; 500 Allied personnel were dead and 4,800 wounded.

What was the motivation of the kamikaze pilots? By the accounts of those who remain, and their officers who assigned them, they had an attitude to death characteristic of many martyrs. First, they believed that obedience gave meaning to self-sacrifice. They had come to the point when to give up one's life for one's country was the highest honour. Secondly, they believed they were not going to die at all. Their souls would go to Yasakuni, a special place for those who die fighting for their country; a special place also reserved for the Emperor. As one said, 'Even if you did die, you felt you would still be alive to describe it.' The widows of these men paid their respects and went to honour their 'god-like' husbands.

But it wasn't always quite so straightforward for the pilots. People who interviewed them subsequently found that a different, more sombre mood sometimes emerged. Some appear to have brooded about their death, complaining that the waiting went on for ever. Others said it felt as if they were being sentenced to death. Still others questioned whether they had been in their right mind when they volunteered. They rejoiced for the camera, but harboured doubts off camera. They dealt with such feelings by reattributing any emotions to things other than the fear of dying. One pilot said that at the time he'd find himself crying in the night, but not because he was frightened. He couldn't say he really ever knew why he was crying. Perhaps it was because most kamikaze pilots never reached the age of 20.

Concluding remarks

Can suicide be rational? There is little doubt it can. Durkheim argued strongly in favour of this position in 1897, and there is no reason to disagree. Many endorse the aims of those societies that promote euthanasia as a rational, compassionate end to life. Many others have no difficulty accepting that there are situations, as in wartime, when there is a very thin line between those prepared to put their lives at risk for the good of their country and those who go out on a suicide mission. As soon as a society, a nation or a subculture, gives permission to its members to kill on its behalf, it will find many volunteers, and as we shall see, violence against another and against oneself have similar psychodynamic and biological roots.

Chapter 7

PSYCHODYNAMICS, BIOLOGY AND GENETICS

There is no one reason why people kill themselves. Suicide is the final common pathway for many human problems. But there are also biological factors, and some of these may have a genetic component. I shall now build upon the discussion of psychiatric, social and psychological perspectives on suicide (Chapter 3) and parasuicide (Chapter 5) to review psychoanalytic and biological perspectives.

Psychoanalytic perspectives

The starting-point for psychoanalytic work on suicide and parasuicide is Freud's 1917 paper, *Mourning and Melancholia*, the aim of which was to draw a comparison between severe depression and the normal experience of mourning following loss. In suicide, the life instinct is overcome by more powerful forces, leading to a reaction that is an even more extreme form of the self-deprecation found in depressed people. Mourning is a normal means of coping following loss of a loved person (the 'loved object'). However, people who have lost others on whom they depended too much for their own sense of self (a 'narcissistic object-choice') find the experience of loss impossible to tolerate. The anger of normal grief is, for these, a rage of murderous proportions. Identification with the lost object (internalization) means that the object that is to be murdered becomes part of the ego.

If one listens patiently to a melancholic's many and various self-accusations, one cannot in the end avoid the impression that often the most violent of them are hardly at all applicable to the patient himself, but that with insignificant modifications they do fit someone else, someone whom the patient loves or has loved or should love . . . So we find the key to the clinical picture: we perceive that the self-reproaches are reproaches against a loved object (individual) which have been shifted away from it on to the patient's own ego . . .

There is no difficulty in reconstructing this process. An object-choice, an attachment of the libido to a particular person, had at one time existed; then owing to a real slight or disappointment coming from this loved person, the object-relationship was shattered. The result was not the normal one of a withdrawal of the libido from this object and a displacement of it on to a new one, but something different . . . it was withdrawn into the ego. In this way, the object loss was transformed into an ego loss.[1]

Since outwardly directed reproaches towards the lost object are not possible, they turn into self-reproaches and the wish to harm oneself. When the rage is sufficiently intense, it will lead to strong urges towards self-destruction.

If the love for the object – a love which cannot be given up though the object itself is given up – takes refuge in narcissistic identification, then the hate comes into operation on this substitutive object, abusing it, debasing it, making it suffer and deriving sadistic satisfaction from its suffering.

It is this sadism alone that solves the riddle of the tendency to suicide which makes melancholia so interesting – and so dangerous . . . No neurotic harbours thoughts of suicide which he has not turned back upon himself from murderous impulses against others . . . The ego can kill itself . . . if it is able to direct against itself the hostility which related to an object and which represents the ego's original reaction to objects in the external world.[2]

In a later discussion of suicide, Freud introduces the concept of the death instinct (Thanatos). He defined this as a drive, commonly seen in nature, to reinstate the former state of affairs, the return of all organic or living matter to its inorganic unorganized state. This view sees life as a preparation for death, with the death instinct as a drive to its end. Freud uses the concept to explain why the super-ego develops such a harshness towards the ego in melancholia.

We find that the excessively strong super-ego which has obtained a hold upon consciousness rages against the ego with merciless violence, as if it had taken possession of the whole of the sadism available in the person concerned. Following our view of sadism, we should say that the destructive component had entrenched itself in the super-ego and turned against the ego. What is now holding sway in the super-ego is, as it were, a pure culture of the death instinct, and in fact it often enough succeeds in driving the ego into death.[3]

At times Freud expressed uncertainty about the status of the death instinct he had invoked, saying he did not know how far he believed in it and would not seek to persuade others. However, he continued to find it a useful idea, eventually changing the concept of masochism from being simply the opposite of dominant aspects of sadism to a primary instinct in its own right; a basic drive towards subjection and submission, and in the most extreme form a drive to embrace death. (Chapter 9 will show how many of the same ideas have emerged in sociobiology.)

Later psychoanalytic writers have built upon Freud's observations. Menninger asserted that every suicide had three elements: the wish to kill (originating in the death instinct), the wish to be killed (originating in the super-ego's masochistic need for punishment), and the wish to die (originating in a relatively fundamental desire to return to the womb). Such approaches emphasize the aggressive nature of suicide, but careful attention to the fantasies of suicidal patients shows that aggressive impulses are not always the most prominent.

Patients speak about a wish to join a dead relative with whom they identify strongly. These reunion fantasies are not readily explained simply on the basis of self-directed aggression. They appear to result from libidinal rather than aggressive wishes, pleasurable rather than masochistic fantasies. Other patients have fantasies about rebirth following their own death, a rebirth they can hasten by destroying this self (compare the examples of martyrdom in Chapter 6). Still others appear to be looking for a sense of mastery, or even omnipotence over an impossible situation, and their death is the only element in life that they feel they have retained control over. Some believe they will still, in some sense, be present after their death to 'see what happens next', and, in a spirit of revenge that is sometimes present as part of suicidal thoughts, able to experience pleasure in the distress their death might cause others. The inconsistency between death as escape into oblivion on the one hand and a continued existence in which the pain of others can be experienced on the other is not apparent to the suicidal person in their confusion.[4]

Object-relations approach

Freud had suggested that suicide was an attack on the love-object, now lost, that had been internalized. Melanie Klein extended these ideas, suggesting that the person was motivated by the wish to preserve the good aspects of the internalized object (now a valued part of the self).[5] The inwardly directed attack was therefore aimed mainly at the bad part of the object. Since aggression mainly arose from the death instinct, there was a danger that such destructive forces might destroy a good object. Guntrip developed these ideas further, distinguishing between depressive suicide and schizoid suicide.[6] Depressive suicide comes about as the result of hatred redirected towards the self from the hated and loved object (as Freud had argued). By contrast, schizoid suicide comes about when the person finds themselves facing the loss of self, and begins to fantasize about death as a path to rebirth.

Early in a child's development, it is in a symbiotic relationship with its mother and the child's idea of self and of mother are not yet differentiated. Later there will come inevitable separation and individuation, where self and object are differentiated. What happens if this transition is not completed satisfactorily? One outcome might be that the person will tend to become involved in relationships where the other party is not treated as a separate and unique individual, but as part of the self. This choice of friend or partner has been called 'symbiotic object-choice' corresponding to the 'narcissistic object-choice' in Freud's writings.[7] Suicide, according to this analysis, involves not only ridding self of bad internal objects, but the fusion with the earlier 'symbiotic mother' of pre-individuation infancy.

The hypotheses about suicidal behaviour that invokes fantasies about return to infantile dependence on the mother have been extensively developed by attachment theorists. According to Bowlby,[8] infants respond to even brief separations with distress, and if such separations and returns are not predictable or controllable, there develops a style of anxious and insecure attachments. These styles, resulting from the breakdown of the reciprocal interaction between child and primary care-giver, may persist, and can even affect the way the child, when grown up, relates to his or her own children.

Secure attachments in infancy are the primary means by which the child learns to regulate his or her own emotions. In the absence of mature self-regulatory structures, such children come to depend too much on others, or ideas about others that have been internalized, for comfort. Such a person will become over-sensitive to abandonment; vulnerable to crises of aloneness which give way to self-contempt and murderous rage. Suicidal behaviour in this context can be seen as an interpersonal act, an (albeit maladaptive) means of procuring attachment, signalling distress to others in the environment and punishing them for their actual or perceived rejection of the person.

John Maltsberger[9] summarizes the sorts of ideas about death that might be apparent in the suicidal person:

1. Suicide is a gateway leading into a dreamless sleep (nothingness).
2. It will effect a reunion with someone or something which has been lost.
3. It will be a way of escaping from a persecutory enemy, interior or exterior.
4. It will destroy an enemy who seems to have taken up a place in the patient's body or some other part of him or herself.
5. It will provide a passage into another, better world.
6. One can get revenge on someone else by abandoning him or her or by destroying his or her favourite possession (one's own body), and one can then watch him or her suffer from beyond the grave.

An underlying theme is the idea that one's body is a prison from which suicide promises an escape – particularly true of those who suffer physical pain. Maltsberger advises therapists to assess the extent to which their suicidal clients have lost the capacity to tell whether or not their own body is a part of themselves. 'Does he feel at home in it and take it for granted as an integrated self aspect, or does he experience it as an alien cage in which he is confined, a cage belonging to, or even identified with, someone else?' This aspect of the psychodynamics of suicide takes us a long way from simply seeing such death as an expression of anger turned towards the self. Importantly, it raises the theme of escape. The notion of escape is important because it builds bridges to other approaches to suicide. Meanwhile inescapable stress has biological consequences, which might be triggered by stress that is *believed* to be inescapable (which introduces psychological mechanisms).

Biological approaches

From the brain, and from the brain only, arise our pleasures, joys, laughters and jests, as well as our sorrows, pain, grief and tears . . . It is the brain which makes us mad or delirious; inspires us with dread and fear, whether by night or day; brings sleeplessness, mistakes, anxieties, absent-mindedness, acts that are contrary to our normal habits. These things that we suffer from all come from the brain, including madness.

So wrote Hippocrates, who lived between 460 and 377 B C. He had, as this quote from his book *On Sacred Disease* shows, an approach to mental disorder that feels very modern.

To understand the possible role of the brain in general and suicidal depression in particular, we need to understand the role of neurotransmitters. Neurones (nerve cells of which there are billions in the brain) typically consist of a cell body, dendrites (finely branched structures connected to the cell body), and axons. Electrical impulses are transmitted from one neurone to another by means of neuro-chemicals which bridge the gap at the point of contact between one cell and the next (the synapse). Across this synaptic gap or cleft, neurotransmitters such as dopamine or noradrenalin (norepi-nephrine) travel, released from one neurone and triggering an electrical impulse at the 'receptor' of the next neurone. Brain scientists have so far discovered over fifty different types of neurotransmitter, and each of these may act alone or in combination with others to serve different pathways in the brain.

One is at once able to see a number of ways in which the delicate balance of brain activity could go wrong. First, there may be too much or too little neurotransmitter present at the synapse. Secondly, the receptor of the 'receiving' neurones may be too dense or too sparse, so that even a normal amount of neurotransmitter has too much or too little effect. Thirdly, there may be other neurochemicals that may block or excite the action of another, either inhibiting the neurone from firing as it should or facilitating its action.

For many years it has been believed that depression is associated with a depletion of certain neurotransmitters. Most interest has focused on norepinephrine and serotonin. A reduction of the activity in brain pathways which rely on these neurochemicals may be responsible for the changes in appetite, sleep and energy levels in depression. Antidepressant medication was thought to work by making more neurotransmitter available at the synapse, by blocking the reabsorption ('reuptake') into the presynaptic neurones. This relatively simple theory has always had a number of difficulties, the major problem being that the action of the antidepressant in blocking reuptake is relatively quick, but antidepressants take ten days to two weeks to have their therapeutic effects. Another problem is that more careful measurement of norepinephrine has shown it is not reduced in depressed patients, and may even be increased in some.[10]

Interest has therefore shifted away from simple ('too little neuro-transmitter') theories to consider instead the changes that take place in the density and sensitivity of the receptors – how well these are able to respond to the amount of neurotransmitter available. Such changes at the receptor site take longer, and may explain why antidepressants take so long to begin to alleviate mood. It is now believed that antidepressants alter the complex interaction between different inhibitory and facilitatory pathways.

In suicidal behaviour, the neurotransmitter serotonin has been thought to be involved. Evidence comes from a number of sources. Low levels of the product of the metabolism of serotonin (the 'metabolite', 5-HIAA) have been found in the cerebrospinal fluid (CSF) of suicide attempters, measured after a lumbar puncture. Asberg and colleagues[11] found this was true of people who used more violent means to harm themselves, consistent with parallel findings that reduced levels of serotonin, or reduced metabolism of serotonin (not the same thing), are found in violent offenders – those who take their anger out on others. Low levels of 5-HIAA in the cerebrospinal fluid are associated with suicidality and impulsivity both on behavioural and self-report measures, both in depressed people and in patients with personality disorder, schizophrenia and alcoholism, and in impulsive violent offenders.[12] This has given rise to the suggestion that serotonin affects tendencies to act with impulsive aggression rather than being associated with the direction of such aggression. Studies suggest that the serotonergic involvement is with trait (permanent predisposition) rather than state (transient, situation-specific) features. Thus some people have a life-long tendency to behave in an impulsive way. Then, if depression produces a further temporary lowering in brain serotonin, there will be increased tendency to act impulsively in response to negative events.

If violent suicide is associated with abnormalities in the serotonin pathways in the brain, might this be detected at post-mortem? Establishing the facts remains extremely difficult. The method by which someone has died (overdose, carbon-monoxide poisoning) can affect the physical state of the brain at death, and the delay before post-mortem also affects the chances of discovering subtle differences between suicide victims and controls. Error can also creep in through factors such as abnormal diet, or drug and alcohol use.

However, most researchers agree that some sort of association between serotonin function and violence (either internally or externally directed) exists.[13] Relevant to this is the finding that murderers have a suicide rate several hundred times greater than people of the same age and sex who have not committed murder, and that people found guilty of violent and impulsive crimes, such as arsonists, have low serotonin levels and a very high incidence of violent suicide attempts. Crimes that are premeditated are not so closely associated with serotonin levels, emphasizing once again the importance of impulsivity.[14] Of course, all these groups tend to share other psycho-social risk factors such as early loss, disrupted family background, alcohol and substance-abuse problems. What has not been established yet is whether biochemical studies have accounted for variance in the suicide statistics that cannot be accounted for in these other ways.

The fact that biological findings have crossed diagnostic boundaries (serotonin involvement is associated with violent suicidal behaviour in depressed people, those with a diagnosis of schizophrenia, alcoholics and those with a personality disorder) implies that suicidality should be assessed and treated in its own right, rather than relying on the treatment of the psychiatric disturbance in which it occurs. Another advantage of the biological approach is that it would provide a means by which genetic influences might be mediated.

Genetic influences

Suicidal behaviour is more common in the relatives of completed suicides, suggesting a genetic component, but people related to each other commonly share much more than genes. They also share a similar environment, with all its stresses and difficulties. Furthermore, if a suicide has occurred in a family, there is the possibility of later imitation, and a feeling that the family is 'tainted' with a suicide history which makes other members more likely to see this type of death as a way out of difficulties they themselves encounter.

Since identical twins share the same genetic make-up, such twins should be more alike with respect to suicidal tendencies than non-identical twins. Unfortunately, the evidence is contradictory. Roy and colleagues[15] found that identical twins had a concordance rate for suicide of 13.2 per cent (the percentage of twins who show the same behaviour as their other twin), compared with a concordance rate of 0.7 per cent in non-identical twins. However, a study presented at the World Congress of Psychiatric Genetics in Cardiff in 1995 found no evidence of any difference between identical and non-identical twins. To date, there is insufficient evidence to resolve this discrepancy. The balance of evidence still favours higher concordance rates for suicide in identical twins.

A major single gene effect is unlikely. More likely is a multiple gene which leads to an increased risk of suicide, but needs environmental triggers. These other effects are likely to outweigh the genetic effects. Most twins, even in Roy's study, were 'discordant' with respect to suicidal behaviour. Also, most of the suicides in the twins who were concordant had psychiatric disturbances known to be associated with suicide. If genes are involved, it remains to be seen whether what is inherited is a suicide gene (most unlikely) or a predisposition to psychological disturbance.

The studies most likely to be helpful are those that look for adoptees who commit suicide in later life. It is then possible to tease apart biological from environmental influences, by looking at the suicide rate in biological versus adopted relatives. Such a study has been done by Schulsinger and colleagues in Denmark on a national sample of individuals adopted between 1925 and 1948.[16] They identified 57 people who were adopted and later committed suicide, and studied the suicide rate in their adoptive and biological parents, siblings and half-siblings (269 relatives in all). They selected a control group of people who were adopted but had not committed suicide and studied a total of 269 of their relatives too.

The incidence of suicide in the biological relatives of the control group was 0.7 per cent compared to an incidence of 4.5 per cent (6.5 times higher) in the biological relatives of those who committed suicide. In the adoptive relatives of both controls and suicides, there were no suicides at all. Further study of the sample showed that whereas depression (unipolar and bipolar) was higher in the biological relatives of the suicide victims, the highest incidence of suicide was in relatives of those who had a diagnosis of brief affective reaction, a term given to brief emotional disturbance often including an impulsive suicide attempt precipitated by a stressful life event. This gives a clue to what the genetic predisposition might be, adding weight to the idea that it is the inability to inhibit an impulsive reaction to stress that is involved. Such a personality predisposition crosses the boundaries between different types of psychiatric disorder.

Depression, schizophrenia, alcoholism or personality disorder might all have been candidates as carriers of a genetic loading for suicide, since they all carry an increased risk of self-harm behaviour. But the fact that suicide does not discriminate between the diagnoses throws doubt on this possibility. I have suggested (page 64) that it was not the diagnosis *per se* but an individual's perception of their symptoms as aversive and uncontrollable that was important.

The next generation of research on serotonin is likely to have to address several pressing issues. What is the effect of chronic stress on the serotonergic system and on impulsivity? What is the relationship between alcohol and impulsivity? Alcohol disinhibits a person and makes them act in a more dangerous way, but also lowers serotonin. It remains unclear whether this disinhibition comes from the serotonergic effect rather than the disinhibiting effect of alcohol itself. It is possible that alcohol's effect on impulsiveness is simply short-term, whereas that of serotonin is longer-term.

Progress in this area is unlikely to be fast. First, changes in serotonin function may only be a marker for another causal factor, and even if it were decisively established that it was linked to certain forms of suicide, both suicide and altered serotonin function may be caused by this third variable. Secondly, decreased serotonin function may represent the brain's attempt to compensate in one pathway for an increase in serotonin activity elsewhere, or to compensate for a problem in another neurotransmitter system. Thirdly, since all the data on serotonin function comes from correlations between known suicidal behaviour and biological function, we do not yet know whether there are any changes in serotonin function that precede such behaviour. Therefore no inferences can yet be drawn about the predictive value of knowing about serotonin function in an individual prior to suicidal behaviour.

A final problem is that biological studies have to date been done in isolation. They have been concerned to establish links between brain systems and behavioural tendencies such as violent or impulsive behaviour, without asking what the psychological (e.g. information-processing) and social (e.g. acute and chronic stress) factors involved in such behaviour might be, or what the neuropsychological mediators of such behaviours are.

Following a review of this material, Seymour Kety concludes:

We cannot dismiss the possibility that the genetic factor in suicide is an inability to control impulsive behavior, while depression and other mental illness, as well as overwhelming environmental stress, serve as potentiating mechanisms that foster or trigger the impulsive behavior, directing it toward a suicidal outcome. In any case, suicide illustrates better than any of the mental illnesses ... the very crucial and important interactions between genetic and environmental influences.[17]

Concluding remarks

A common theme emerges from both psychodynamic and biological approaches to suicide: the theme of escape from a situation that is seen as inescapable in any other way. From the dynamic perspective, the roots of this inescapability are to be found in the type of attachments formed early in life. In some theories, these are seen specifically as over-narcissistic, but it is common ground between many of these theories that the result of these early experiences is that loss or threatened loss of important relationships later in life produces an intolerable feeling of abandonment and interpersonal failure. Loss at any stage in life produces a mixture of protest, anger, anguish and despair. Such loss is associated with biological changes, and the serotonin system in the brain may act as an important link in the chain of events connecting uncontrollable events with impulsive and aggressive responses, whether directed at others or at oneself.

Neither psychodynamic nor biological theories make a clear distinction between impulses that drive someone *towards* suicide as an option on the one hand, and factors that *remove the obstacles* to such behaviour on the other. A wish that one could escape a hopeless life situation or escape one's mental anguish might provide sufficient push towards suicide, but it is equally important to understand the factors that take away the usual reasons for living or remove the barriers to dying. One such barrier might be the fear of death. We have seen how this can be reduced by a feeling that death might not be the end. It might also be reduced by exposure to real or fictional accounts of suicidal behaviour in books, magazines, television and radio.

Chapter 8

THE EFFECT OF THE MEDIA

My teenage son and I were clearing up the back garden. I was clearing parts of a tree which had been trimmed some time before, and he was sawing them into logs. He remarked that it was exactly a year ago since he had last been sawing logs. When I expressed surprise at his accurate memory, he said he remembered the date clearly because it was the anniversary of Kurt Cobain's death by suicide. Kurt Cobain was the lead singer of the band Nirvana. He had harmed himself in the past and finally shot himself, having left a long suicide note. When such a high-profile suicide occurs, people want to know what effects the death has on all the fans.

The debate about whether accounts of suicides (whether fictional stories or actual suicide) cause people to imitate them has a long history. In the eighteenth century Goethe was accused of encouraging suicidal behaviour by the publication of his novel *The Sorrows of Young Werther* (1774), in which a young man ends his life by shooting himself in the head.

The book had a tremendous influence on attitudes to romantic suicide and coroners all over Europe began to believe that the Werther effect was influential in bringing about suicides by lovelorn young people. The book was accused of sentimentalizing self-destruction, but whether or not it produced imitative suicides, it certainly produced imitative poetry and literature. The sentimentalization of death which followed such literature inspired pity for those who committed suicide and helped to erode the revulsion suicide had formerly inspired. The result was that many became concerned that suicide would spread by imitation.

Émile Durkheim agreed that 'no other phenomenon is more readily contagious', but he did not agree that imitative behaviour would affect suicide rates when they were calculated over a longer-term period.[1] However, evidence from several studies suggests that imitative suicidal behaviour can and does take place.

Evidence for imitative effects

In the first of a series of papers, David Phillips of San Diego University, California, examined the monthly suicide rates in the United States for the period 1947–68.[2] After correcting for the effects of seasonal fluctuations and linear trends, he found that suicide rates were higher just after a heavily publicized suicide story. The more publicity devoted to the story, the greater the increase in suicides, this increase occurring mainly in the geographical areas where the story was publicized.

Similar work by Brian Barraclough and colleagues in the United Kingdom examined seventy-six deaths by suicide or undetermined in the Portsmouth area over the three-year period 1970–72.[3] They also looked at newspaper reports about suicide inquests recorded in a local newspaper which reported 80 per cent of inquests on suicides and was read by 70 per cent of the adult population. Over the few days following the newspaper report of a suicide verdict, they found an excess of observed suicides which was statistically significant for males under 45.

Do television reports of suicides have a similar effect? Phillips and colleagues examined the US daily mortality figures for the period 1972–6 in relation to national TV news coverage of suicides.[4] They identified seven suicide stories which had been featured on National TV news (e.g. Christine Chubbuck, the talk-show hostess who shot herself while on the air on Monday, 15 July 1975). Following five out of the seven suicide stories, there was an increase in the daily mortality figures for deaths by suicide.

A spate of suicides occurred on the Viennese underground system in the 1980s. Between 1980 and 1984 there had only been nine suicides in total on the underground system. However, in 1986 one or two suicides were followed by dramatic reporting of the events, and several other (apparently copycat) suicides followed, so that in 1986 alone thirteen suicides occurred and a further nine in the first few months of 1987. Reporting restrictions were introduced and the number of suicides on the underground reverted to more normal levels (three in 1989 and four in 1990). Such events appear to show that reporting of real suicides can have a contagious effect.[5]

Fictional portrayals

Does this effect generalize to suicides or attempted suicides shown in fictional stories on television? To examine this question, Phillips turned to soap operas shown during 1977 on US television. Since the soap operas attract a larger audience than any other sort of television programme (40 per cent of all US homes with televisions are tuned to at least one soap opera in any week), he assumed this was likely to be a large potential source of behaviour which people might attempt to model.

Phillips identified nine separate weeks in which one or more soap operas carried a story in which a character committed or attempted suicide. From the US daily mortality statistics, he then examined whether there had been a rise in suicides in those particular weeks. As control periods, he took the weeks before, correcting for trends and eliminating public holiday periods and periods in which there had been an actual suicide publicized in the media. The results showed a rise in suicides in the latter part of the weeks in which suicidal behaviour was depicted in a major soap opera in eight out of the nine periods. For some fictional portrayals, however, the data is not always so clear cut.

The 'Angie' myth

An estimated 14 million watched the episode of the soap opera *EastEnders* on British TV on the evening of Thursday, 27 February 1986, and 9 million watched the repeat showing during an omnibus edition the following Sunday. The Thursday episode included an overdose by one of the main characters (Angie) together with alcohol (neat gin). Although the overdose involved several bottles of pills, the programme had also shown this character buying one of the bottles from a newsagent – a bottle of aspirin. The supposition was that this was an overdose with analgesics, and that, like many overdoses in real life, it arose out of a difficult interpersonal situation in which the 'husband' had been unfaithful. Following that programme and the omnibus edition on Sunday (in which the actual overdose was not shown though all the other elements were present), a large number of attendances for deliberate overdose at Hackney Hospital and St Bartholomew's Hospital in London were claimed. A letter to the *Lancet* reported that the number of patients admitted to Hackney Hospital during that week was far in excess of the average for the previous ten weeks, and of the average for that week for six out of the previous ten years.[6]

On close inspection the 'copycat' effect was less certain. Stephen Platt examined data from sixty-three hospitals for the period and for a comparable control period the previous year.[7] Although he found an increase in all women, the increase was not especially prominent in women in the 30–40 age group which he hypothesized might have been most closely associated with a model in that age range. He also found an increase in both sexes over 45. He concluded, however, that these were freak results owing to the fact that the control period for 1985 had witnessed a slight *decline* in the number of parasuicides within these categories, so this was not a particularly good baseline period against which to judge the 'rise' in the 1986 figures.

Platt also found a significant correlation in the *opposite* direction to that predicted between the viewing figures for different regions and the increase in overdoses attending hospitals. The increase in overdoses was lowest in London, which had the highest viewing figures, and highest in the Yorkshire and the north-east, in which a smaller proportion of the population watched the programme. For these reasons his conclusion was 'case not proven'.

With some colleagues, I also investigated the Angie phenomenon. We examined in detail the numbers attending the departments that had made the original claim at Hackney and St Bartholomew's Hospitals. We examined data for the period up to and including the dates of the broadcasts and for the same periods for two control years.[8] We also not only compared the number of 'imitative' cases with the numbers of people attending in control years, but looked for any trends which might have contributed to an apparently large number in the target period. For both hospitals, overdose attenders in the fourteen days after the broadcast were higher than those in the corresponding period for the two control years, but the rise in numbers began well before the programme was shown, in December in one hospital, January in the other. Analysis of daily data showed no evidence of unusual short-term changes within the fortnight after the programme. We concluded there had been no copycat effect.

Do these findings mean that no imitation ever takes place? Clearly that cannot be concluded on the basis of this study. There remains enough *prima facie* evidence to suggest caution when editors decide what to print or to show. Other studies, which have provided a more rigorous 'natural experiment', indicate that fiction can be powerful. Arnold Schmidtke showed how a fictional portrayal of a young man's suicide on a railway line could have an imitation effect on viewers.[9] He studied the number of railway suicides in the seventy days after the fictional episode was broadcast and found an increase. The suggestion that this was indeed imitation was reinforced by the finding that the suicides most often occurred in people of the same age and sex as the fictional character. Furthermore, the numbers of suicides correlated with the audience figures. The broadcast was repeated by the television authorities and Schmidtke found, once again, an increase in suicide. In total, his report estimated that an extra sixty suicide deaths occurred as a result of this fictional episode.

Criticisms of imitative research

Research on imitative suicidal behaviour has, however, been surrounded with controversy. There are three sorts of criticism. First, that there is very little theory which can explain some of the anomalies in the data. For example, some of Phillips's work found a lag of three days before 'imitative' behaviour became apparent, but no theoretical account has been given for this phenomenon. Further-

134

more, in the sort of 'macro' research that looks only at the gross numbers of suicides and only at whether a suicide story has occurred or not, there is no attempt to match the properties of the media stimuli with the set of behaviours that qualify as an imitative response. Many of the studies, for example, have not followed Schmidtke and looked at whether the age and sex of the suicide victims correspond to the age and sex of the person who commits suicide in the news or soap opera story.

Perhaps more serious than a lack of good theory is the possibility that at least part of the phenomenon is a mere statistical artefact. When one group of researchers re-analysed data from Phillips's 1982 soap opera study,[10] corrected some dating errors, increased the sample size, and used a more reliable regression analysis, they failed to replicate Phillips's results.[11]

Others have pointed out different sources of bias in imitative suicide research. These suggest that both the overall increase and the pattern of lags in the data are explained if one takes into account the fact that more suicides happen on some days of the week (Monday and Tuesday) than occur on others. Introducing a control period which also includes this day of the week may not help if, along with the increased average number of suicides for this day, there is also an increase in the variance of the data. This aspect of the data makes it more probable that one will make a statistical error using conventional statistical significance levels, claiming an effect when there really is none.

If one examines the same weeks that Bollen and Phillips used in their 1982 study, but looks at the following year when no suicide story was published, one finds evidence for increases which mimic those found by Phillips, even though it could not have been imitative behaviour.[12] However, in reply to this criticism, Phillips and Bollen returned to their data and eliminated these statistical problems. They found it did not affect their results. Furthermore, in a subsequent study Phillips[13] examined the daily fluctuation of a large number of teenage suicides during 1973–9 in relation to news or feature stories on the major TV networks. Using statistical analyses that corrected for the day of the week, month of the year, yearly trends and holidays, they found a mean increase per story or feature of 2.91 in the number of suicides. They also found a significant correlation between the number of news bulletins that featured a story and the increase in the subsequent seven-day period in suicides. Taking into account all previous criticisms, they also looked at similar time periods for the year before and the year after, and found there were no effects when there had not been a suicide story or feature article. Taken together with data from other researchers in very different contexts (such as the railway suicides reported by Schmidtke), there can be little doubt that imitation does occur.

Mechanisms of imitation

Much of our behaviour is learned by copying the behaviour of others. This is especially true when we are in situations where we do not know the right thing to do. Such processes determine children's behaviour much of the time, but are found later in life, too. Uncertainty may be the key to when modelling is most likely to occur in suicidal behaviour. It is when prior suicidal feelings are accompanied by feelings of uncertainty about what to do that imitation will be most likely to increase the probability of suicidal behaviour. If the model is attractive or famous, the imitative effect will be stronger because their behaviour will resolve more of the uncertainty about suicide as the right course of action. Indeed, Phillips has found that the increase in copycat suicide is greater if more prominence is given to it. Other researchers have found that celebrity suicides in the United States produced imitative behaviour only if the celebrity was famous enough to rate the front page of *The New York Times*.

Concluding remarks

There is compelling evidence that imitation is a factor in increasing risk of suicide. However, there is little evidence that such effects occur in isolation from all the other vulnerability factors. Imitation may take the form of suicide or of parasuicide, and may follow real or fictional accounts in the media. Seeing others commit suicide, especially someone with whom there is a strong identification, may lower the barrier to suicide in certain circumstances. However, the overall effects on the suicide rate are relatively small, and we need therefore to ask why imitation does not have a larger effect.

The first, most obvious reason is that most people are not in the 'vulnerability window' that gives them a strong motive to die. Decreasing barriers to suicide are simply irrelevant for the majority. But the second reason takes us back to the example of Kurt Cobain. Although there have been some suicides by his fans that appeared to imitate his death, many of these occurred a considerable time afterwards, so the role of direct imitation is questionable. The puzzle is why there have not been more. I believe the answer lies in the fact that the death of such an idol, though it upsets many fans, can unite them in mourning. At the very least, many followers of his music have a major topic of conversation, which acts as a source of bonding. The increased social support countermands the tendency to imitate. It follows that imitative suicide is more likely to happen in those individuals who are loners, or are temporarily outside their social group. Obsessing about the death in isolation, without the social support of others, is most likely to result in imitative suicidal behaviour.

Do any recommendations follow from this for media presentation of suicide? The following suggestions are based on those of Gould:[14]

1. Detailed descriptions of methods of committing suicide or parasuicide should not be given, nor shown in fictional portrayals, since these will demonstrate possible means for those who are suicidal.
2. Physical consequences of parasuicide, where this has occurred (e.g. paralysis, brain damage) should not be minimized, but neither should such harmful consequences be dwelt upon, which might attract those who seek victim status.
3. If the victim had prior mental health problems, these should not be ignored. Many stories refer to life circumstances or philosophies as if these were sufficient precipitants. (See Chapter 6, where Arthur Koestler's suicide is discussed (pages 111–12), and it is pointed out how reports of his death failed to focus on his long-standing psychological problems.)

4. Simplistic psychological notions, such as 'pressure', should not be used. Many people have such pressure, but few commit suicide, and such references belittle the complexity of the situation. Similarly, simple motives such as 'getting even' or 'becoming famous' should be avoided.

5. Where possible, stories should avoid emphasizing the attractive qualities of the deceased in such a way as to make the suicide a part of this attractiveness.

6. Such stories should be accompanied by details of what help is available, together with hotline numbers (such as the Samaritans or other befriending agencies).

7. Extensive or unnecessary repeated coverage of such events should be avoided.

8. There should be ongoing discussion between those working in the media and mental health experts in which the evidence for such imitative effects are kept under review.

Chapter 9

THE CRY OF PAIN

In the United Kingdom each August teenagers receive their end of school examination results from schools and colleges. Often the grades obtained are critical in determining whether the person is able to go to the college or university course of their choice. In 1994, when the Advanced Level (the end of school public examination) results came out, a talented pupil from a village in Norfolk killed herself. She felt that her grades (a B, a C and two D's) were not good enough to win her a place on the physiotherapy course she hoped to do. On the day she collected her results, she told friends she wanted to be alone, but then let herself into her cousin's empty cottage and hanged herself.

What can explain such a rapid escalation of suicidal depression? She was popular and talented, had hobbies and appeared happy-go-lucky. It particularly surprised people since she had fought back after a riding accident two years before in which she broke her back and seemed to be a survivor. Hindsight in such cases can be very deceptive, and it is unwise to imagine that such a rare event might have been predicted. However, such a tragedy serves as a reminder to be vigilant for those who may be (a) especially sensitive to feelings of failure and (b) likely to conclude they are trapped if they do fail. At the time, several commentators suggested that her case should signal a danger that the education system had become too dominated by a league-table culture that emphasized academic performance as the sole criterion of success. The example of Japan was thought to be another warning.

The high rate of suicide among teenage students in Japan is often linked to the highly competitive nature of the education system. Pupils as young as 12 often attend cramming schools in attempts to improve marks so that, eventually, they will win a job with a top company. A further consequence of such a dominance-subordinance environment is the high rate of bullying, or *ijime*, between pupils. Such bullying is often the actual precipitant of a suicide. In December 1994, an emergency Cabinet meeting in Japan was called to discuss bullying in schools. It was becoming clear that it could go to extreme lengths, but was being under-reported by schools, who feared criticism for allowing it to occur. The meeting took place against the background of the suicide of two 13-year-old boys. One of them, from Nishio, in the prefecture of Aichi, had hanged himself. He left a four-page suicide note giving details of the beatings and extortion he had suffered for over a year. He had been repeatedly dunked in a river until he feared he would drown, and forced many times to give money. 'These days they bully me so hard and demand large sums of money although I have none. I can't stand it any more.'

The Education Ministry was forced to admit that a large part of the problem stemmed from the highly competitive nature of the education system. In a special report in December 1994, they called on teachers to be more aware of pupils' stress levels and competition between them in examinations. Little guidance was given, however, in how teachers could assess whether students were suffering in this way.

The use of exam success as the sole criterion of self-worth produces individuals who feel ashamed of their 'weakness' and trapped by their apparent failure. The feeling of humiliation and 'weakness' acts as a barrier to sharing the fear of failure with peers or family. The feeling of humiliation is exacerbated by feelings of loneliness, and each mood feeds on the other in a vicious spiral of despair.

These themes are illustrated by another situation that came to light relatively recently. Around fifty suicides in the United Kingdom each year are among people found shop-lifting and awaiting a court appearance. They are most often people who had no financial need to shop-lift. There is, for them, an overwhelming feeling of shame and humiliation. If the case comes to court, the verdict will often reflect the judgement that the person is suffering a psychological problem that needs psychological intervention rather than punishment, but many commit suicide before the case comes to court.

Interpersonal disputes can involve combinations of the same emotions. A woman in her mid-forties took a massive overdose soon after she discovered that the man she planned to marry in a few weeks (having lived with him for several years) had unilaterally cancelled the arrangements. Without her knowledge, he had sent notes to all the guests to say the wedding was cancelled. He came to visit her in hospital, but only to give her ring back, and tell her to collect her stuff, which he had left in suitcases on the front doorstep. Her overdose was not lethal, and she lived. But her crisis threatened to last for some time, and while it did so, she remained at serious risk of further suicidal behaviour.

Biological, psychodynamic and social aspects may be combined in explaining such behaviour. Individuals are sensitive to signals from their social environment of threats both to their rank within the group and their acceptance as part of the group. Events signalling threat to rank or group similarity are seen, by the person, as signs that they are a 'loser'. Like the woman whose wedding was cancelled, such people have lost a battle. Such 'loser' status we know as reduced self-esteem, and it triggers evolutionarily 'old' biological patterns in the brain. This affects mood and produces further hypersensitivity to social information, resulting in a vicious circle that appears to confirm the individual as a 'loser'. In the early stages a 'reactance' pattern is shown, in which the individual 'protests' against the threatened loss. At this stage, 'low intent' suicidal behaviour may occur. In the later stages of response, despair and apathy may be seen, and serious attempts at suicide may occur. Occasionally, however, a person may experience a catastrophic increase of suicidal impulse in response to loss or failure, and an unexpected suicide occurs.

Knowledge of brain function is not all we need to explain such behaviour. We need rather to understand what environmental and psychological 'signals' bring about biological changes in brain function (see pages 123–6), and, in turn, what effects such biological changes will have on the way we think and act. For example, psychosocial stress is a critical factor in bringing about biological changes. Long-term stress in both animals and humans can have profound effects on patterns of endocrine and neurotransmitter function. There is increasing evidence that repeated stress in life can bring about changes in messenger RNA and DNA, and there is a renewed interest in mapping the effect of such changes on psychological function.[1]

Depression can be seen as the response to the long-term threat posed by constant frustration and disappointment, by the loss of people, things and status. Such frustrations and losses may result from constantly being put down by society, or receiving insufficient help or support. In considering how we can explain suicidal behaviour in a way that takes full account of biological, psychological and social processes, a helpful starting-point is ethology. Ethology is the study of animals in their natural habitat. The approach has been influential in such important theories as that of Bowlby on attachment. There are a number of different ways animals and humans respond normally to losses: (a) by energizing behaviour to try and secure the rewards in other ways; (b) by switching to alternative sources of reward; and (c) by giving up. These can become distorted in catastrophic ways that cause the individual to believe he or she is trapped, and to begin to think of ways of escaping. Suicidal behaviour is best seen as a cry of pain – a response elicited by this situation of entrapment – and only secondarily as an attempt to communicate or change people or things in the environment.

Conservation-withdrawal

The Australian psychiatrist Robert Goldney was one of the first to take an ethological approach to suicidal behaviour, employing Engel's ideas[2] about 'conservation-withdrawal'.[3] This refers to a biological system which responds to stress by reducing activity, raising barriers against stimulation and conserving energy: a sort of hibernation. This pattern may follow a prolonged period of heightened arousal where the organism has attempted to cope by over-engagement and over-activity. When the organism falls into the state of conservation-withdrawal, the signs that are visible in the social group have a signal function, warning others of a loss of supplies and of exhaustion. The intended outcome is to 'ensure the supply' and 'retain the object'.

This, Goldney notes, has striking parallels with the reports of those who take overdoses: they want to escape, they do not know whether they want to live or die, they cannot stand the pressure any longer. Schneidman (1964) has pointed out how many see a connection between death and sleep, and this can be found in the reasons people give for suicidal acts.[4] They want to 'pull the bedclothes' over their heads, or 'go to sleep for a long time'. The fact that alcohol abuse and suicidal behaviour often go together can be linked to the innate mechanism of 'conservation-withdrawal'. Alcohol also represents an attempt to react to the stresses of life by reducing the demands on consciousness by shutting out external stimuli. When such attempts to bring about temporary oblivion with alcohol fail, then other mechanisms for conservation-withdrawal come into play. The fact that alcohol reduces the fear of the possible negative consequences of any behaviour, when applied to suicidal acts, renders them all the more likely.

Many suicide attempts can thus be seen as a wish for temporary relief. The attempt may represent a conservation of energy, a raising of the barriers to the outside world, or at least an attempt to re-exert control over it. Although the idea of conservation-withdrawal fits in some respects, it seems to apply best to the later stages of response to uncontrollable stress, when the individual has given up hope, become despairing and apathetic. It does not capture the more active 'protest' aspects of some suicidal behaviour, which, I shall argue, arise at an earlier point in the process.

Evolutionary approach

Recent research helps us to go into more detail about the types of biological mechanisms that may be involved in depression and suicidal behaviour. This has been drawn together by Professor Paul Gilbert,[5] who suggests we look to the animal kingdom for hypotheses about the evolutionary primitive mechanisms that might influence human behaviour. He is particularly concerned to explore the concept of defence and safety.

People differ widely in what they find threatening: the fear of a physical illness such as a heart attack, the fear that others will criticize them, the fear of being overwhelmed by emotion when describing past trauma, the fear that people will 'find out' one's weaknesses. Gilbert suggests that defence and safety may be fundamental psycho-biological organizing systems that guide the development of inter-personal schemata and strategies. Non-threatening environments promote creativity, co-operation and affiliation. Threatening environments inhibit flexibility and exploration, producing more stereotyped, automatic responses. This has implications for suicidal behaviour, and how it is linked with inflexibility in cognitive processes such as memory and problem solving. The most important 'unsafe' environment for most humans, however, is not exposure to predators or physical harm, but exposure to unfavourable social comparison. Thus we need to explore further the evolutionary significance of social comparison in determining rank and status within social groups.

The animal kingdom shows many examples where social groups survive because of the smooth operation of social processes whose functions are (a) so that sexual partners are chosen (intersexual selection – where one sex attracts and chooses a partner) and (b) so that potential rivals are excluded (intrasexual selection – where members of a single sex prevent other members of the same sex from gaining access to potential partners). An important aspect is rank and status within a social group that shares the same territory. High-ranking individuals explore more, have more erect posture, and are less timid than low-ranking individuals across a number of species.

Changes in rank can bring about changes in biological systems (e.g. in levels of testosterone), but more importantly for understanding depression and suicidal behaviour, in levels of the neurotransmitter serotonin. What evolutionary function do such systems have? An important study in 1984 by Michael Raleigh and his colleagues at the UCLA School of Medicine, Los Angeles,[6] investigated the connection, in colonies of adult male vervet monkeys, between social rank and blood levels of serotonin. They found that dominant animals (judged by observation of how many encounters a male monkey won over its peers) had much higher levels. If the dominant animal lost its position, however, there followed a reduction (of some 40 per cent) of blood serotonin levels. This occurred whether loss of status happened naturally or was experimentally produced by removal of the dominant male. In either case, the male that then became dominant experienced an increase in serotonin to the same levels characteristic of the previous dominant male.

Such biological systems seem to be involved in regulating fights and challenges in a group by establishing a hierarchy of rank. It is important for an animal that is likely to lose encounters not to compete continually, so expending valuable resources in challenges that cannot be won. On the other hand, some contests may be worth fighting. The ranking determines who is likely and who unlikely to be beaten. There has evolved a large number of signals used by animals to communicate challenge, attack and submission. Submission, when triggered, involves a menu of behaviours signalling that no further threat to the victor is intended. Further challenges are inhibited by this mechanism. Neither party need waste further resources on establishing relative rank. Furthermore, the signalling that goes on in animal groups means that animals may not actually have to fight it out.

Out of this research comes the study of analogous behaviour in humans. Although such extrapolation has to be done with extreme care, the analogy between observations of social groups in animals and humans is justified so long as they are used to set up *hypotheses* rather than coming to *conclusions* about human behaviour. How best to proceed? First, we can observe that humans appear sensitive to, and make rapid judgements about, one another's rank and status. The social comparison process may be done on the basis of another person's size of house, or make of car, or quality of clothes. Indeed, we have invented games which explicitly ascribe rank, such as the role-playing games played by increasing numbers of people during the 1980s and 1990s. Players are allocated characteristics in various dimensions: size, strength, skill, previous success, weapons, allies, etc. The outcome of encounters between competitors is determined by their ability to use and to conserve these 'attributes'.

Social biologists refer collectively to these attributes, when observed in animals, as Resource Holding Potential (RHP). Ritual encounters between two members of the same species result in comparison of relative RHP, and the loser will back off. As the hierarchy becomes established, the amount of fighting reduces. Gilbert suggests that the human equivalent of RHP is self-esteem. Self-esteem is an estimate of one's ability to secure important goals such as a desired job, or partner. It is damaged by unemployment, by failure in love, and by aggression from others, as in school by bullies or in the home by family members who use psychological or physical violence.

Paul Gilbert suggests that dominance hierarchies have evolved through stages. First, they were territorial, where fighting was designed to create space for territorial ownerships. Subsequently, territories gradually dissolved and success in the dominance hierarchy became associated with other forms of social success; it was a dispenser of useful resources. Dominance, however established, creates inhibition in subordinates. Since that time there have been large changes in the importance of affiliative behaviour, particularly alliance building (see next section), which requires approach rather than inhibition. This results in the fact that, today in humans, rank is often (though not always) determined by things such as perceived popularity, beauty, talent, etc. Gilbert maintains that when individuals lose rank, then the defensive systems of escape, etc., become activated. The means of acquiring rank and status may have changed, but the feeling when one loses has not. Submission in humans continues to involve giving up claims on resources.

Being 'in' with the group

In addition to helping to determine rank by looking for signs of RHP, social comparison can also judge the extent to which one is succeeding in gaining favourable attention from other members of the group. Unlike RHP, which is to do with ranking, this is concerned with judgements about *sameness* v. *difference* from the reference group. Gilbert calls it Social Attention Holding Power. It conveys status by attractiveness rather than by aggressive displays of strength over weakness. It is concerned with receiving signals that one is attractive to others and/or needed by them.

In clinical practice, one may observe two types of problem when individuals are over-concerned with whether their company is rewarding to others. First there are those who appear to be sustained exclusively by *receiving* attention from others. They are sensitive to any signs that these sources of attention may be under threat of being switched off. They feel abandoned when this happens, and are likely to become demanding of others' attention, seeking reassurance that they are still loved. In therapy, they may say, 'No one really loves me,' or 'All my friends are sick of me.'

Secondly, there are those who appear to be sustained by their ability to *give* attention to others and be needed by them. People who seek helping roles in various organizations may fit into this category. They are often held up as examples to the group, as people who 'can't do enough for others'. They are welcome to most groups they join, since they often appear to have boundless energy. There is little wrong with this except when 'being needed by others' is the sole source of their satisfaction in life. If so, they become vulnerable when other members of the group or family make it clear they no longer need their help. In this case, the person may feel depressed, for they know no other way of relating to people other than to help them. When depressed, they do not doubt that others love them, but rather they say, 'I am a burden to others'; and in the most extreme cases, 'They would be better off without me.' Their 'black and white' (dichotomous) thinking makes them conclude that there are only two possibilities: either they are a *help* to others or they are a *burden* to them.

Social comparison and psychopathology

Whether attempting to compare resources for ranking using RHP or to evaluate the extent to which one fits in with the group (the amount of Social Attention Holding Power), the effects of social comparison run deep. It is the comparative effect, not the absolute effect, that determines the amount of stress or depression. During the Thatcher/Reagan years, politicians used to answer the accusation that a large gap had opened up between rich and poor by saying that, although the rich had indeed become richer, the poor had little cause to complain since they had not become much poorer, if at all. However, this takes no account of the fact that people's mood and their psychological (and sometimes physical) health are determined by social comparison. Absolute levels of deprivation are higher in war, but cases of suicide and depression fall because all are perceived to be suffering together – social cohesion goes up. Similarly, absolute levels of deprivation are higher in underdeveloped countries than in most Western countries, but there is no excess of suicides and depression in these poorer countries.

This explains some of the discrepancy in the debate about suicide and unemployment. There is little doubt that being unemployed is an extra risk factor for suicidal behaviour, but overall rates are sometimes found not to fluctuate with the unemployment rate as one might expect. Research by Stephen Platt and colleagues in Edinburgh shows that this confusion arises partly from the fact that unemployment has less capacity to cause depression and suicide if the person perceives everyone else to be in the same boat.[7] It is not absolute levels of poverty and employment which are important in physical and mental health, but distribution of inequality.[8] It is the conclusion that, compared to others, one is a failure, unwanted or powerless, which increases vulnerability to emotional distress.

Involuntary subordination

In Paul Gilbert's *Depression: The Evolution of Powerlessness*,[9] he draws an important distinction between voluntarily giving up and moving on, and involuntarily being defeated. In the latter case, the individual is trapped and feels they have no alternative. Involuntary subordination is an important aspect of depression, which may arise from a person being forced to be subordinate and take a submissive role. This takes us back into social rank theory. The dimension of rank (whether one is dominant or subordinate in a group) may be more significant in the cause of depression than previously thought. When depressed, people seem to feel an increased need for recognition and prestige. They worry about how they are succeeding in relation to others, evaluate themselves as inferior or second rate, feel weak and ashamed about such weakness. The usual summary term for such a constellation of symptoms is 'low self-esteem', which sums up the sense of subordination, the perception or reality of negative social comparison.

The value of the concept of involuntary subordination is that it sums up what many see as the cause of increased depression in women relative to men: that it is often a consequence of enforced subordinacy. To protect themselves (and often their children), women are forced to take a submissive role, increasing self-blame so as to reduce the likelihood of counter-aggression from their partner. Consistent with this, researchers in London (Bernice Andrews and Chris Brewin) found that women being abused by their partners blamed themselves for their partner's violence. However, this was only true if they were asked about it while still in the relationship. If asked after they had moved out of the relationship, they blamed their partners. So far as we can see, their self-blame while still in the relationship felt genuine to them; they were not consciously telling lies as a protective strategy. As Gilbert suggests, in a context where one partner is criticized and disempowered, an evolutionary primitive inhibitory system comes into play and this system gives rise to the symptoms we know as a depressive state.

Such an evolutionary primitive mechanism may come into play even if there is the *perception* of low status, failure and weakness.[10] A person may be pursuing unrealistically high goals, so their perfectionism itself may give rise to the perception that they are failing, weak or subordinate. They invent for themselves a punitive environment. They feel they have failed, then feel trapped by such failure, since there seems no way out of their situation. Occasionally a single failure can activate these depressive mechanisms very suddenly with devastating effect, as we see by the cases of school 'failure' and suicide reported at the start of this chapter. Suicide following bullying is an example where the more long-lasting stress of being trapped gives way, eventually, to this most extreme form of escape.

Cry for help or cry of pain?

In the past, many authors have seen suicidal behaviour (especially attempted suicide) as a 'cry for help'.[11] That is, the suicidal behaviour is seen as motivated by impulses towards preservation rather than self-destruction. Stengel[12] wrote that suicidal behaviour functions as an alarm system, possibly even as a social releaser in the Lorenz/ Tinbergen sense.

Schneidman spoke of 'cessation', breaking this concept into sub-categories of 'intentioned, subintentioned, unintentioned, and contraintentioned'.[13] Each categorization attempts to capture the prevailing sense that suicidal behaviour varies in its 'seriousness' (hence a general classification used by many clinicians into 'gestures', 'ambivalent' and 'serious'). Certainly in the past it seemed that classification into two main groups appeared to be justified: first, the depressed, alienated group with a high risk of death; secondly, a group whose act is highly operant (behaviour maintained and modifiable by its consequences). This is consistent with Beck's conclusions that the two most salient dimensions along which such behaviour can be judged is the 'escape' motive and the 'communication' motive.

Unfortunately, even within this overall classification, the motivation for suicidal behaviour is complex. Writing in 1966, Kessel took exception to those who thought that all suicidal behaviour was consciously or unconsciously motivated by the wish to die.[14] He accused suicidologists of deceiving themselves: 'in the fact of the obvious and the simple, they cleave to the complicated, fortified against the evidence by the concept of unconscious ambivalence'. Kessel is right to be suspicious of any theory which assumes, a priori, that self-harm behaviour must always have suicidal intent, and that, if not found, then it is 'latent'. However, such sweeping statements take little account of the complexity of motivations for those who do kill themselves. The fatality of the outcome should not be seen as the only determinant of the factors that motivate the behaviour.

It may be better to assume that most suicidal behaviour, whether the outcome is fatal or not, has some element of the Janus face –

mixed feelings about the will to live and the will to die. As we know, even within the general population, many people have at some time felt suicidal. Given that the lifetime risk for clinical depression is 20 per cent, and that suicidal feelings are a common accompaniment to such depression, it makes little sense to dismiss those who actually harm themselves as not serious, or to dismiss the pressure to escape that the person feels.

For these reasons, the cry for help, which many have misinterpreted as a lack of genuineness, is better seen as a cry of pain. Suicidal behaviour can have a communication outcome without communication being the main motive. The behaviour is elicited by a situation in which the person feels trapped. As with the animal in a trap that cries in pain, the fact that the behaviour affects the behaviour of other members of the species does not mean that the only motive for the cry was to seek help. Suicidal behaviour may be overtly communicative in a minority of cases, but mainly it is 'elicited' by the pain of a situation with which the person cannot cope – it is a cry of pain first, and only after that a cry for help.

The 'cry for help' idea, though originally intended to be a neutral theory about suicidal behaviour, has outlived its usefulness. It has become limited to non-fatal suicide attempts (parasuicide) and thus contributed to a widening of the gap between fatal suicide and parasuicide. Also it is almost always used pejoratively, or at least to imply that a certain suicidal act was not so serious, but 'merely' a cry for help. Such behaviour is never 'merely' anything.

Some self-harm may not be motivated by a wish to die, but most shares with suicide the wish to escape from an otherwise unbearable situation. The difficulty many authors have got into is to define completed suicide as the core behaviour that needs to be explained, and parasuicide as its pale reflection. Instead, if one defines *entrapment and helplessness in the face of actual or threatened loss* as the basic dimension, it becomes easier to see that all self-harm falls somewhere along the dimension, whatever the outcome. Such feelings of being trapped are fuelled and maintained by biological and psychological changes. They appear completely impervious to intellectual argument, as Alvarez found:

... mere intellectual recognition did no good, and anyway, my clear moments were few. My life felt so cluttered and obstructed that I could hardly breathe. I inhabited a closed, concentrated world, airless and without exits. I doubt if any of this was noticeable socially: I was simply more tense, more nervous than usual, and I drank more. But underneath I was going a bit mad. I had entered the closed world of suicide, and my life was being lived for me by forces I couldn't control.[15]

Entrapment

I suggest the sense of *entrapment* is central to suicidal behaviour. In the case of the A level student with which the chapter began, there was an unpredicted and sudden surge of such feelings of 'no escape'. In most cases, however, the entrapment is a longer-term state, first because external causes of stress are themselves long-term (e.g. the person is trapped by bullying peers or partners). But it may be prolonged also because the person has grown up in an environment where he or she could exercise very little control, where others had all the power, so the person has learned over a long time period that the only possible response option is to submit. The person is thus extra-sensitive to social threats, and their world constantly seems to present fewer alternatives for action, whatever the reality. The result is long-term demobilization, a biological state involving chemical changes.

The depressed person effectively 'takes themselves off the list' of those who might threaten the more powerful. This is akin to the low-risk low-gain strategy of some animals, a strategy that involves internal inhibition of any behaviour that would appear to challenge those higher in the dominance hierarchy. Gilbert suggests that the downturn into depression may involve the activation of these inhibitory mechanisms of 'no challenge'. At the extreme, they are associated with not only reduced aspiration but also abnormally low aspiration: feelings of worthlessness, uselessness, powerlessness; and lack of interest in engaging in any social behaviour that might involve taking even minimal risks. Depression is the biological assignment of 'loser' status. It signals to oneself and others that one is not prepared to take on challenges or fight for resources.

The benefit in the animal kingdom is that the risk of losing fights is minimized, but the cost is that the chance of dominating others is lost. In the case of bullying in schools or armed services or prisons, however, the competitive nature of the institution appears to encourage the bully to continue to torment the subordinate long after the weaker one has given up. The inhibitory mechanisms designed to protect the loser from further losses fail to work. At such times the risk of suicide is increased.

Entrapment – evidence from history

One benefit of the entrapment model is that it helps to explain historical data. Take, for example, the increased risk of suicide that children and young people suffered in the late Middle Ages and early modern period. It appears the best explanation for this is the violence with which children were mistreated and the fact that such brutalized boys and girls had nowhere to turn. They therefore killed themselves to escape.

MacDonald and Murphy[16] give the example of a 12-year-old girl called Agnes Addam who went horse-riding with a girlfriend in 1565 and dirtied her clothes. She started to return home but then became seized with terror over what her father would do to her when he saw she had spoilt her clothes. She rushed into a pond and drowned herself. Another example was a boy who in 1729 was frightened after he threw a piece of glass at his brother. He knew he would receive a severe beating from his father and hanged himself in the outhouse. A third example was the 13-year-old son of a Hackney tradesman who was victim of a cruel practical joke. He lost his hat after his father had threatened to beat him within an inch of his life if he lost his new one. The boy's sister had overheard the threat and as a joke hidden the hat. When the boy found it was missing, he hanged himself for fear of the beating.

The situation was compounded because when young people left home in their early teens to work as servants or apprentices, the law forbade them to flee the homes of their masters and mistresses. This only encouraged many such masters to mistreat them and abuse them in a miserable way. Only the most flagrant brutality was regarded as sufficient grounds for leaving a master. Neither could those boys or girls who ran away expect much sympathy from their parents if they returned home. A 12-year-old lad called Daniel Rose was miserable after having been apprenticed to a weaver and returned home. They warned him and sent him back to his master. He left the house that evening and was found dead the next morning. He had hanged himself in his master's garden.

Girls who found themselves pregnant would also be likely to kill themselves. In some cases girls made pregnant by their master found themselves isolated both from their master and mistress and their parents. Since there was no way out, suicide was common.

Running through these stories are the elements of helplessness and the impossibility of escape, and particularly fear of punishment. We see the same in contemporary societies in the fear of punishment that comes in a school system which is institutionalized in the penalties society exacts for lack of success at exams. Similarly we see it with the fear of bullying which is often the origin of suicidal thoughts in people serving in the army, navy or air force. Finally we see it dramatically illustrated in the suicide of those in prison, especially young people on remand, who can escape neither the prison nor the terrible fear that they will be bullied there.

Self-harm and suicide: connections

High-suicide-intent self-harm and completed suicide do not require a different theory from that needed to explain less serious suicidal behaviour. The less serious behaviour represents the early active 'protest' stage of response to threatened loss of rank, response to threatened entrapment. It is later, after repeated exposure to social comparison resulting in 'loser' status or 'non-belonging/abandoned' status, that the more severe manifestation of conservation-withdrawal emerges: self-denigration, worthlessness and despair, and with them the high suicide intent. Low intent parasuicide can thus be seen as the 'reactance' (the increased activity in response to threatened loss) which precedes the 'helplessness' (the decreased activity in response to actual loss) associated with high intent-to-die suicidal behaviour.

The recent rise in younger males attempting and committing suicide can be related to reduced role both through loss of employment opportunities and loss of opportunities of long-term relationship. This latter effect arises from the increases in divorce and family breakdown. In later life, separation or divorce or living alone can reactivate such feelings of being 'less-favoured' together with the feeling of being a 'loser'. Such are the components of Durkheim's 'anomie' that he saw as closely associated with suicide. We can now see how such anomie, a sociological concept, relates to the psychological concept of social comparison, which itself relates directly to evolutionary old biological sub-systems, each having a generally adaptive function, but sometimes producing a maladaptive outcome. Social comparison has two important elements: ranking (upwards v. downwards) and similarity to others (like v. unlike). Those who are depressed and 'anomic' feel both *inferior to* and also *different from* others.

Thus low self-esteem is a biologically old tendency that may be activated relatively early in life, and reactivated at times when individuals are, or imagine themselves to be, defeated, powerless and failing to meet the challenges of the world of work or of interpersonal relationships. How is the gender effect to be explained within the 'entrapment' model? Historically, women have been given roles in society in which they have less control, e.g. in earning power, control over resources, in jobs even when working. In Western society, women are likely to attribute their failures to themselves, and attribute their successes to luck or to other people or circumstances. Women have thus explored the boundaries of 'no control' more than have men. When the trap begins to close, they are more likely to see it closing. The result is that they take action earlier than men. The cry of pain comes earlier in the entrapment process. At this early stage, people are more ambivalent about dying, and use less lethal methods. The historic tendency for women to be more likely to attempt suicide, but less likely to commit suicide, is explained by this 'time course' model. In the past, men did not show self-punitive behaviour at this stage. However, having not reacted to threatened loss and entrapment early on in the sequence, they miss out on the important benefits that earlier cries of pain may bring, and are more likely to move, in the extreme cases, to helplessness and social isolation. When the trap closes, the effect is more catastrophic.

For men, with less opportunity for receiving care (fewer social support networks) and less opportunity for care giving (fewer caring roles), the expectation of no escape feeds directly into a sense of hopelessness and the possibility of suicidal behaviour as the escape route. As men become increasingly marginalized in the job market, they may experience, as women have always done, more uncontrollable aspects of life at a younger age. The effect will be that they, too, show suicidal behaviour at an earlier stage in the entrapment. This may be why the numbers of young men are beginning to exceed the numbers of young women in parasuicide statistics.

Concluding remarks

If social signals switch on old biological scripts of defeat and submission, then antidepressants may switch off these processes to give the person more energy to explore other response options, with reduced sensitivity to signals of social loss and failure. Equally, psychotherapy may help the person recognize their patterns of thinking that see every situation as potentially threatening, every encounter as win-or-lose. In this way, the person may learn to modify their aspirations, to accept things how they are so as to see better how they may change. The limits of such interventions are set by the persistence of a real state of powerlessness arising from, say, bullying by other students, or domination by a violent partner. However, psychotherapy has often been able to empower people to change relationships, to move away from non-supportive or threatening individuals, to change the external factors that normally conspire to keep them trapped.

How far a person finds alternative escape routes may depend on an important psychological factor, a person's memory of their own past history. There is evidence that autobiographical memory may be so affected that it reduces the ability to solve current problems and restricts their view of the future. The next chapter will consider this aspect in depth, for it promises to provide a way in to break the vicious circle of biological and social influences on suicidal feelings and behaviour.

Chapter 10

MEMORY TRAPS

I have suggested that a major factor in suicide and parasuicide is the feeling of being trapped – trapped by both circumstances and one's own thoughts and feelings. The psychological aspect, the thoughts and feelings, were seen as important in worsening the effects of the external realities. Though people rarely think themselves into a hole, once there, thoughts about their own helplessness often maintain the depression and prevent them climbing out. One response to these thoughts is to view them as the symptoms of underlying depression. When the depression clears up, or is treated, they will stop.

In one sense this is true. We know that such negative and hopeless thoughts go up and down with depressed mood. We know that, when a person takes antidepressants, the thoughts may lose their grip, given time. However, if the antidepressants are stopped, the risk of becoming depressed remains. Once a person has been clinically depressed, they remain at an increased risk of becoming depressed again. In 50 per cent of cases, the depression returns within two years. For those who have been depressed more than once in the past, the risk of recurrence is 70 per cent. The thoughts return, the helplessness returns. The pills have clearly not dealt with the underlying vulnerability to becoming depressed and suicidal, much of which may stem from a person's memory of the past.

The importance of memory is hard to overstate. Memory provides us with all our knowledge about who we are, what we have been through in the past: happy times and sad times. It is on the basis of our memory that we make predictions about the future. If our memory is biased or faulty, then our predictions are also likely to be biased and faulty. Our self-esteem also depends on memory. Self-esteem is based upon our past successes and failures, and how successfully we have navigated a path through the world so far.

Depression is one of the major vulnerability factors for suicidal behaviour and depression does not only affect mood, it affects memory as well. Memory provides the key to understanding how, when someone feels under pressure from their life circumstances, they begin to feel trapped in a mental cage from which they appear unable to escape. First, memory can be biased so that it tends to retrieve only negative events. Secondly, memory can be over-general. Instead of recording specific events, a person tends to lump together events of the same type or category without distinguishing between them. The story of how this memory problem was discovered is interesting in its own right.

Memory bias – the horse race

I am writing this paragraph on the train on the way to a meeting of the British Association for the Advancement of Science. As I gaze out of the window at the mountains of North Wales on my right and the sea on my left, my mind wanders. I see a sandy beach, empty but for a lone figure and his dog. It triggers a memory of me walking along a similar beach many years ago with my own collie dog. Such triggering of memories happens constantly, whether we are day-dreaming or engaged in conversation. Many of the triggers are fairly neutral and ambiguous. A man, out with his dog, might be 'peaceful' or 'lonely'. In other words, seeing something like that might trigger memories of positive or negative events from our past.

When something triggers or 'cues' memory, the event seems to come to mind immediately. This is not the case. There is a small time-lag between the cue and the event coming to mind. During this brief interval there is a race between a number of events which the same cue could trigger. This same cue can activate a range of memory fragments, each of which could be completed by a number of different memories. Some psychologists have likened memory retrieval to a horse race. Whichever event gets to the line first wins, and when it wins, that is the event that comes to mind.

It is now known that such a 'horse race' occurs between positive events and negative events from the past. One can imagine positive memories as a white horse, and negative memories as a black horse. My seeing the man and his dog activated a pleasant memory of long ago; the white horse won. But one effect of depressed mood is to bias memory so that the black horse wins much of the time. Had I been depressed, the sight of the man and the dog might have brought to mind the day I had to take my dog to the vet to be put down, when he was very old and grey and ailing. Further, the depression would have suppressed any happy memories of subsequent dogs, thus allowing me to conclude, unhappily, that I have never had a dog as wonderful again.

Some of the first experiments on depressed mood memory bias phenomena were performed by Professor Alwyn Lishman at the Institute of Psychiatry in London and by John Teasdale and colleagues at the Warneford Hospital in Oxford. Lishman concluded that patients who were more depressed in mood found it easier to recall negative events, but a problem with this early study was that the apparent mood memory 'bias' might have arisen because the people who were more depressed had fewer positive events in their lives.

To avoid this problem, John Teasdale took student volunteers who were not depressed and experimentally manipulated their mood using a Mood Induction Procedure. All subjects started by being randomly allocated to different mood groups, so that results could not be explained by differences in the number of positive and negative events in their lives. The earlier effect was replicated, with the additional finding that negative mood did not so much speed negative events as slow down the recall of positive events.[1]

Taking the analogy of a horse race, the finding that depression does not seem to work by speeding up the black horse is important. In psychotherapy for depression, it will not be sufficient for a client to work to make negative events less accessible. The therapy will need also to increase the availability of more positive aspects of the past. There is abundant evidence that depressed people have suffered a great deal of genuinely negative life events and chronic difficulties. Given the real difficulties of these people's actual experience, the effect of their mood on memory is to place an additional burden on them by making it difficult for them to remember those positive events, the recall of which might alleviate some of the distress.

When I and my colleagues began our research on suicidal behaviour in the early 1980s in Cambridge, we wanted to find out what turns a crisis into a suicidal crisis and thought bias in memory a good candidate. Perhaps some people, at certain points, became so dominated by negative memories that their past seemed nothing but a string of failures, disappointments and arguments. We set out to see if this bias operates in people who are feeling suicidal, even if they are not clinically depressed. We were to find something about their memories more significant than the memory bias we expected.

Memory in suicidal patients

In research of this sort, it is important to obtain as accurate a measure as possible of how fast people are in recalling events from their past. We also wanted to measure the time people took to recall events, so we followed previous research in giving patients words one at a time, a task reminiscent of the word-association test pioneered by C. G. Jung. But instead of responding with the first word that came to mind, participants were asked to respond with the first memory that came to mind. By giving some positive and some negative words as 'cues', it is possible to examine how long people take to recall positive and negative events.

The first patient I gave the task to was a young woman in her early twenties who had been kept in hospital following an overdose. She was still quite sad and hopeless, but had no hesitation in volunteering, saying she was glad of someone to talk to. I had carefully prepared my questionnaires and memory tasks, choosing five positive words and five negative words to use as memory cues. The words – *happy, safe, interested, successful* and *surprised*; and *sorry, hurt, clumsy, angry* and *lonely* – were chosen because a colleague at Cambridge had used them in a memory experiment on a large number of non-depressed people. These had found no difficulty in responding to the words with events from their lives.

I had typed each word on the top of a piece of paper, and printed the instructions on the top of the first page. These asked the person to look at each word in turn, and to write down an event from their past which the word reminded them of. The event could be recent or have happened a long time ago. It might be important or trivial.

I timed how long it took this first participant to start writing in each case. She responded to each word. Later I found that to the cue word 'happy' she had written 'my father'; to the cue word 'sorry' she had written 'when I do things wrong'; to 'surprised' she had written 'when my brother plays tricks on me'. This was not what was supposed to have happened. She was supposed to be recalling specific events, but one response was a person (her father), and the rest were summaries of many events.

We tried the task with one or two other patients (who, like all the others, had recently taken an overdose), and seemed to get similar results. Perhaps asking them to write down their memories was the problem. We changed to reading out the words and asking for a verbal response, which we then wrote down. Then we could prompt them if they started to produce such general responses. Things did not improve. Perhaps the instructions were not being understood. We started to give more detailed instructions and asked people to recall specific events, defining them clearly as events that happened at a particular place and time and lasted less than a day. We gave some practice words until the person was able to produce a specific memory and repeat the instructions back.

The first consistent result to appear[2] was that the suicidal individuals do indeed take much longer to retrieve positive events from their lives, though they are not much quicker than non-depressed controls at retrieving negative events (see Figure 18). In this respect they behaved like the depressed subjects in the studies mentioned earlier. But the feature that particularly interested us was the cause of the delay in retrieving a specific positive memory. It was because they persisted, despite all our prompting, in retrieving an inappropriately general memory when the cue word was first given.

Table 7 shows some of their responses compared with the responses of control participants, who were either people from the Applied Psychology Unit Subject Panel in Cambridge or non-psychiatric patients from the same hospital wards as the overdose patients. Control participants respond to the cues by giving specific memories

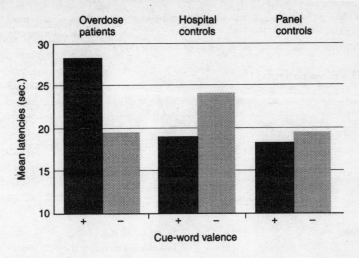

Figure 18. Mean latency to respond to cue words with specific autobiographical memories (from Williams and Broadbent, 'Autobiographical Memory in Attempted Suicide Patients, *Journal of Abnormal Psychology*, 1986).

as asked, but overdose patients are much more likely to respond by giving a general memory which summarizes a number of events. They do this equally for positive and negative memories.

The mechanism of memory retrieval

Memory for events in one's life is hierarchically organized, with the 'upper' layers containing general memory information that can act as pointers to the more specific and detailed 'lower' layers. Thus these upper layers act as intermediate stages in the laying down and later recollection of events. When we try to recollect an event, we first find an 'upper layer' general description. This is then used to search the 'lower layer' memory database for an appropriate candidate memory. For example, in response to the cue 'happy', people generate an intermediate description based on the implicit question, 'What sort of people, activities, places make me happy?' This 'upper layer' description may be such things as 'gardening' or

Table 7. Responses to cue words given by overdose and matched control subjects (from Williams and Broadbent, 'Autobiographical Memory in Attempted Suicide Patients', *Journal of Abnormal Psychology*, 1986).

Overdose patients

Cue	Latency (secs.)	Response
Happy	3	Being with John.
	9	The night he told me he loved me.
Sorry	26	Sorry if I've hurt anyone, any time.
	35	Arguments.
	53	This week-end, Friday.
Safe	3	Being in my flat.
	12	Just when I'm sitting there.
Angry	10	A lot of the time.
	23	A lot of people make me angry.
	35	Racial prejudice.
	46	I went to a party once – this Nigerian wasn't allowed in.

Control subjects

Cue	Latency (secs.)	Response
Happy	18	When I went to see my daughter in her new house.
Sorry	42	When I went to see my sister after her husband had had a heart attack.
Safe	6	After reaching home after driving a long way (from Yorkshire).
Angry	7	Very angry after I found that my older son had been misbehaving.

'my girlfriend' or 'drinking in pubs with friends'. It appears that suicidal and depressed patients get stuck at that intermediate stage, and cannot use the general descriptions they generate to help them retrieve specific examples.

Why do they abort the search for a specific memory at this intermediate stage? Further research suggests that this may be partly because of the traumatic nature of some past event or events, so that the search is stopped as a way of defending against the pain of remembering.[3] However, this would not explain why such people are as likely, or even more likely, to give a generic memory in response to positive cues, i.e. when the memory system is searching for a positive event.

Maybe patients become caught up at the intermediate description level – a phenomenon called 'mnemonic interlock'. Evidence suggests that whenever the memory system attempts to retrieve an event using a personal description, the description itself simply tends to activate other general self-descriptions (as illustrated in Figures 19 and 20). In these figures, one can see the cue word 'sorry' elicits the intermediate description, 'When I've hurt someone.' Instead of proceeding to generate possible memories which fit the general description (e.g. the specific memory of the time he received a letter telling him his partner was leaving), the description activates further self-descriptive summaries such as 'arguments' and, 'I always hurt people I love.'

We begin to see how an event can become a 'final straw' for suicidal behaviour. The final straw is not simply one extra source of stress. It is rather any extra source which activates this network of intermediate, self-referent descriptions, causing mnemonic interlock.

Mnemonic interlock in depression

To return to depression, to see whether depressed people who are not currently suicidal have similar difficulties, recall that the early work on memory in depression was concerned only with the probability or latency of negative versus positive memories; with the

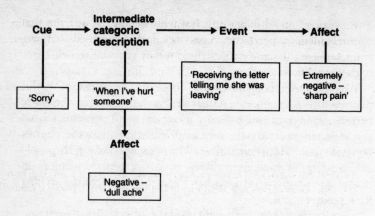

Figure 19. Stages in retrieval of specific autobiographical memory.

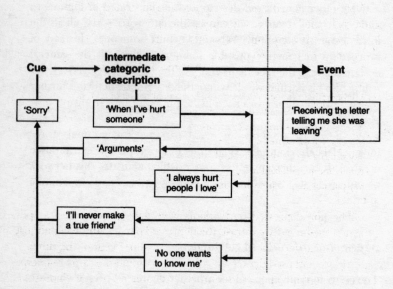

Figure 20. Effect of aborting search for specific memory results in many iterations of intermediate stage, resulting in over-elaborated self-descriptive categories ('mnemonic interlock').

'horse race' model of memory. It was not concerned with the quality of the memory produced. Some indication that depressed people might have the same difficulty was found in a study carried out by Richard Moore as part of his doctoral thesis at Cambridge.[4] He asked depressed people questions about their past, focusing on times when they felt supported (either in practical terms, or emotionally) by a neighbour, friend, family member or partner. Eight positive and eight negative scenarios were presented (see Table 8) to depressed people and matched volunteers who were not depressed.

Table 8. Scenarios used to cue memories (from Moore, Watts and Williams, 'The Specificity of Personal Memories in Depression', *British Journal of Clinical Psychology*, 1988).

My brother/sister criticized me.
A neighbour helped me with some practical problem.
My partner caused some practical problem.
A neighbour caused some practical problem.
My best friend reassured and encouraged me.
My partner reassured and encouraged me.
My best friend criticized me.
My brother/sister helped me with some practical problem.
My partner criticized me.
My best friend helped me with some practical problem.
My brother/sister caused some practical problem.
A neighbour reassured and encouraged me.
My best friend caused some practical problem.
My brother/sister reassured and encouraged me.
A neighbour criticized me.
My partner helped me with some practical problem.

The non-depressed participants gave general memories 21 per cent of the time. By contrast, the depressed participants were almost twice as likely to give general memories (38 per cent of the time).

Moore had used depressed volunteers. Would the same phenomenon be found in people who met criteria for major depressive disorder? Jan Scott and I tested the autobiographical memory of twenty in-patients with major depressive disorder.[5] We compared depressed patients' memory with twenty controls, matched for age, educational level and performance on a semantic processing speed task which had been found sensitive to drugs. We discovered that the speed with which they recalled positive and negative memories from their past was biased. They were much slower to recall positive events (confirming the earlier researches on memory and depression). As we had anticipated, depressed patients were much more likely to respond with over-general memories. A research clinic in Belgium recently replicated this result.[6]

The origins of over-general memory

Developmental psychologists have shown that retrieval of events in a summary, over-general form is a normal developmental phase before specific-event memory emerges at the ages of 3 to 4.[7] Before this time children are likely to answer questions about what has happened, say, at their nursery school or kindergarten, with a general reply (such as, 'On Tuesdays we have orange juice'). This occurs even when unique events are arranged for children at playgroup (e.g. a person visiting dressed as a witch). Following such an interesting event, questioning on the subsequent day shows the children do not have very good specific memory for it.[8]

Further research reveals that the children do have some memory for the event, but eliciting details takes very careful questioning. It is not the young child's preferred method of retrieving events in their life. Could it be, then, that some children never adequately get beyond this method of retrieval? It is possible that stressful events at around that time have the two effects alluded to earlier: making specific events too traumatic to remember in detail and causing the child to be self-focused. Such self-focus means that attempts to recollect events (even positive events) causes mnemonic interlock and he or she aborts the search. A small amount of circumstantial evidence points in this direction.

Willem Kuyken and Chris Brewin, working at the Institute of Psychiatry in London, studied autobiographical recall in fifty-eight depressed women.[9] Comparing their retrieval patterns with a matched control group, they were able to replicate our earlier findings on the effects of depression on generality of recall. However, of even greater significance was their finding that many of these women (64 per cent) had been sexually or physically abused in childhood and adolescence. The women who had been sexually abused had even greater difficulty in recalling specific events from their past, despite the fact that the abused situations were not the events being asked about nor the events the women retrieved.

The average age of the women in this sample was 37, and the traumatic events they experienced occurred prior to 17. Despite this large gap in time, many were still having flashbacks of the physical and sexual abuse. Kuyken and Brewin used a questionnaire, the Impact of Events Scale, to assess the extent of the intrusiveness of thoughts relating to the abuse and how much the person tried to avoid these thoughts and images. Dividing those women who had been abused into high and low scorers on the Impact of Events Scale showed that those still suffering intrusive thoughts, and trying to avoid such flashbacks, had particular difficulties in retrieving specific events from their past, either positive or negative.

These data suggest that general memory may serve as an indicator that emotionally disturbing events have not yet been emotionally processed. In a sense, this is unsurprising. Emotional processing involves being able to return voluntarily to specific details of events, sometimes to give a greater sense of control over them, sometimes to generate alternative explanations and accounts of them (e.g. to shift the blame away from oneself). Generic memory prevents this emotional processing from taking place.

The consequences of over-general memory

Therefore what sort of variables *are* likely to make a person suffering from chronic problems decide to make an attempt on their own life? Why this person; why now? The mnemonic interlock means that any one small event (the final straw) can activate a network of summary self-descriptive memories. Whether these are positive or negative, they are still likely to have damaging consequences. In the case of negative memories, the person's mind is quickly dominated by global self-referent descriptions such as 'I've always been a failure,' 'Nobody's ever really liked me.' But even mnemonic interlock around positive events may have damaging effects. The person has no speedy access to specific positive events which would allow him or her to generate specific ideas for how to bring about similar positive events in the future. This is likely to undermine attempts to solve current problems, to increase hopelessness, and thereby finally to lengthen any episode of depression.

General memory and problem-solving

If the word 'happy' simply brings back a summary memory – 'There were lots of happy times when I lived at home' – the summary memory does not deliver especially good hints for what to do about current unhappiness. The much-loved home may have broken up, and the resulting conclusion may be, 'I cannot be happy.' Over-general positive mnemonic interlock can be as damaging as negative mnemonic interlock. By contrast, those able to retrieve specific events, positive or negative, are more likely to be able to generate alternative problem-solving strategies for current problems. Those who, when given the cue word 'happy', are able to remember a specific event when they lived at home, such as, 'Going out with a friend to the cinema, where we met Jan and Pete and went back to their house for a coffee,' are more likely to find in this some hints for what to do about their current unhappiness: the event, the cinema, the friends, the coffee, etc.

The hypothesis that over-general memory impairs problem-solving ability has been tested in a study by Julie Evans, working with the parasuicide counselling team at Kidderminster General Hospital in England.[10] They contrasted the memory performance of people who had recently taken an overdose with carefully matched control patients who were in hospital for surgery. As well as using the autobiographical memory tests, they assessed problem-solving ability using the Means–Ends Problem Solving Test (MEPS). In this test, individuals are given the beginning and end of a story and asked to fill in the middle section. The five items used in the study are shown in Table 9.

Table 9. Situations used from the Means–Ends Problem Solving Test (used by Evans, Williams, O'Loughlin and Howells, 'Autobiographical Memory and Problem Solving Strategies of Parasuicide Patients', *Psychological Medicine*, 1992).

---

1. Someone who loves his/her partner very much, but they have many arguments, after one of which the partner leaves.

2. Someone who had just moved to a new neighbourhood and didn't know anyone, though he/she wanted to have friends in the neighbourhood.

3. Someone who sees a person of the opposite sex, eating in a restaurant, and to whom they are attracted.

4. Someone who is having trouble getting along with the foreman on his/her job.

5. Someone who comes home after shopping and finds that he/she had lost a watch.

Earlier work using this task with depressed patients[11] had found that problem-solving was more difficult for depressed patients, but had not examined the link between problem-solving abilities and memory function. What it had done, however, was to propose a scoring system of the MEPS task to take into account the effectiveness of the solutions people generated. An example of this scoring system is given in Table 10.

Not only were depressed patients unable to produce as many alternative means of solving the problems as were non-depressed controls, but when they did generate a possible solution, it was less effective, i.e. less likely to produce the desired outcome. Julie Evans found both that overdose patients produced fewer ways of solving the problems, and that what they did produce were generally less effective solutions. Were these difficulties associated with difficulty in retrieving specific memories? The result confirmed, as predicted, a significant correlation between the effectiveness of solutions and the generality of autobiographical memories.

The results were consistent with the hypothesis that deficits in memory may play an important role in blocking access to effective solutions to current difficulties, increasing the sense of helplessness

Table 10. Ratings of effectiveness of problem solutions (from Marx, Williams and Claridge, 'Depression and Social Problem-solving', *Journal of Abnormal Psychology*, 1992).

In order to illustrate the scoring for effectiveness, and to illustrate the range of this dimension, two examples representing the extreme poles of the scale, from

1 = 'not at all effective' to
7 = 'extremely effective'.

These ratings are made by independent judges.

The following examples are taken from the situation: 'trying to make new friends in a new neighbourhood':

> I wouldn't know what to do in that situation. I have always had someone to go out and make friends for me. I can't imagine what to do. (Rated 1 – Not at all effective)

> First thing is to introduce herself to the immediate neighbours, explaining that she had just moved in, possibly inviting the people for a coffee anytime, and also if they seem interested in her, if they invite her, making it clear that she intends to take it up anytime. Chatting to people in the local shops, joining clubs, offering to be helpful in some ways, e.g. baby-sitting, gardening for old people. One tactic would be to get a dog and take it for walks – that's easy to get in contact. Similarly, if she has children, it's easy to get in contact. Inviting people round for dinner or drinks. (Rated 7 – Extremely effective)

and entrapment. To understand how all-pervasive this effect of memory can be, one only has to realize that such memory problems also feed forward into a person's view of the future.

General memory and hopelessness

Hopelessness has been seen as the critical factor mediating between depression and suicidality. Hopelessness about the future appears to combine so lethally with depression as to produce suicidal ideas and behaviour. Hopelessness has been found to predict repetition of parasuicide six months later and completed suicides up to ten years later. If over-general memory is seen as a significant effect on future suicidal behaviour, then we need to examine its effect on people's attitude to the future.

With my colleague Andrew MacLeod, I began to investigate the components of hopelessness (see page 94). We were particularly interested in looking at the effect of over-general memories on how specifically or vaguely a person imagined the future. We reasoned that an important element in hopelessness was that people cannot imagine any future with certainty, either positive or negative.

One experiment asked people to remember times in their life when they had been either unhappy or happy. We cued them with sentences such as, 'Try to remember an event in your life when you were in tears,' or, 'Try to remember an event in your life when you were laughing.' Similarly we asked the subjects on another occasion, 'Try to think of a time in the future when you might be in tears,' or, 'Try to envisage a time in the future when you will laugh.' We coded the specificity of future images into three levels (Table 11).

Patients admitted to hospital following an overdose were compared with matched medical patients and matched non-hospitalized volunteers. The results were as predicted. Overdose patients were more vague than controls in descriptions of future and past. Furthermore, subjects who were less specific about past and future were more hopeless about the future. General memory can undermine the very process by which a person constructs a specific future for themselves, and thereby allows hopelessness to grow and develop without hindrance.[12]

General memory and persistence of depression

Finally, if these memory deficits affect both problem-solving and levels of hopelessness in this way, then one might expect that people who have such a problem will have unusually prolonged episodes of depression, since they will not have the resources to take advantage of any breaks in mood that other treatments (e.g. antidepressants) might bring about. Can we therefore improve our prediction of how long depression lasts by taking account of how patients perform

Table 11. Ratings of specificity of future image (from Williams *et al.*, 'The specificity of autobiographical memory and imageability of the future', *Memory and Cognition*, 24, 116–25).

Try and picture a situation in the future where:

... 'you make a mistake'

general	intermediate	specific
'I'll always be making mistakes'	Perhaps giving a friend the wrong advice	My law exams in October

... 'someone pays you a compliment'

general	intermediate	specific
'A friend could'	'Someone at work may say I've lost weight'	'Next week from my husband when I have my hair cut again'

when asked about their autobiographical memory? Is it the case that two people equally depressed will have different prognoses, depending on the level of specificity in their memories? This is an important question. We know it is the longer-lasting depressions which are most likely to lead to suicide.

Some results from the early literature on psychotherapy process are consistent with the hypothesis that specificity of recall affects rate of progress in overcoming emotional problems. One early investigation examined taped transcripts from over a hundred sessions of group psychotherapy with hospitalized patients of various diagnoses. It found that clients who described current feelings and life situations in a concrete and specific way were more likely to make progress in therapy.[13] Does non-specificity therefore have a predictive effect on the course of depressive illness?

With the help of colleagues, Andy Brittlebank, Jan Scott and Nicol Ferrier, we examined this question in some seriously depressed patients admitted to a psychiatric unit in Newcastle upon Tyne.[14]

When admitted, patients completed the Hamilton Rating Scale, widely used to measure the severity of depression, and the Autobiographical Memory Test. Each patient was followed up after three and seven months. The more over-general in memory the patients were at admission, the worse their Hamilton Depression Scale scores at both three and seven months. Dividing patients at admission into high and low over-generality in response to positive cues (found to be the more sensitive indicator), we examined the outcome at seven months for each sub-group. Of nine patients who were 'over-general to positive cues', only one had recovered. Of ten patients who were 'specific to positive cues', eight had recovered. These results suggest that this aspect of memory is a powerful determinant of how long the depression lasts. It appears that for depressed people who have this additional problem, their mood will appear more pervasive and durable, with the result that these individuals will feel more helpless, and less motivated to engage in activities which might otherwise lift their mood.

These results show the importance of memory in contributing to the trap from which the suicidal person wishes to escape. The past is dominated by generalities, which undermine the ability to see an effective way to solve current problems. If this were not bad enough, the memory problem has an additional effect on how the future is viewed, contributing to the feeling of vagueness about the future. Non-specificity about past and future is significantly associated with hopelessness, that aspect of depression which most points towards suicidal behaviour as an option. As we will see in Chapter 12, a major characteristic of successful treatments for suicidal feelings and behaviour is that they induce the person to be very specific about the past, often with the use of diaries to record daily events.

Concluding remarks

This chapter gives an account of work in progress. Our aim is ultimately to explain why some people take drastic action to harm themselves or end their life. We need a theory which can relate to other perspectives: sociological, psychiatric and biological. We need a theory which promises to specify the nature of the final common pathway leading from depression to hopelessness, then to suicide. We now feel in a better position to understand why some people are more vulnerable to suicidal behaviour than others.

An inability to be specific in retrieval of personal memories may signal a history of negative events, a history which is unprocessed and still has power to interrupt the present with intrusive thoughts. Such general memories lead to a situation in which people are vague about the future and fail to produce good effective problem-solving alternatives. It sets the context against which the final straw, that event which produces a global summary of the emptiness of one's life, may have its devastating consequences. If life circumstances are the factors that put a person in a cage, it is memory that springs the door closed.

Chapter 11

THE PRIMARY PREVENTION OF
SUICIDAL BEHAVIOUR

In assessing what scope exists for preventing suicide, one of the most obvious measures would be the more sensitive assessment of suicide risk by health professionals. Depression is a frequently occurring psychiatric disorder and most depressed patients are treated in general practice. Training primary-care professionals to recognize depressive symptoms and treat them appropriately is a potentially important prevention strategy. Evidence suggests that 50 per cent of sufferers are not recognized by their general practitioner as suffering major depression. A further 10 per cent are subsequently recognized, and of the 40 per cent not recognized half will remain depressed. Twenty per cent of the original sample, therefore, are still depressed and not recognized six months later.

There are a number of reasons why depression is missed in the context of a GP's clinic. The patient may present somatic symptoms and physical problems; may feel there is a stigma about presenting psychological problems, compounded by a belief that the doctor does not have time to listen to their psychological problems. There is also some evidence that depression is more likely to be missed if it is of recent origin, where the symptoms are atypical, the depressed mood is less severe and the patient has less insight into their own symptoms. A picture emerges of a complex interplay of factors which result in the primary-care worker not spotting depressed symptoms.

Depression and hopelessness are clearly associated with suicidal ideation and behaviour. If depression is going unrecognized, then suicidal ideation is also likely to go unrecognized. Implicit blame is often put on the physician or mental-health professional who has failed to pick up the signs, yet it is never quite so simple. Data from twenty years ago seemed to suggest that between 50 and 80 per cent of people who commit suicide had seen a doctor up to one month prior to death. More recent reviews suggest that only 20 to 25 per cent of those committing suicide have seen their GP or other health-care professional in the week before death, and 40 per cent in the month before. It is likely that the decrease in suicide among the older population and the increase in younger men accounts for this change. Young men are much less likely to visit their doctors than young women or older men.

Identifying scope for improvement in the recognition of depressed symptoms in general, and suicidal symptoms in particular, need not be associated with blaming the primary-care physicians for not spotting them in the first place. We need to understand more about the interpersonal processes that govern the interaction between doctor and patient. These were studied by David Coombs and colleagues at the University of Alabama,[1] who examined the consultations between care-givers (physicians, psychiatrists, psychologists and mental-health counsellors) and patients who had subsequently attempted suicide up to three months later. Thirty-six of the fifty patients studied (72 per cent) had, by their own accounts, sought professional help for depression or suicidal thinking in the three months prior to the episode. However, according to the patients' own reports, they made direct reference to suicidal thinking in only 23 per cent of all consultations. How much this was because of reluctance to talk about these feelings, and how much a result of the professional failing to ask the right questions, is an open question. According to the professionals' reports, they said they asked about suicidal feelings in 48 per cent of cases.

Coombs also wanted to see whether people were less likely to report depression and suicidal feelings to physicians than to mental-health professionals. They found they were much less likely to disclose symptoms to the physicians. This confirms that a major determinant of what is talked about is the context of the visit. Even when a person *intends* to communicate emotional and psychological distress, once they enter the context of the physician's surgery, the evidence of physical medicine all around them elicits talk about their physical symptoms rather than their psychological difficulties.

Another indication of how the interpersonal context determines what takes place between health professional and patient is a finding about how the age of the patient determined outcome. Patients of 55 or older were not asked at all about suicidal thinking. Given that these patients are the most vulnerable for completed suicide, it seemed a surprising result. One possible explanation is that older people are more likely to express problems through physical symptoms. Another is that care-givers feel more reluctant to ask about psychological symptoms of people older than themselves. Social mores that dictate respect for older people and their privacy may be a more powerful determinant of professionals' behaviour than previously thought.

The Gotland study

If people do seek help, what evidence is there to suggest that any appropriate help at all can be given? In 1989 an important study by Rutz and colleagues in Sweden investigated the possibility that recognizing and treating depressed patients in the primary-care setting would affect rates of suicidal behaviour.[2] They conducted their study on the island of Gotland, which has a population of 56,000, a single psychiatric department and eighteen GPs. In 1983 and 1984, all the GPs attended two education programmes given by the Swedish Prevention and Treatment of Depression Committee. The aims were to increase their knowledge of diagnosis and treatment of depressive disorders. Interestingly, the study monitored suicide rates not because it was thought these would decrease, but because of worry that they might increase if more cases of depression were inappropriately treated in general practice rather than being sent to the psychiatric department.

The resulting suicide rates for 1982–5, shown in Figure 21, reveal a significant decline on the island of Gotland compared with the rates for the same time period on mainland Sweden. However, a 1992 report showed that this effect was only temporary, owing to the fact that some of the doctors who had been trained subsequently left the island.[3] The authors concluded that there was a significant effect from their intervention, but that the educational programme needed to be maintained if it was to continue to have an impact.

They also showed that training GPs increased the appropriate use of antidepressant medication, with a parallel decrease in the use of hypnotics, sedatives and major tranquillizers. There was also a decrease in patients taking sick leave from work. These results suggested that the benefits of such a training programme were likely to generalize beyond simply the treatment of the symptoms of depression which were its primary focus.

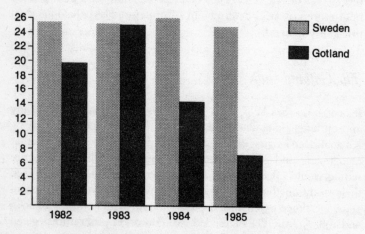

Figure 21. Suicide rates in Gotland and the mainland of Sweden, during and after systematic education of Gotland GPs on diagnosis and treatment of depressive disorders.

Criticism of the Gotland study

The interpretation of the Gotland study has been controversial. Because it was not a randomized trial (with a control group of GPs who did not receive the training), some have said its results should be treated with extreme caution. The reduction in suicide rate may have happened by chance. Other critics have gone further, and said that even the published results give a misleading impression. A letter to the *British Journal of Psychiatry*, claiming that the numbers committing suicide on Gotland had started to fall well before the education programme was introduced,[4] included a graph showing a reanalysis of the data. The graph seemed to show a long, slow decline in the suicide rate before the education programme was begun. Because the study is the only one of its type, it is important to consider this last criticism with particular care.

Reply to criticism

In fact, the writer of the letter had made a simple but critical error in his reanalysis of the Gotland data. Instead of examining the suicide rate year by year, he had calculated a five-year moving average. Taking a moving average of such data is a well-recognized method of 'smoothing' a graph so that trends may be seen more clearly. In the procedure, a 'window' of consecutive points in a series (between two or five points usually) is taken, and the average used as a new data point. So, a five-year moving average takes data points from years 1, 2, 3, 4 and 5 for the first data point; years 2, 3, 4, 5 and 6 for the second; 3, 4, 5, 6 and 7 for the third, and so on. The five-year 'window' is moved across the data and the graph is smoothed.

However, if an intervention is introduced, the moving window must stop at the last data point *before* the intervention. Otherwise the window is gradually contaminated by more and more data points from the intervention phase. To illustrate this, consider the dummy data in Figure 22, which clearly show the effect of an intervention. Figure 23, however, shows what happens to this graph if a five-year moving average is applied which does not stop when the intervention starts. The baseline data is contaminated increasingly by the data from the intervention phase, giving the wrong impression that the rate of the behaviour in question started to decline before the intervention – precisely the mistake made in the critical letter.

Figure 24 shows the smoothed means of the Gotland data retaining a five-year moving average but stopping the window prior to the intervention. As can be seen, the intervention follows three successive drops in the smoothed graph (of 1.9, 1.2 and 2.7 per 100,000 respectively). In this sense, the author of the critical letter was right to point out some reduction in the suicide rate prior to the intervention phase starting, but his error made this reduction seem much greater than it was. The first post-intervention data point is 7.0 per 100,000, lower

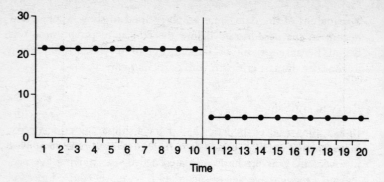

Figure 22. Dummy data illustrating effect of hypothetical intervention to reduce death-rate.

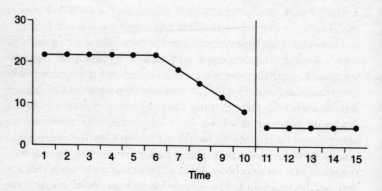

Figure 23. Graph illustrating effect of applying five-year moving average to data in Figure 22 if moving average is not stopped prior to intervention.

again than the last point prior to the intervention – a much larger drop than that between any two prior data points.

Of course, without a controlled study, the Gotland data remain preliminary. But the implications for suicide prevention by GPs cannot be ignored. Nevertheless, it is right to point out that such intervention may be extremely difficult to achieve.

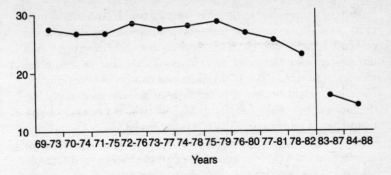

Figure 24. Graph showing the smoothed means of actual Gotland data retaining a five-year moving average but stopping the window prior to intervention.

Primary care and primary prevention: some cautions

We have seen that physicians sometimes miss the seriousness of depression, treating the single symptom of insomnia or agitation without checking for other symptoms. However, it remains painfully true that the chances of a GP successfully spotting a suicidal patient are relatively low, given that there is likely to be a suicide only once every four to five years among his or her patients. Because of the 40 per cent rate of contact of suicide victims with their doctors in the month prior to suicide, this means that a GP is likely to receive a consultation from somebody in the month before they commit suicide only once every eight to ten years. This makes it an extremely rare event compared with the large proportion who consult their doctors with emotional problems.[5]

Some have suggested that just because suicide is rare does not mean the doctor should not test for it. If a GP sees a child with a fever, he or she will test for meningitis, although this is also very rare. By analogy, it is suggested that the GP should spend some time testing for suicide risk. However, physical tests for rare diseases are not a fair analogy. Physical tests often produce a greater certainty of diagnosis, and even if they do not, an 'at risk' result may warrant further, more specialist testing. Yet even if a health professional used every available measuring instrument to assess suicide risk, the evidence suggests that he or she would successfully detect only half the people who are going to commit suicide. For this number, moreover, he would 'detect' an enormous number of false positives. His clinic would be full of people whom he suspected might kill themselves, but who, the statistics show, will not actually harm themselves. Taking the analogy of a radar screen, the doctor is being expected to perceive an image on the screen which will occur three or four times in a professional life, against the background of many similar images occurring at every daily surgery.

The general problem of prediction: sensitivity and specificity

Why is prediction so difficult? If we take the common predictors of suicide (see Table 12), we find a number of factors that we feel should help identify those most at risk.

There are two problems in predicting such behaviour: sensitivity

Table 12. Predictors of suicide.

Mental disorder, especially depression
Alcohol or drug abuse
Suicide ideation, talking and planning
Prior parasuicide
Lethal methods
Isolation, living alone, few social supports
Hopelessness
Being white male
Suicide in the family (modelling, genetic loading?)
Work problems, unemployment, high-risk occupation
Family and marital problems
Stress and negative life events
Problems of affective control (anger, impulsivity)
Physical illness

('not having many misses') and specificity ('not having false positives'). An assessment device needs to have adequate sensitivity (i.e. a high hit rate for 'true positives', predicting suicide and getting suicide). It must also have adequate specificity, predicting the true negatives (predict no suicide and get no suicide).[6] The issue of specificity is particularly significant because of the low base rate of suicidal behaviour. Thus, even in a highly selected group, there will be more people falsely identified as at risk (false positives) than correctly identified as at risk (hits). When trying to predict suicide the problem is even greater.

Pokorny, in a prospective study,[7] followed up almost 5,000 in-patients. The predictive model identified 35 out of the 67 subsequent suicides but at the cost of over 1,000 false positives. Whichever analysis Pokorny used, he found the result was a false positive rate of 25–30 per cent. Over 1,000 people would have been put on the vulnerable list, but not have committed suicide. Perhaps more worrying was the 44 per cent false negative rate. This means that of the people who did commit suicide, 44 per cent would have been allocated to the 'low risk' category.

This pessimistic message is reinforced by the suicidologist, Ronald Maris.[8] He points out that so-called 'high risk' groups are not, after all, at that high a risk of suicide. Take the statistic that 15 per cent of those who have been patients in psychiatric units with a diagnosis of major depression will commit suicide. They are at a greatly increased risk compared with the general population. Yet even they will commit suicide at a group rate of some 1 per cent per year over a period of about thirty to thirty-five years. For every hundred patients in the 'suicide high risk' category, only one will actually commit suicide in any one year, and we cannot be sure which one, or when. The question of 'when' is one of the most difficult to answer.

Timing

It is clear that assessment of suicidal risk cannot merely be done at a single point in time, on the basis only of predisposing (and pre-existing) vulnerability factors. Changes over time need also to be taken into account. Are there any indications about what the vulnerable times might be?

Times of change in circumstances appear to be most vulnerable. For example, in prison populations, the first twenty-four hours is the most risky time. Over 50 per cent of prison suicides occur in the period immediately following incarceration. As Maris points out, the vulnerable times for psychiatric patients are also times of change: a move out of hospital, whether on a week-end pass or at discharge, or even a move within the hospital to another unit; or change in symptoms, such as an improvement in activity, sleep and appetite that may precede a change in mood and hopelessness; changes in social, family or living arrangements.[8]

This is an under-researched topic, so any theory must be speculative. Nevertheless we can narrow the possibilities. I suggest that any disruption to a settled routine triggers a state in which the individual reviews goals and plans. They start to compare current circumstances to goals – what they would like to be the case. The review includes an assessment of their own energy and ability levels needed to achieve these goals. If the individual estimates they do not have the energy or resources to reduce the gap between current reality and future goals, they are in danger of feeling even more hopeless.

The change in circumstances that can trigger such a review may be subtle. It may be a change in the external environment, or a change in the 'internal' environment, i.e. in a person's mood state. But however it has been triggered, once the review has started the individual may find it very difficult to switch it off. The ruminative habits of thought in such circumstances can produce, for the individual, extremely pessimistic self-assessment, and further catastrophic downward spirals in mood. These are the critical periods for suicidal thoughts and behaviour, when the availability of the means of suicide becomes an important factor.

Availability of means

The devastating effect of the availability of lethal substances is illustrated by the case of a brilliant Cambridge postgraduate student who killed himself with a lethal injection early in 1995. He had been the best A level biology student at his home school. At Cambridge, he performed as well as his early school career had promised, coming top in all subjects in the university examinations out of all the medical students in his first and second years. At 24 years old his tutors thought him one of the brightest students of the past decade. It was clear he was heading for a brilliant academic career, and he started on a course that would eventually give him not only a medical qualification but a PhD as well.

But his private life was not going so well. According to friends and tutors, he loved a woman who did not love him. His work seemed no compensation for such unrequited love. He was quite a private person, but nobody expected the devastating effect this would have. At a party in Cambridge one Saturday night he appeared cheerful, and may have gone home briefly before going to the laboratory. It was there that the availability of lethal substances had its effect, for none of his friends or tutors doubted that, had he been able to get over his acute feeling of desperation, the weekend would have passed and he could have recovered his composure. But the laboratory contained chemicals used on animals in research – substances lethal if used in an unsafe manner. They were at hand when he felt at his worst, and suicide was the result.

Clinicians and researchers have had little doubt for some time that if help and protection are available during a period of suicidal crisis, and lethal methods are not to hand, the crisis may pass and the person not commit suicide. It may not even be help that is needed, but simply distraction at a critical moment. One person who put the muzzle of a revolver into his mouth and was feeling for the trigger, suddenly heard his children laughing and running through the hall. 'That snapped me out of it. The suicide impulse lasted only a moment – but that's all it takes,' he reported later.

The basis for expecting that availability of lethal methods makes a difference is this: if the preferred method is not there, the motivation to search for an alternative may not be high enough to prompt such a search. The suicidal feelings may pass without being acted upon. If this seems difficult to understand, we only need recall that suicide occurs in the context of hopelessness and despair. If a single opportunity appears to present an escape, yet that escape route is blocked, the despair may turn into hopelessness about suicide as an effective solution. The 'Russian roulette' aspect of suicidal motivation produces a sense of not caring 'whether I live or die'. If a person has effectively 'allowed the Fates to decide', then their verdict in favour of staying alive may be passively accepted. But if, at that moment, the person has access to lethal methods, the outcome will be suicide.

Of course, a person determined to kill him or herself may take many steps to ensure success, including taking themselves away to a place where they will not be interrupted. Even where this does not occur, the family or friends of a suicidal person cannot be on hand twenty-four hours a day. To try to be constantly present in this way would put so much pressure on a relationship it would be unsustainable. Nevertheless it is possible to try to ensure that lethal means of suicide are unavailable for those attempts that are more impulsive. The problem is knowing which threats to remove.

In *Savage God*, Alvarez quotes the views of Seneca, who said that the means of committing suicide are everywhere: each precipice and river, each branch of each tree, every vein in the body will set a person free. Alvarez disagreed: 'No one is promiscuous in his way of dying. A man who has decided to hang himself will never jump in front of a train. And the more sophisticated and painless the method, the greater the chance of failure: I can vouch, at least, for that.' If true, this means that a health professional may ask someone who is suicidal what they have thought of doing, and try to ensure that these means are removed.

Research evidence

The preventative effect of removing such lethal means has been demonstrated many times. The most commonly cited example is the fall in suicide rates during the 1960s and 1970s in the United Kingdom as domestic gas was detoxified. In 1948–50, poisoning by domestic gas accounted for 41 per cent of male suicides and 60 per cent of female suicides. By 1970, only 16 per cent of males and 9 per cent of females used domestic gas in suicide. Death by this method had completely disappeared by 1990. It has been estimated that the detoxification of domestic gas has prevented approximately 6,700 deaths by suicide.

Similarly, there was a decline in the suicide rate in Australia in the late 1960s and early 1970s, an effect directly attributable to legislation to reduce amounts of barbiturate and other sleeping pills. Before the mid 1960s, drug overdose was the most common form of suicide in Australia. Up to this time, a hundred to three hundred tablets or capsules of sedative sleeping pills, such as barbiturates, had been available, making suicide by their use extremely easy. In July 1967 it became illegal to prescribe sedative hypnotic drugs, particularly barbiturates, in greater quantities than twenty-five tablets or capsules. Statistics for Australia showed that restricting barbiturates in this way made the suicide rate fall in ensuing years.

However, the reduction in overall rate from the unavailability of one method may gradually bottom out and alternative methods become more common. In England and Wales this occurred with the use of car exhaust replacing domestic gas. Car exhaust now accounts for 35 per cent of male suicides in England and Wales, compared with 31 per cent who hang themselves and 14 per cent who take poisons. The pattern for females is slightly different, with self-poisoning remaining the most common method (44 per cent), followed by hanging (23 per cent) and vehicle exhaust (13 per cent).

The increase in vehicle exhaust deaths parallels the increase in motor vehicle use in the past twenty years. In fact it slightly *exceeds* the rate of increase in car usage, but this may be owing to the fact that within the car market there has been an increase in the proportion of hatchback models, which makes suicide by this method easier. Some have advocated changes to exhaust-pipe design, to make it more difficult to attach a hose, though ultimately it may be more useful to install safety cut-out switches in cars to switch off the engine in response to high levels of fumes. In any event, as emission controls on car exhausts are adopted by more and more countries, we can expect to see a reduction in suicide using car exhaust in the coming years.

Dangerous weapons

Suicide rates using firearms are, of course, another indicator that availability of means is important. Guns are used in over 50 per cent of cases in the United States compared to only 3 per cent in Great Britain. In the United States the impact of availability has focused on the strictness of gun legislation from state to state. Lester (1989) found significant correlations between 'gun control statute strictness' and rates of suicide over the forty-eight continental states (see Table 13).

Table 13. Correlation between gun control strictness and suicide rates across forty-eight American states.

Suicide method	Correlation	Significance
Poisons	−.07	ns
Hanging/strangulation	.15	ns
Firearms	−.52	$p < .001$
Other (e.g. drowning)	.43	$p < .01$

Although stricter gun laws correlated with few suicides by firearms (suggesting that making the method less available will reduce fatalities), there was also an association between lower firearm availability and the use of alternative methods (though not poisons or hanging). Despite this, there are reasons to think that availability *is* important. The positive correlation between strict gun laws and alternative methods in Table 13 does not tell us the overall *level* of suicide by these other methods. Indeed, other work by Lester[9] has shown that the *total* suicide rate is *lower* in states with strict gun control laws. It appears Alvarez is right: only a few suicidal people switch to an alternative method for suicide. People seem to have a preferred method they would use to kill themselves, and are unlikely to deviate from this when actually suicidal. This is important clinically, for depressed patients, when not very suicidal, may agree to get rid of the means of killing themselves that they know they might use later when feeling worse.

Dangerous medication

Other evidence of a link between suicide and availability of method is shown by the correlation between the number of prescriptions given out for sedatives, sleeping pills and tranquillizers, and the rate of suicide by self-poisoning. These data for 1969–90 for England and Wales are shown in Figure 25.

Prescribed mood-altering drugs, such as tricyclic antidepressants, account for 15 per cent of all suicides. Figure 26 shows the relative toxicity of some common antidepressants. Some suicides may therefore be prevented by the prescribing of relatively non-toxic antidepressants. One problem with prescribing safer antidepressants is that they are more expensive, and difficulty in predicting who is most vulnerable to suicide at what point in time means there might have to be a general switch to these newer substances to bring about a reduction in the suicide rate. Such a switch would mean that the cost per life saved would be very high indeed. On the other hand, use of these safer antidepressants in those known to have a higher risk of suicide (psychiatric patients, those with a history of self-harm, etc.) appears an important potential development.

A clear relationship between prescribing patterns and the deaths by these drugs can be found. The clear implication is the need to give patients at risk medication for a few days only and/or give the medication to another family member to keep. Neither of these preventative strategies has been systematically studied.

There are even more deaths attributable to analgesics, anti-fever and anti-rheumatic medications, many of which are available without prescription. Ten per cent of all suicide deaths by overdose are caused by an overdose of paracetamol and 5 per cent from aspirin. However, nearly all patients (94 per cent) who take an overdose take the first drug they can obtain. Few (only 20 per cent)[10] are found to know about the toxicity of a drug or what quantity would be lethal. Many wrongly believe that aspirin and paracetamol, because freely available from the pharmacist, are relatively non-toxic. In France paracetamol is not allowed to be sold in greater quantities than 8 grams (16 × 500 milligram tablets) and there are very few fatal paracetamol overdoses.

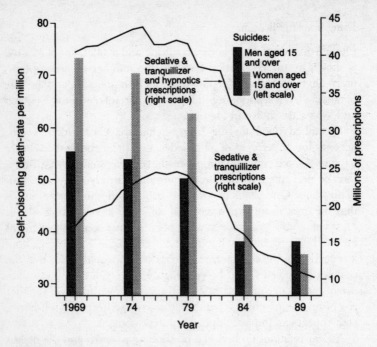

Figure 25. Self-poisoning death-rates by sex and number of GPs' prescriptions for sedatives, tranquillizers and hypnotics, 1969–90, England and Wales. (Crown Copyright, reproduced with permission of HMSO.)

Dangerous jobs

A final piece of evidence that availability of lethal means is important comes from the sort of jobs people do. The only thing the professions most vulnerable to suicide (veterinary surgeon, dental practitioner, pharmacist, farmer and medical practitioner) have in common is access to lethal means of self-killing. Recent evidence suggests that the nursing profession is also vulnerable. Between 1988 and 1992, nurses accounted for a greater number of suicides than any other occupation and over 5 per cent of all female suicides. This is wholly consistent with the 'dangerous jobs' explanation, since nurses know about the lethality of drugs and have ready access to them.

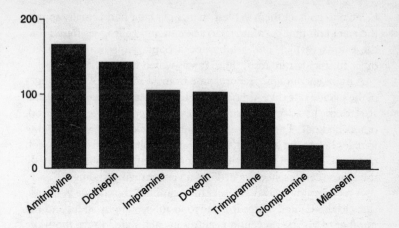

Figure 26. Estimated incidence of death from overdose of antidepressants in England and Wales. Figures are for single drug fatalities per million patients. (From the publication of the Office of Population Census and Surveys for the period 1977–84.) (NOTE: (a) These data need to be treated cautiously. Some antidepressants are more likely to be prescribed where the suicide risk is greatest. For this reason, they may be more likely to feature in overdose statistics. The effect of such distortion on the figures remains unknown. (b) Mianserin is now only rarely prescribed because of the risk of blood disorders.)

Samaritans and suicide prevention centres

Between 4 and 7 per cent of people who commit suicide in the United Kingdom have had past contact with the Samaritans, but how recent these contacts are is not clear. For many years there has been a debate about whether suicide prevention centres and organizations significantly affect the suicide rate. What is not in dispute is that there is a great need for such centres and organizations, as shown by the extensive use made of them. However, even though people know where to turn for help, when they are very suicidal they may not act on this knowledge. One study conducted by Greer and Alderson in 1979[11] found that of those patients who attempted suicide, 72 per cent had sufficient knowledge of the Samaritans to be able to contact them yet less than 2 per cent had actually sought their help on that occasion. Barraclough and colleagues found that those towns which had established a Samaritans branch did not differ in suicide rate from those towns which had not.[12]

A more encouraging report came from an analysis of the changes of the suicide rates in 226 cities in the United States between 1968 and 1973. Some had developed suicide prevention centres over the period, others had not. There was a reduction in suicide rates among white females below the age of 25 in those cities that had introduced such centres. Given that this was just the sort of client who most frequently used those centres, here indeed was an encouraging finding.

A recent study by David Lester has examined the change in suicide rates in the United States from 1970 to 1980, state by state, and the number of suicide prevention centres in each state in 1970 (both the absolute number, and the number per capita of the population).[13] He finds a significant negative correlation: that is, the greater availability of such centres, the greater the reduction in suicide rate. The largest association was between the change in suicide rate among women and the number of suicide prevention centres (−·54), but there was some indication of a preventative effect for both sexes in certain age bands (15−24; 45−64; and 75+). If these results are generalizable to other time periods and other places, they will represent an important advance.

The pattern of use of such services itself provides interesting insights. Callers to the Samaritans in the United Kingdom were more likely to be female until 1995, when the number of male callers exceeded those of females for the first time. The suicide statistics show that males are much more likely to commit suicide than women, but for many years this ratio was in the opposite direction for parasuicidal episodes, with young women more likely than men to attempt suicide. However, for the first time in the mid 1990s, hospitals around the United Kingdom and Ireland independently reported that men were now equal to or exceeding women in the number of parasuicides.

Parallel data from the Samaritans is unlikely to be coincidence. It is much more likely that we are witnessing a major change in the socio-demographic characteristics of suicidal behaviour in the 1990s.

School-based intervention

Following the rapid increase in youth suicide in the United States in the 1980s, many school-based suicide intervention programmes were introduced. Their aims were to increase awareness of the problem of suicide, to provide information about the help available and to encourage suicidal teenagers to come forward and seek it. Wherever such programmes were evaluated, however, they had little or no effect.[14]

Such education programmes target a relatively low-risk audience. The suicide rate among teenagers in school, though increasing, is still low compared with the general population. Indeed, such programmes might not reach those adolescents most at risk, such as regular truants. More seriously, the risk profile of a potential teenage suicide patient is still not fully known. This means that the warning signs as taught may not be representative or accurate.

A further study[15] has assessed the impact of suicide prevention programmes on teenagers' attitudes and knowledge about suicide, with evaluation based on a questionnaire completed before and after exposure to the programme. Even before the programme, most students had a sound knowledge of the issues relating to suicide: the warning signs; the fact that suicide threats should be taken seriously; and that vulnerable individuals should be helped in consultation with responsible adults. But where the research found attitudes that would be considered inappropriate (e.g. that suicide could be a reasonable solution to problems), the education programmes did not change them.

Chapter 8 reviewed the evidence suggesting an increased risk of copycat suicidal behaviour if vulnerable people were exposed to examples of people who harmed themselves. Given this risk, school-based suicide awareness programmes would need to be shown to be clearly effective in reducing the risk of suicidal behaviour for them to be justified. Such effects have not been shown. It is possible that any benefits of such programmes are offset by the fact that they de-stigmatize suicide. By portraying it as an understandable response to stress, the intervention may actually backfire by encouraging an unrealistic, romantic view of suicide, increasing the chances of imitation.

Concluding remarks

Given all this information about who is most vulnerable and what are the most dangerous circumstances, can we estimate the possible effects of making changes? Gunnell lists all the potential effects of suicide prevention strategies for the United Kingdom.[16] Most strategies, he concludes, would have uncertain effects. However, he estimates that a 4 per cent reduction in suicide rates could be achieved by GPs prescribing safer antidepressants; that increased care around the time of discharge from psychiatric hospital could reduce the rate by 2 to 3 per cent; that improved safety measures around places such as bridges and undergrounds/subways where there is a great risk of suicide would save between 1 and 3 per cent of lives; that taking steps to prevent car exhaust being used for suicide, together with the general introduction of catalytic converters, would probably reduce the suicide rate by 7 per cent. Reduction of access to guns (which account for 3 per cent of all suicides in England and Wales) might reduce the suicide rate by a further 1 per cent. The total, a reduction of 15 to 18 per cent, would represent over 700 lives saved in England and Wales alone each year.

The evidence strongly suggests that, for any individual, suicidal impulses come in waves. This implies that if such impulses can find no ready expression, they may pass without the person having harmed themselves. The precise timing of such compelling suicidal urges remains unpredictable, but further research should focus on times of change and how such changes can be prepared for so they do not bring about a life-review process that sends the person's mood spiralling out of control. Meanwhile, if suicide occurs, there will always be some who feel they should have seen it coming: family, friends, health professionals. Hindsight is a painful but pointless source of grief. Instead, primary prevention needs to focus on general measures to reduce the number of 'invitations to suicide' in the environment.

Chapter 12

SECONDARY PREVENTION: THERAPY FOR SUICIDAL FEELINGS AND BEHAVIOUR

What more may be done to prevent further suicidal behaviour once a person has harmed him or herself? Several studies have confirmed that the following six factors predict repetition of parasuicide in the year following an episode: previous parasuicide, previous out-patient and in-patient psychiatric treatment, not living with relatives, previous diagnosis of personality disorder and problems in the use of alcohol. What emerges is the fact that even having a large number of psychosocial difficulties still does not predict further suicidal behaviour in over 50 per cent of the sample. Even in this highly selected group, there will be more people falsely identified as 'at risk' than correctly identified. Nevertheless, therapists are faced with an increasing number judged to be at risk of suicidal behaviour. We need to know what skills are required and what special issues raised in therapy with suicidal clients.

Vigilance for suicidal expression

Although, as we have said, depression is often associated with suicidal thoughts, not all depressed people are suicidal: it is when depressed people also become hopeless that they are most likely to feel suicidal. Therefore a primary goal of therapy with suicidal clients must be (a) accurate assessment of their state of hopelessness; (b) vigilance for further changes in level of hopelessness; (c) reduction of current state of hopelessness; and (d) reduction of vulnerability for future states of hopelessness. Two other important factors must also be assessed: (e) how stable is the client's life situation (both objectively and subjectively to the client), especially their interpersonal relation-

CRY OF PAIN

ships (by far the most common precipitant)? (f) How impulsive is the client? Given that two thirds of parasuicide episodes are contemplated for less than an hour beforehand, impulsiveness may be considered an important vulnerability factor.

The client may arrive at the conclusion that life is intolerable through combinations of the errors in reasoning described in depression. In *dichotomous thinking* (black/white, all-or-nothing thinking), there is no perceived middle path – just the extremes. *Selective abstraction* consists of the selecting out of small parts of a situation and ignoring others, e.g. a tutor's report on an essay gives much praise, but mentions at one point that the introduction is too long: 'He doesn't like my essay' would be selective abstraction. In *arbitrary inference*, a conclusion is inferred from irrelevant evidence, e.g. an individual phones a boy/girlfriend and no one answers. The conclusion: '(S)he's probably out with another partner' would be an arbitrary inference (if inferred on those grounds alone). *Overgeneralization* is concluding from one specific negative event that other negative events are therefore more likely, e.g. failure at maths means failure at everything. Finally, *catastrophizing* is to think the very worst of a situation.

Many of the errors of logic which underlie such beliefs and assumptions are exactly those found in depression. The danger with suicidal clients is that they act so decisively and violently on their beliefs. Often this process takes place in only a few minutes. First, their thinking about their problems is dominated by the distortions described; then they react to these thoughts as inescapable facts and take proportionately drastic action. Because this is a process – however swift – intervention to prevent acts of deliberate self-harm may be aimed at different stages.

If someone expresses suicidal ideas, it is important to determine what method is contemplated, how familiar the client is with the lethality of medicines, and the availability of methods (e.g. firearms). The therapist will need to be vigilant for verbal or mood cues which might indirectly signal suicidal intent. Verbal expressions of hopelessness provide the best clue (see Chapter 5). Not all depressed clients are hopeless, and there is an accumulating body of evidence to suggest that hopelessness is the factor that turns depression into suicidal depression. Sudden changes in emotion in either direction may also signal impending suicidal behaviour.

A framework for therapy

Suicidal intent is a continuum. There is a balance between the intention to live and the intention to die, and even relatively insignificant chance factors may tip the balance. Tipping the balance against suicide involves building a bridge to the next session, if possible, by getting the client to see the next episode of suicidal feelings as an opportunity to note in detail how they feel, so as to bring this information to the next session. The therapist might encourage the client to agree to make explicit the pros and cons of living and dying.

Dealing with hopelessness will involve careful assessment of the contribution of the reality of the life situation of the client and of the interpretative biases the client may be using to evaluate it. For many there will have been real failures and/or real rejection experiences which must not be minimized by the therapist. But the depression may also have made them select the most catastrophic interpretation of these life situations and of their implication for the future. In this case the questions are: What biased conclusions may be blocking hope? What alternative behaviours and choices are realistically available? 'Alternative therapy' can be used, in which the person uses their imagination of a crisis situation to generate within the session some of the same hopelessness and despair typically felt outside the therapy situation. Under these conditions, the person attempts to generate some alternative coping responses.

Assessing suicidal intent and the probability of repetition

If a therapist is seeing a client immediately following a suicidal episode, he or she will need to assess suicidal intent and the probability of repetition. Assessment of suicidal intent is best made on the basis of the circumstances surrounding the episode and the client's own report (as outlined in Chapter 4). The more the behaviour approximates to suicide (e.g. precautions taken against discovery, etc.), the greater the assumed intent. Whether the actual medical risk should be taken into account remains a controversial issue. Over a large number of cases there is a significant correlation between actual lethality and suicidal intent, but it may be difficult to infer intent from the medical lethality in an individual case. Some clients (especially those not used to taking pills) may believe that relatively few pills are lethal. Actual physical risk would then be no guide to what may in fact be a very serious suicidal attempt. There is also, however, the obvious but often overlooked point that the correlation between actual physical lethality and intent is much stronger in cases where the client is knowledgeable about the lethality of drugs available to them.

Finally, the therapist ascertains how actively suicide is being considered. Modifying some of the items from the Suicide Ideation Scale of Beck is helpful as a basis. The following questions are useful in that they converge relatively quickly from general issues about problem-solving to the specific issue of suicide. The therapist asks (a) whether they feel their problems can be overcome; (b) whether they have any current ideas or fantasies about dying; (c) whether they find ideas about suicide going through their mind; (d) whether they expect to make an attempt on their life; (e) whether they are actually planning such an attempt; (f) whether they expect to put their plan into action, and how imminently; (g) whether anyone would care if they carried out such a plan.

Some common problems

A number of questions arise during therapy with suicidal clients. Two are worth considering at this point. First, since many of these clients have severe real-life problems, is not their hopelessness understandable? Secondly, might not consideration of reasons for dying precipitate a suicide attempt?

Reality-based hopelessness is indeed often found. Many clients have real problems that must not be minimized by the therapist. On the other hand, some people appear able to cope with apparently unbearable problems without becoming suicidal. Why? Possibly because depressive hopelessness is not the same as normal sadness. Financial hardship and interpersonal chaos may reasonably cause a great deal of anger, frustration and sadness. However, a person becomes depressed and suicidal when their sadness changes to a situation in which the person tells themselves, 'I'm to blame,' 'I've never succeeded at anything in my life,' 'If my love leaves, I am nothing.' People under great stress – stress which has understandable consequences on mood – need all the coping resources they can muster. What they do not need is a constant stream of negative thoughts and images to convince them they are a bad or worthless person who could never be forgiven. Therapy may be conceived as enabling the person to discriminate between realistic and depressive hopelessness so that the real problems can be faced realistically.

As to whether focusing on problems in therapy precipitates suicidal wishes by increasing reasons for dying, making these factors explicit is more likely to be therapeutic. If the client believes there are overwhelming reasons for dying, it is not beneficial to proceed with therapy as if these reasons did not exist. Objective definition of the problems (reasons for dying) is only the first step to deciding which are solvable and which are not; what might be done about those that are; evaluating the evidence for and against each reason for living and for dying; and discussing why some reasons are weighted in the client's mind more or less heavily than others. There is no evidence that explicit discussion of such issues increases suicidal intent. Indeed, clinical experience suggests the converse.

Problem-solving therapy

In reviewing the evidence on factors leading up to suicidal behaviour, a common factor has been the presence of stress factors with which the person feels unable to cope, and from which they wish to escape. This has led many to adopt a generic problem-solving approach in therapy for suicidal clients.[1] Poor problem-solving has been targeted because of the belief that such deficits may be a final common pathway for many psychological difficulties. This assumes that, whatever the psychological problem, whatever the diagnosis, poor problem-solving will be present as a contributor, whether as a vulnerability factor, a precipitating factor, or most importantly for therapy, a maintenance factor.

Problem-solving therapy has certain key characteristics. First, it has a well-planned rationale which provides an initial structure that guides patients to the belief that they can control their own behaviour and thereby their own emotional problems. Secondly, it provides clients with the motivation and the training in skills to feel more effective in solving problems in their life. Thirdly, it emphasizes the independent use of these skills by the individual outside the therapy context, and provides sufficient structure so that he or she can attain the independent use of them. Finally, it allows patients to attribute improvement in their mood to their own increased skilfulness and not that of the therapist.

To proceed with such therapy, the first need is to specify which aspects of problem-solving are impaired. Problem-solving involves several steps,[2] the first being general orientation to a problem. People have to be able to recognize that a problem exists. The second is problem definition: they have to be able to articulate the problem as precisely as possible, and what their goals are for each problem. This may involve breaking down the problem into different parts. The next stage is to generate as many alternative solutions as possible. During this stage, the person has to inhibit the tendency to prejudge which potential solutions might work and deal with the tendency for their hopelessness to overwhelm them. Then comes the need to weigh up the advantages and disadvantages of implementing each alternative, and to devise ways to test out some of them. Later the person has to be able to evaluate the effects and learn to congratulate him or herself if some progress has been made, even if such progress is the discovery that some aspects of the problem cannot be solved at present.

There is little doubt that depressed and suicidal patients find such problem-solving difficult. They do not generate as many alternative solutions as non-depressed and non-suicidal people, and what alternatives they do generate tend to be less effective and more passive. During a crisis, when a person faces obstacles to important life-goals that seem insurmountable through usual methods of problem-solving, there follows a period of intense disorganization. The upset caused can result in many abortive attempts at solutions, which only serve to increase the feelings of crisis.

Keith Hawton and Joan Kirk have developed a brief 'Problem Solving Treatment' that has been used in several studies in Oxford.[3] It starts with careful assessment of the situation as the therapist:

1. Identifies the client's problems.
2. Identifies the client's resources – assets and supports.
3. Obtains information from other sources.
4. Decides whether problem-solving is appropriate.
5. Decides on practical arrangements – who will be involved, the likely number of sessions, duration, timing, etc.
6. Establishes a therapeutic contract – including the client's and therapist's responsibilities in problem-solving.

The first step is probably the most important. During a suicidal crisis, everything in a client's life can seem overwhelming to them and to their therapist. It may be difficult therefore to collaborate in articulating as accurately as possible all the things that are going wrong. Yet the aim remains to draw up a problem list. On the list, agreed between client and therapist, each problem is clearly described. Often this will be very difficult. People's problems may not seem easy to describe clearly. The therapist will then need to help the client be more specific (e.g. 'What is it about x which is difficult?' 'Could you go into more detail about the problem you are having with y?'). Only if sufficient specificity is achieved at this stage can concrete strategies to cope with the problem be identified.

Hawton and Kirk offer the following helpful check-list of potential problem areas:

1. Relationship with partner or spouse.
2. Relationship with other family members, particularly young children.
3. Employment or studies.
4. Finances.

5. Housing.
6. Legal.
7. Social isolation and relationships with friends.
8. Use of alcohol and drugs.
9. Psychiatric health.
10. Physical health.
11. Sexual adjustment.
12. Bereavement and impending loss.

The next step in assessment is identifying the client's resources, their assets and strengths, using other sources of information where relevant. This is much easier if the problems have been clearly articulated at the outset. The central question is: 'How have you coped in the past when this sort of thing has happened?' The therapist will discuss some of the reasons why previous ways of dealing with the crisis are no longer available, evaluating as objectively as possible what resources remain, despite the feelings that all options have been closed off. As in all such therapies, the therapist's role is to help the client clarify things for him or herself, not to enter into arguments about availability of resources.

Having agreed a problem list, there are several steps to be taken in problem-solving treatment, steps made explicit to the client so that the process is entirely transparent. (The statements in brackets have been suggested as useful *aide-mémoires* for clients to use in such treatments.)

1. Decide which problem(s) to be tackled first. (*What is my main concern at the moment?*)
2. Agree goal(s). (*What do I want?*)
3. Work out steps necessary to achieve goal(s). (*What can I do?*)
4. Consider the possible consequences. (*What might happen?*)
5. Decide tasks necessary to tackle first step. (*What is my decision?*)
6. Carry out task as homework. (*Now do it!*)
7. Review progress at next therapy session, including difficulties encountered. (*Did it work?*)

During the next session, client and therapist make use of the information gained from the last homework to decide on the next step. This clearly depends on what progress was made, and will lead to further agreement about subsequent tasks. Further goal(s) may need to be agreed, or problems redefined for further loops around the sequence.

There are a number of other techniques used in problem-solving therapy, including some that are common to cognitive therapy. These include:

Brainstorming techniques: is an approach in which a client suggests as many solutions as possible, without evaluating the potential usefulness of any. The aim is to generate a list without premature dismissal of alternatives as 'useless', which simply inhibits further problem-solving.

The therapist may suggest some possibilities if the client finds it difficult to generate solutions. Hawton and Kirk advocate the deliberate suggestion of some extreme or even humorous solutions to facilitate the involvement of the client in the process. They suggest that including extreme solutions can lead the client into unexplored avenues and produce other novel solutions.

They give the example of a client called Mary, who was helped to brainstorm possible solutions to her problem of her mother, who she felt was intrusive, constantly visiting or telephoning at inconvenient times. This was the list, which included some deliberately extreme solutions:

1. Ask her not to visit or telephone any more.
2. Ask her to reduce her visits and telephone calls.
3. Leave the country.
4. Change telephone number and go ex-directory.
5. Discuss the problem with the mother.
6. Do nothing and accept the status quo.

After Mary examined the advantages and disadvantages of each solution in detail, she decided that discussing the problem with her mother, previously seen as impossible, was the most appropriate thing to try first.

Examining alternatives: using 'two-column' or 'pros and cons' technique (simply writing down the advantages and disadvantages, including likely outcomes, of each possibility, giving relative weightings if appropriate). Sometimes the best course of action becomes clearer as a result of this technique, or it shows how much further information is needed to give further weight to one or another alternative.

Cognitive rehearsal: is the detailed rehearsal in imagination of carrying out a particular task, including details of steps taken, the consequences of each step, and any accompanying thoughts and feelings. Since the person in this technique imagines completing the task, it can be useful for helping a client develop confidence in attempting a task, in identifying possible blocks to progress not previously obvious.

Activity scheduling: involves the deliberate setting of time aside to attempt particular tasks or actions. Tasks can be split up or graded into simpler sub-tasks early on in therapy, gradually building up to the assignment of whole tasks. While completion of a task is the main goal, the person decides in advance how much time can be allocated, and keeps to that time, even if a task is not completed. In this way, the person may make some helpful observations about how well they are able to estimate how long different tasks may take. Clients are also encouraged to make time for breaks in their schedule, to give time for reviewing progress and for self-reward. Subsequent treatment sessions will involve examining to what extent the person was able to carry out assigned tasks, learn from any problems encountered, then plan a new schedule in the light of what is learned.

Hawton and Kirk point out that problem-solving may not be appropriate in every case, or at every stage in the crisis:

The fundamental decision which determines if problem-solving is currently applicable for a patient concerns whether the person is so severely disabled by psychiatric symptoms or disorder that he or she cannot at present be expected to take responsibility, even with the support of the therapist, for managing the problems that require attention. For example, a patient with marked retarded or agitated depression is very unlikely to be able to engage in the steps necessary for problem-solving until there has been some reduction in the severity of the affective disturbance. Similarly, when a person is in a severe state of crisis, especially if suicidal, problem-solving will usually be inappropriate until the level of disorganization and helplessness which often characterizes such a state has been reduced. Attention to exacerbating factors (e.g. sleep disturbance, lack of supports) can often bring this about, following which problem-solving may then be very appropriate.

Evaluation of problem-solving approaches

Early studies using these types of approach have used both out-patient treatment sessions and sessions conducted in the client's own home. In these early studies, repetition rates were not reduced. Of course, other benefits of such treatments have emerged. One such study[4] used task-centred case-work (nine sessions over three months) and compared it with normal psychiatric out-patient visits. At four months' follow-up, the psycho-social treatment group showed significantly fewer social problems and were better at handling personal relationships and social transitions than the other group. In addition, they were less lonely and better at coping with their own emotional distress as well as with practical difficulties in their lives.

However, this study, and others like it, was not able to show an effect on repetition. This is for two reasons. First, the treatment produces most positive benefits in those less likely to repeat the attempts as judged by the vulnerability indices (pages 78–9). Simply put, one can divide suicidal individuals into those likely to respond to psycho-social intervention and those unlikely to respond (because of their chronic psychological/psychiatric and social problems). The problem in these therapy studies is that those most likely to respond are also more likely to have been suffering an acute crisis which has now passed and are therefore unlikely to repeat parasuicide. This leaves the 'non-responder' group, who are always going to be difficult to treat using short-term psycho-social treatments.

This pessimistic conclusion may be premature.[5] One possible future strategy for therapy research is to examine those clients who are at greatest risk for repetition. This is important on two counts. First, it is targeting those most in need of help. Secondly, with an increased probability of repetition of parasuicide, one may more clearly see whether a treatment is working. Might a larger scale, more complex treatment package work more effectively? Such a treatment has been developed by Marsha Linehan in the University of Washington.[6]

Dialectical Behaviour Therapy (DBT)

Linehan's Dialectical Behaviour Therapy (DBT) combines weekly individual and weekly group therapy over a one-year period. It uses treatment strategies from behavioural, cognitive and supportive psychotherapies. Thus behavioural skills training, contingency management, cognitive modification and exposure to emotional cues are combined and balanced with supportive techniques such as reflection, empathy and acceptance. The behavioural/problem-solving component focuses on enhancing capability, generating alternative ways of coping, clarifying and managing contingencies, all with the emphasis on the 'here and now'. Secondly, DBT focuses on the dialectical aspect both of the client's experience and the therapy, e.g. the client may be experiencing feelings of anger very intensively, yet may continuously invalidate those feelings by saying he or she ought not to feel angry. This only increases the amount of emotional disturbance in a vicious circle, which quickly escalates to the point where the client feels their affect is completely out of control. Within the general orientation of the therapy, the dialectical focus lies in its emphasis on balancing acceptance of the sources of stress that exist in the environment on the one hand with the need to change them on the other. The theme is encouraging clients to see things clearly, as they are, and to step back from them temporarily to see what things may be changed.

The individual therapy (lasting one hour each week) stays within a strict agenda and prioritizes themes related to parasuicide. Thus, for example, if any parasuicidal act, threat or thought has occurred since the previous therapy session, that will be the priority for the current session. Therapist and client will then investigate in great detail the circumstances surrounding each suicidal 'episode', even if there was no overt suicidal behaviour. To help this process, the client keeps a record of the use of prescribed or non-prescribed drugs, and of the intensity and frequency of suicidal urges and bouts of depression. Finally, the client records whether there has been self-harm in the previous week. No suicidal behaviour, no matter how apparently insignificant, is ignored. Linehan believes this is an important keynote of the therapy. She asserts that newly trained therapists too easily avoid explicit discussion of these suicidal thoughts, threats and behaviour. The client needs to learn that help for other problems can only be discussed when the self-harm behaviour has been brought under control.

Once the suicidal behaviour or thinking has been discussed in therapy, or if there has been no episode during the previous week, the second priority within a therapy session is to deal with 'therapy interfering behaviours' such as non-adherence to agreed goals, not filling in the homework records, or non-attendance. These are again subject to a detailed functional analysis within the context of therapy. The emphasis throughout is on teaching clients how to manage emotional crises rather than reducing the trauma or withdrawing from them.

These individual therapy sessions are supplemented by weekly group therapy, which lasts for two and a half hours a session, focusing on (a) interpersonal problem-solving skills, (b) distress tolerance and reality acceptance skills, and (c) the skills of emotional regulation. Discussion of individual crises is discouraged during group sessions, clients being referred to their individual counsellors for help with these.

In a study to assess the effectiveness of the therapy, forty-four clients were treated. Each met criteria for borderline personality disorder (see page 98). In addition, each had at least two episodes of parasuicide in the previous five years, at least one of which occurred in the previous eight weeks. Clients were randomly allocated to receive either DBT or Treatment as Usual (TAU). The client group were women, aged between 18 and 45, and were excluded only if they met criteria for schizophrenia, bi-polar disorder, substance dependence or learning disability (mental handicap); or if they declined to agree to the study conditions, including the agreement to give up psychotherapy if they were assigned to the DBT group. Linehan's 1991 report gave the results for the period while the clients were in therapy. A later report gave the details of what happened in the following twelve months.

Looking first at the data for the period of the study (twelve months), the results showed that DBT significantly reduced parasuicide episodes over the year (see Figure 27). The TAU control group had a median of 9 parasuicide episodes over the year, compared to the DBT group's 1.5. During the final four-month period, over 60 per cent of the TAU were still having parasuicide episodes, whereas only 25 per cent of the DBT group were showing such behaviour. Ninety-six per cent of the TAU group had a parasuicide episode during the year in question, compared to 64 per cent of the DBT.

It is always possible that some of these differences emerged because of the DBT group's unwillingness to report parasuicide episodes that had in fact been taking place. However, there was independent evidence from hospital records that these results were not subject to reporting biases. For example, DBT clients spent a median of seventeen days whereas the control group spent a median of fifty-one days in psychiatric hospital over the year. Furthermore, the parasuicide episodes of the control group were likely to incur greater medical risk than those of the DBT group. Comparing risk for just those control subjects (n = 10) and DBT (n = 5) who needed medical treatment for a parasuicide, the difference in medical risk was significant.

Follow-up of DBT for suicidal behaviour

The promising data of the 1991 report only provide details of the effect of treatment while it continued. Remarkable as these treatment gains are, it was still an open question whether any of them would

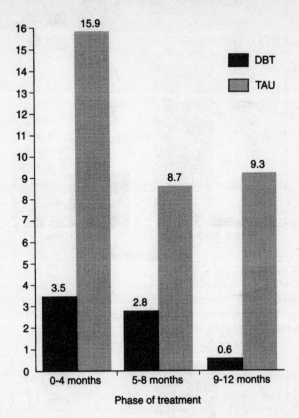

Figure 27. Number of parasuicidal acts in borderline personality clients at three phases of treatment (in Linehan, Armstrong, Suarez, Allmond and Heard, 'Behavioural Treatment of Chronically Parasuicidal Borderline Patients', *Archives of General Psychiatry*, 1991).

be maintained once the therapy finished. The follow-up study was therefore of great interest.[7] It was a naturalistic follow-up, and therefore did not prevent people from returning to treatment if they wished. Control clients were able to continue to receive psychotherapy in the community. DBT clients, although required to take a 'two-month vacation' from their individual DBT therapists, could continue in psychotherapy thereafter if the therapist was agreeable.

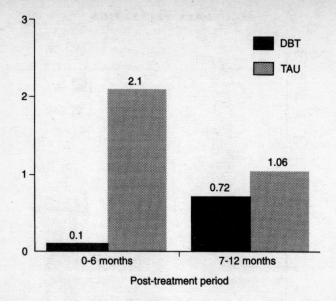

Figure 28. Mean number of parasuicidal episodes in year following acute DBT treatment of borderline personality disorder clients (from Linehan, Heard and Armstrong, 'Naturalistic Follow-up of a Behavioural Treatment', *Archives of General Psychiatry*, 1993).

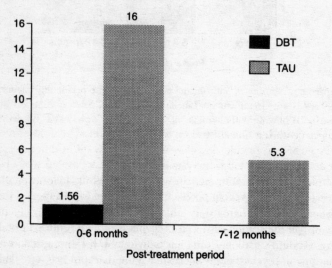

Figure 29. Mean number of days in psychiatric hospital in year following acute DBT treatment of borderline personality disorder clients (Linehan *et al.*, art. cit., 1993).

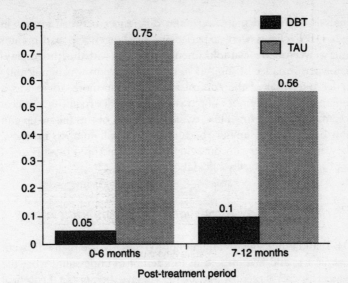

Figure 30. Mean number of medically treated parasuicidal episodes in year following acute DBT treatment of borderline personality disorder clients (Linehan *et al.*, art. cit., 1993).

Seven subjects (35 per cent) took this option. This contrasts with 55 per cent who continued with psychotherapy in the control group.

Follow-up assessments were made at six months and twelve months following the end of the experimental treatment year. Subjects were asked about the frequency of their parasuicidal behaviour and any medical treatment that resulted. Results showed that over the entire year the repetition rate for parasuicide was lower in the DBT group (26 per cent) than the control group (60 per cent). The difference in number of parasuicide episodes was mainly owing to difference in the first six-month follow-up phase (Figure 28).

There was also a difference in the number of psychiatric hospitaliz-ations between DBT (11 per cent) and control (40 per cent), mostly because of a difference that emerged between the groups in the second six-month follow-up phase (Figure 29). During this period none of the DBT groups were hospitalized, contrasting with a mean of 5.3 psychiatric hospital days for the control group. Subsequent analysis confirmed there were also differences between groups in that DBT clients were experiencing less anger and had greater interviewer-rated social adjustment. Consistent with this, the employment performance of subjects in the DBT group was significantly better than that of the control group. Furthermore, there was a difference in the number of parasuicide episodes requiring medical treatment (Figure 30). Thus, while the results of this follow-up can only be seen as preliminary because of the small numbers involved, they are clearly very encouraging for this structured psycho-social approach to chronically suicidal clients.

Psychological mechanisms underlying therapeutic change

DBT and other such treatment approaches involve many different techniques, and it is important to attempt to understand what the critical aspects of therapy may be so as to give therapists a theoretical framework to orientate themselves within the therapy. Research on the psychological processes mediating hopelessness and suicidal behaviour would suggest that any successful therapy will need to affect the global and undifferentiated cognitive style in such clients, which tends to be activated whenever any change triggers a ruminative review of their lives. The tendency of clients to recall events in their lives in a generalized, undifferentiated way is associated with an inability to problem-solve, both in terms of the number of alternatives people can generate and the effectiveness of those alternatives. Furthermore, the study by Julie Evans[8] found that the more angry the clients, the less they could retrieve specific events from their past, and the less effective were the problem solutions they produced on the Means–Ends Problem Solving Test. A similar pattern of correlations was found for the hopelessness levels of the clients.

These results suggest that non-specificity of memory and difficulties in emotional regulation are closely related in producing and exacerbating suicidal crises. The therapy appears to be successful in making the link between thoughts, feelings and behaviour more explicit. Might the therapy be helping the person become more specific in their encoding and retrieval of events in their lives? Examining

Marsha Linehan's description of her therapy, this appears likely. She points out that it involves 'an exhaustive description of the moment-to-moment chain of environmental and behavioural events that preceded the suicidal behaviour ... Alternative solutions that the individual could have used are explored, behavioural deficits as well as factors that interfere with more adaptive solutions are examined, and remedial procedures are applied if necessary.' If true, future research will find that those clients who respond least well to treatment will be those who are not able to recall events in this more specific way. Such memory problems prevent them generating effective alternative solutions to their problems.

Another important feature of all these therapies is that they give the person a sense of control over their lives. Since a major problem with suicidal individuals is the tendency to generalize from one situation that is uncontrollable to other situations that are potentially solvable, and simply assume there is nothing they can do about a new situation, a self-fulfilling prophecy ensues. They do not try because they 'know' there is nothing they can do. When the problem does not resolve, they take this as evidence that they were right. Of course, after a lifetime of stressful events, such a conclusion may be quite understandable for some, but it is often applied too generally. Any therapy able to give clients a sense of control over events in their lives is likely to be helpful.

What is the minimum intervention one might make with those who are vulnerable to suicide to give them a sense of control? A possibility is to let such people know they have control, at least over the help they can receive; that they are able to contact the emergency services at any time, and they will be seen. This was the aim of an innovative UK study in Bristol: the Green Card Study. The approach, pioneered by Professor Gethin Morgan and colleagues, involves giving people following a first parasuicide a Green Card. It is explained that possession of the Green Card gives the person the right to telephone or personal contact, even admission to hospital, at any time (day or night) should the need arise, provided that the person possessing the card had not repeated the suicidal behaviour on the same occasion. A total of 212 patients were randomly allocated, either to receive the usual psychiatric and social aftercare (n = 111) or to receive a card in addition to the usual help (n = 101).[9] Twelve people in the TAU control group (10.8 per cent) harmed themselves again over the following year. By contrast, only five (5 per cent) who had the Green Card did so. Although these results are not statistically significant, they do offer hope that a larger study might find the Green Card a helpful adjunct to existing treatments. Of considerable interest was that, whereas many might have predicted that making such an open commitment to suicidal people was dangerous since services might have been inundated with requests for help, this did not occur. Only 15 of the 101 who had the Green Card made contact with the psychiatric service over the year, the majority by telephone. Some got in contact more than once, but even the total number of contacts was only 19, of which 4 involved face-to-face interviews. In half such contacts, a single episode of discussion was enough to deal with the problem. Only in one case was there a request for readmission to hospital.

There needs to be some caution in generalizing these results. We have seen (page 77) that the pattern of parasuicide has changed during the 1990s, with more men being admitted following self-harm than ever before. Whether a Green Card will be effective for this new group of suicidal clients remains to be seen.

Concluding remarks: the future of secondary prevention research

What does the future of research on secondary prevention hold? Clearly there will need to be replication and extension of previous studies. First, Linehan's pioneering work needs to be extended, to see how well it can be applied in other settings throughout the world, with a focus on both male and female clients (Linehan's study consisted of women only). Secondly, studies of problem-solving and the Green Card need to be extended to include large enough numbers to be able definitively to assess their impact on repetition. Thirdly, the use of such approaches in combination with medication could be investigated. Although psycho-social treatments have developed in isolation from improvements in drug treatments for various psychiatric conditions, there is evidence that the combined use of pharmaco-logical and psychological treatments might be useful. (This has been studied for treatments of depression, where clients clearly do not find the combination of biological and psychological models confusing.) Thirdly, since depression remains the most important final common pathway to suicide, the quest for new and better treatments for depression itself is an important part of the agenda in attempting to deal with suicide. Future work will need to concentrate on the prevention of relapse as a problem in its own right.

Secondary prevention demands a multi-modal approach. Mental health professionals need to be aware of the ease with which suicidal feelings may be missed in a therapy consultation. They need to be aware of the preferred method by which clients would commit suicide if they had the chance, and able to estimate the lethality of the method as well as the probability of carrying out the action. They need to be aware of the risk factors for repetition following parasuicide episodes, but also aware that half the clients who have all these risk factors do not actually repeat within the following year.

The data help us to understand why early studies of treatment interventions were pessimistic. Those clients who might have responded well to treatment tended to be those less likely to repeat the parasuicide episode anyway. That left those who have had a great many psychological, psychiatric and social problems in their lives. Only as studies have started to look at this difficult sub-group have we begun to make advances. In particular, the structured psychological approach of Marsha Linehan, Dialectical Behaviour Therapy, offers an interesting range of methods to be investigated in future research.

Chapter 13

FINAL THOUGHTS

'Anguish is known to everyone since childhood, and everyone
knows that it is often blank, undifferentiated. It rarely carries
a clearly written label that also contains its motivation; when
it does have one, it is often mendacious. One can believe or
declare oneself to be anguished for one reason and be so due
to something totally different: one can think that one is
suffering at facing the future and instead be suffering because
of one's past; one can think that one is suffering for others,
out of pity, out of compassion, and instead be suffering for
one's own reasons, more or less profound, more or less
avowable and avowed; sometimes so deep that only the
specialist, the analyst of souls, knows how to exhume them.'
– Primo Levi, *The Drowned and the Saved*[1]

I have suggested that the key to understanding suicidal behaviour is
to view it as a cry of pain. Suicide comes out of mental anguish. It
is a response to uncontrollable stresses that arise from the environment, or from the uncontrollability of the mental anguish itself.
When an individual first becomes aware that they lack control over
important areas of their circumstances or of their mental life, the
cry of pain may be one of anger and rage: a protest against the
feelings of entrapment. As the person becomes more and more
convinced they have failed, or that they have been rejected or
abandoned, the anger becomes mixed with hopelessness and despair.
A tunnel vision ensues, in which normal escape routes are not
noticed. Offers of help are rejected or misinterpreted. The person
feels more alienated, increasing his or her feelings of anger and
hopelessness, and begins to seek alternative ways of escape. The
likelihood of suicide at such times depends on how overwhelming
such feelings are, whether there have been models among family
or friends or in the media, whether a suitable method is readily

available, how violent or impulsive the person is, and whether drugs or alcohol are available which reduce fear of death and impair judgement.

Completed suicide and parasuicide can be understood as different responses to these circumstances, occurring at different points in the downward spiral into hopelessness. For many years it was thought that suicide and parasuicide had to be qualitatively different behaviours, partly because many who harm themselves say they do not want to die. Their motivation seemed much more complex than a simple wish to die. But motivation for completed suicide is also complex. Because the tragedy of a death by suicide is so extreme, we tend to assume that, when death is the outcome, death has been the predominant motive.

Yet I have also suggested that the predominant motivation in suicidal behaviour is escape. The person feels trapped. They can see no way out of their prison, and take little account of the possibility that some of their feeling of entrapment comes from a biased view of their own past lives that feeds into their hopelessness about the future.

Getting away from seeing completed suicide as motivated only by a wish to die frees us from a punitive view of parasuicide. In the past, we have allowed the question of how much a person wished to die to define the way in which we understand all who harm themselves. We ask ourselves, 'How suicidal was this behaviour really?' If we decide it was not, then we are inclined to dismiss it, get angry about it, see it as 'manipulative', and so on. (Of course, the truth is that those whom we call manipulative have actually *failed* to manipulate us. For we all manipulate each other all the time. We are simply so good at it that no one notices. It is only when we meet someone in whom such attempts are more obvious that we notice it. It is ironic that we accuse them of being manipulative when, in fact, they have failed adequately to hide the social performance in which we all engage.) The problem with the idea of the 'cry for help' is that it fed this dismissive view of self-harm.

Of course, there were other reasons for thinking that suicide and parasuicide were different things. The most important reason was that those who completed suicide on the one hand, and those who attempted suicide on the other, seemed to differ in a number of respects. For example, while suicide, until recently, was predominantly a feature of older males, parasuicide seemed predominantly a feature of younger females. Furthermore, while suicide rates were coming down in the 1960s in the United Kingdom, parasuicide was rising. Such differences between suicide and parasuicide seemed to suggest that different explanations for each were needed. Yet, if we are to see age and sex differences as pointing to different underlying causes, what are we to make of the recent data from the United States and the United Kingdom that show male suicide is rising while female suicide is falling? Here we have the same outcome, suicide deaths, moving in different directions in different sub-groups of the same population.

Instead it is possible that the same underlying set of causes might produce the age and sex differences in suicidal behaviour that are sometimes observed. If suicidal behaviour is best seen as a cry of pain – a response to feeling trapped by uncontrollable external circumstances and uncontrollable internal anguish – then different types of people, older or younger, male or female, take action on these feelings at different points in the sequence of events as the trap is perceived to close. Internal and external stresses give rise to differences in perceived escape potential (i.e. their ability to see a way out; see Figure 31). This, in turn, gives rise to stronger or weaker wishes to die.

At one end of the continuum, a weaker wish to die may not be expressed as a wish to die at all, but rather be seen as seeking temporary oblivion. But such people are best seen as one end of a dimension of lethality that cannot be ignored (see Figure 32). The protest and anger that produce parasuicidal behaviour represent a response early in the sequence of events when escape still seems possible. The despair and apathy that produce more lethal suicidal behaviour represent the response to loss that comes later when the person sees no hope in their situation at all. Even at this stage, however, the presence of social support can ameliorate the intensity of feelings of hopelessness (see Figure 33). Men differ from women in the extent to which they perceive or make use of such supports. This is not simply a question of biology, but of the different ways

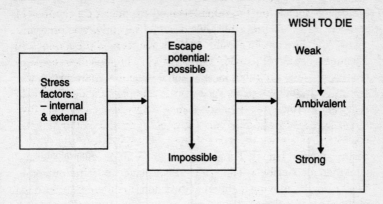

Figure 31. Internal and external stresses give rise to differences in a person's ability to see a way out, causing stronger or weaker motivation to die.

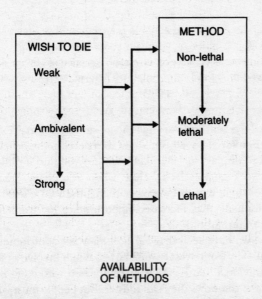

Figure 32. Differences along the dimension of motivation to die lead to different levels of lethality, the outcome depending also on the availability of lethal methods.

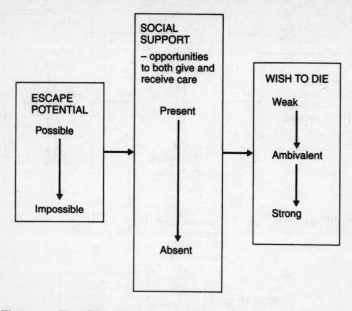

Figure 33. The effect of seeing no escape is moderated by the presence of social support or *perceived* social support. There are gender differences in the perception and use of such support.

in which boys and girls are taught to view emotional expression. Wherever children have been allowed to develop the belief that it is shameful to display one's weaknesses, they will find it difficult later in life to seek support from others when in a crisis. Traditionally boys were taught this attitude more than girls, but we need to guard against implying that increased opportunities for women require adoption of this attitude.

Finally, we have seen that all the important contributors on the causal pathway from stress to suicidal behaviour involve a judgement by the individual (see Figure 34). The person whose life is in crisis needs all the resources they can muster. But people most vulnerable to depression and suicide suffer an additional burden which makes their real problems seem even more aversive, uncontrollable and unsolvable. Biases in their memory prevent them from recalling

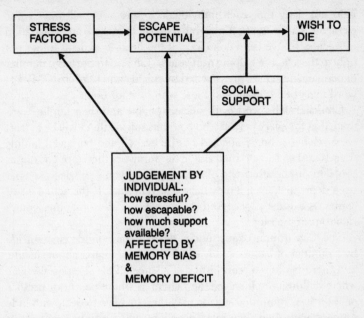

Figure 34. At important points in the causal pathway to suicidal behaviour a judgement by the individual allows scope for bias in estimates of the aversiveness of stress, its controllability, and how much social support is available.

positive aspects of their past and present life. Even worse, when they do recollect events, these are recalled in such non-specific ways as to suggest few ways of dealing with current problems. Furthermore, they induce a non-specific view of the future. Making concrete plans for the future (even for tomorrow or next week) is extremely difficult against the background of such vague and over-general recollection of the past.

The aftermath of suicide

My aim has been to explain something of what I understand of suicide and self-harm. Looking for unifying themes is important, but

I do not deny that each individual circumstance will have some elements that do not fit the overall pattern. In seeking an explanation of suicide, I have been conscious of the need to explain things not only to those in the helping professions, but also to the large number of people whose lives are touched by suicide and self-harm. My last word must be for them and those who care for them.

Clinicians who work with suicidal people and their families estimate that for every person who commits suicide there will be at least six survivors strongly affected by the event – the bereaved family, friends and close workmates. For the survivors there are enormous problems in the aftermath of such a death. Even if the deceased has been depressed, even if they have talked of suicide, the actual death comes as a huge shock. And, of course, suicide sometimes comes right out of the blue.

The huge trauma of any sudden death is compounded in a suicide by a number of factors: many still feel a social stigma about suicide, and there is often a 'conspiracy of silence'. This is especially true where children are involved, and children whose parent or brother or sister has committed suicide may thereby have to deal, with little support, with their own misconceptions and irrational guilt about what has happened. The outcome for children when their parents have separated before one parent commits suicide is worse than for those whose parents are still together.[2]

Even when social support is available, the suicide survivor is less likely to use it than those bereaved by other kinds of sudden death, because of the social stigma and the presence of feelings of personal guilt and shame surrounding the event.[3] Suicide survivors have to cope with their own grief against the background of many 'why' questions: 'Why did they not ask me for help?' 'Could I have done more?' 'Why did I (or someone else) not take the suicide threat more seriously?' Some survivors will blame themselves for not intervening, and endlessly ruminate on what they could have done to prevent it happening. In addition, many feel extremely angry with the deceased. Why couldn't they understand the effect it would have on those left behind?

No answers to these questions can be completely satisfactory, but it may be helpful at some point for survivors to know how suicidal despair reduces a person's ability to ask for help, to accept help if offered, or to understand the effect their action would have on others. We have seen in Chapter 9 that suicide arises from an overwhelming urge to escape feelings of being trapped, and that such entrapment is closely linked with feelings that one has failed. In such states, an individual feels shame and humiliation, so is highly sensitive to anything that might increase such shame. Asking for or accepting help from others will seem to many just such a shameful situation. Even the thought of receiving help from others may increase suicidal thoughts in such circumstances. Further, the deficit in memory outlined in Chapter 10 further exacerbates the situation by blocking recollection of previous times when help was available.

But how can we understand the way a suicidal individual appears to take such little account of the effect of their action on others? Like someone trying to escape from a blazing house-fire, the suicidal person is focused on escape. He or she has tunnel vision, which prevents them imagining what the act would do to others. They are completely self-absorbed. The feelings of other people do not appear in their calculations.

Such catastrophic failure of empathy, the complete breakdown in understanding how others will react, is not well understood. One possibility is that it occurs because, in states of extreme despair, the normal capacity to understand other people's minds is impaired. Recent research in developmental psychology shows that understanding the feelings of others depends on understanding other people's beliefs and intentions, and how they will be affected by things that happen in the world, including one's own actions. Small children develop the ability to take full account of other people's feelings and beliefs as part of their developing language and social communication in the second and third years of life.

I believe that the radical loss of empathy that accompanies suicidal impulses in some people results from impairment of these same psychological mechanisms. Suicidal despair switches off the processes responsible for understanding the beliefs, intentions and feelings of others. Though this will often appear to be a callous disregard for others' feelings (especially close family and friends), it is more likely to be something over which the person has little control.

Making peace with despair

The quotation from Primo Levi with which this short chapter began is taken from his last book, *The Drowned and the Saved*. Levi had survived Auschwitz, and had written of these experiences in his books, *If This Is a Man* and *The Truce*. He was found dead at the bottom of the stairwell of his house in Turin in 1987, and is presumed to have committed suicide. In the quotation, Levi speaks of an anguish sometimes so deep that only the specialist, the analyst of souls, knows how to exhume it.

But what help can an analyst of souls provide? We cannot opt out of trying to answer such questions, no matter how much we would wish to remain silent. When therapies bring hope to those in despair, what is it that they are doing? Of course, they are offering support. They are helping the person to see that perhaps some of their problems are solvable. They are helping the person to gain some distance from the constant propaganda of the mind that would persuade them they are a failure. But I believe these are helpful only to the extent that they allow the person to give up wanting things to be different. As Marsha Linehan points out in her therapy (see page 208), it is about balancing acceptance and change. For when people are in such distress, they become trapped by the idea that, if things were different, then all would be well: if their partner was different; if their job was different; if their house was different; if they themselves were different.

Often, then, the anguish is exacerbated by the search for an escape. In the same way as an animal caught in a trap will only tighten the trap with its struggles, so the desperate search for a way out only drives the suicidal person deeper into despair. The first step in dealing with anguish is therefore to make peace with despair; to take a step back and take stock of the situation. To give permission to oneself to feel whatever it is that one is feeling. This reflects the important insight that it is not the initial feelings of depression and anxiety that cause people the most problems but how they react to them. If a person becomes depressed, they may either see it as a temporary mood which will pass or as evidence that they are worthless. In the former case, the depression may well lift, but in the latter, the self-denigration will cause further depression. There is the danger of a vicious spiral downwards into despair.

Some, such as Ajahn Sucitto, have seen this as a profoundly spiritual question:

It's one that cannot be resolved by trying to make the world into a different place – which tends to be the normal approach. To make peace with despair is a matter of understanding not just where difficulties such as sickness and violence arise, but also how the feeling of being bound to and oppressed by those problems occurs.[4]

Therapies that are helpful are those which allow the person to see their moods as normal, rather than as evidence of their inherent deficiency as a person. They encourage the person to ask not, 'How can I make everything different?' but rather, 'How can I take care of myself right now?' In short, they encourage the person to be gentle with themselves.

NOTES AND REFERENCES

INTRODUCTION

1. A recent example is Sue Chance, *Stronger than Death*, W. W. Norton, New York, 1992. The author is a psychiatrist and a columnist for *The New York Times*, and the book is based on her own experiences when her son committed suicide. It contains extracts from her journal, starting one week after his death, together with poems and other reflections.

2. E. Stengel, *Suicide and Attempted Suicide*, revised edition, Penguin Books, Harmondsworth, 1964.

3. Stengel, *Suicide and Attempted Suicide*, p. 115 (1975 edition).

4. Many authors now refer to any non-fatal suicidal behaviour as 'parasuicide' (with its deliberate agnosticism about motive), since most who deliberately harm themselves say they do not want to die. In this book I use the terms 'parasuicide', 'attempted suicide' and 'self-harm' interchangeably.

CHAPTER I: HISTORICAL PERSPECTIVE

1. H. G. Morgan, *Suicide Prevention: the Assessment and Management of Suicide Risk*, Health Advisory Service, Bristol, 1993.

2. For the data in this chapter I am grateful for Michael MacDonald and Terence Murphy's fascinating study, *Sleepless Souls: Suicide in Early Modern England*, Oxford University Press, 1990, which shows how attitudes and responses to suicide have shifted over the past two thousand years. I have attempted to summarize their review as faithfully as possible, but the interested reader should refer to their book for the data and the careful analysis on which their conclusions are based.

3. MacDonald and Murphy, *Sleepless Souls*, p. 21.

4. *Diary of Samuel Pepys*, vol. III, Swan Sonnenschein, London, 1906, pp. 344−5.

5. Montaigne, *Essayes*, ii, 26−8, 41.

CHAPTER 2: SUICIDE: THE STATISTICS

1. E. Durkheim, *Le Suicide*, Alcan, Paris, 1897; *Suicide*, trans. by John A. Spaulding and George Simpson, Free Press, New York, 1951.

2. P. Sainsbury, J. Jenkins and A. E. Baert, *Suicide Trends in Europe*, World Health Organization, Copenhagen, 1981, ICP/MNH 036.

3. Until the 1960s it remained possible that the different overall rates merely reflected different levels of stringency by the authorities in different countries. In an important paper, P. Sainsbury and B. M. Barraclough showed this was not the case: see 'Differences between Suicide Rates', *Nature*, 220 (1968), p. 1252. They examined the suicide rates of immigrants to the United States from eleven countries, and found that such immigrant populations retained the suicide rate from the country of origin.

4. S. Platt, 'Epidemiology of Suicide and Parasuicide', *Journal of Psychopharmacology*, 6 (1968), pp. 291–9.

5. M. Weinstein and P. Saturno, *Economic Impact of Youth Suicides and Attempted Suicides*, DHSS publication no. (ADM) 89-1264, Department of Health and Human Services, Rockville, Maryland, 1989, pp. 4-/82/4-89.

6. J. Charlton, J. S. Kelly, K. Dunnell, B. Evans, R. Jenkins and R. Wallis, 'Trends in [Factors Associated with] Suicide Deaths in England and Wales', *Population Trends*, OPCS, London, 1992, pp. 10–16 and 34–42.

7. M. Buda and M. T. Tsuang, 'The Epidemiology of Suicide: Implications for Clinical Practice', in S. Blumenthal and D. Kupfer (eds.), *Suicide over the Life Cycle: Risk Factors, Assessment and Treatment of Suicidal Patients*, American Psychiatric Press, Washington, DC, 1990.

8. MacDonald and Murphy, *Sleepless Souls*, p. 247.

9. J. Harry, *Sexual Identity Issues*, Report of the Secretary's Task Force Report on Youth Suicide, vol. 2, DHSS publication no. (ADM) 89-162, Department of Health and Human Services, Washington, DC, 1989, pp. 131–42.

10. C. L. Rich, R. C. Fowler, D. Young and M. Blenkush, 'San Diego Study: Comparison of Gay to Straight Males', *Suicide and Life Threatening Behavior*, 16 (1986), pp. 448–57.

11. D. Shaffer, P. Fisher, R. H. Hicks, M. Parides and M. Gould,

'Sexual Orientation in Adolescents Who Commit Suicide', in *Suicide and Life Threatening Behavior*, 25 (1995), Supplement, pp. 64–71.

12. See P. Muehrer, 'Suicide and Sexual Orientation: a Critical Summary of Recent Research and Directions for Future Research', *Suicide and Life Threatening Behavior*, 25 (1995), Supplement, pp. 72–81.

13. M. Boor, 'Relationship between Employment Rates and Suicide Rates in Eight Countries: 1962–1967', *Psychological Reports*, 47 (1980), pp. 1095–1101.

14. E. Dooley, 'Prison Suicide in Wales 1972 to 1987', *British Journal of Psychiatry*, 156 (1990), pp. 40–45.

15. A case illustrating how important it is not to ignore depression and other accompaniments of terminal illness is cited in J. Scott, 'Cancer Patients', in J. Scott, J. M. G. Williams and A. T. Beck (eds.), *Cognitive Therapy in Clinical Practice*, Routledge, London, 1989.

16. For a study of psychiatric diagnoses as they differed according to age in suicide victims, see C. L. Rich, R. C. Fowler, L. A. Fogarty *et al.*, 'San Diego Suicide Study III: Relationships between Diagnosis and Stressors', *Archives of General Psychiatry*, 445 (1988), pp. 589–92.

17. For detailed statistics, see M. Shafii, J. Steltz-Lenarsky, A. M. Denick *et al.*, 'Co-morbidity of Mental Disorders in the Post-mortem Diagnosis of Completed Suicides in Children and Adolescents', *Journal of Affective Disorders*, 15 (1988), pp. 227–33; Rich, Fowler, Fogarty *et al.*, 'San Diego Suicide Study III'; and, for a British follow-up survey in Edinburgh (1968–85), K. Hawton, S. Platt, J. Fagg and M. Hawkins, 'Suicide following Parasuicide in Young People', *British Journal of Psychiatry*, 152 (1993), pp. 359–66.

18. G. E. Murphy and R. D. Wetzel, 'Suicide Risk by Birth Cohort in the United States, 1949–1974', *Archives of General Psychiatry*, 37 (1980), pp. 519–23; M. J. Solomon and C. P. Hellon, 'Suicide and Age in Alberta, Canada, 1951–1977: a Cohort Analysis', *Archives of General Psychiatry*, 37 (1980), pp. 511–13; R. D. Goldney and M. Katsikitis, 'Suicide Rates in Australia', *Archives of General Psychiatry*, 40 (1983), pp. 71–4.

19. Charlton, Kelly, Dunnell, Evans, Jenkins and Wallis, 'Trends in Suicide Deaths in England and Wales' (see note 6, above).

20. Ibid.

21. N. Kreitman, V. Carstairs and J. Duffy, 'Association of Age and Social Class with Suicide among Men in Great Britain', *Journal of Epidemiology and Community Health*, 45 (1991), pp. 195–202.

22. For the Cross National Collaborative Group reference, see 'The Changing Rate of Major Depression: Cross-national Comparisons', *Journal of the American Medical Association*, 268 (1992), pp. 355–73.

CHAPTER 3: PSYCHIATRIC AND SOCIAL FACTORS IN SUICIDE

1. Durkheim, *Le Suicide*.

2. B. Barraclough, J. Bunch, B. Nelson and P. Sainsbury, 'A Hundred Cases of Suicide: Clinical Aspects', *British Journal of Psychiatry*, 25 (1974), pp. 355–73.

3. S. Platt, R. Micciolo and M. Tansella, 'Suicide and Unemployment in Italy: Description, Analysis and Interpretation of Recent Trends', *Social Science Medicine*, 34 (1992), pp. 1191–201.

4. P. Sainsbury, J. Jenkins and A. Levey, 'The Social Correlates of Suicide in Europe', in R. Farmer and S. Hirsch (eds.), *The Suicide Syndrome*, Croom Helm, London, 1980, pp. 38–53.

5. For recent definitions of 'social support', see G. Brown and T. Harris, *The Social Origins of Depression – a Study of Psychiatric Disorder in Women*, Tavistock, London, 1978.

6. K. Hawton and J. Fagg, 'Suicide, and Other Causes of Death, following Attempted Suicide', *British Journal of Psychiatry*, 152 (1988), pp. 359–66.

CHAPTER 4: ATTEMPTED SUICIDE: THE STATISTICS

1. A. Alvarez, *Savage God, A Study of Suicide*, Random House, New York, 1972.

2. Although true in the individual case, studies of larger numbers have found a correlation between suicide intent and the number of pills taken. More than twenty pills has been found to indicate higher suicide intent. See R. D. Goldney, 'Attempted Suicide in Young Women: Correlates of Lethality', *British Journal of Psychiatry*, 147 (1981), pp. 382–90; K. G. Power, D. J. Cooke and J. S. Gibbons, 'Life

Stress, Medical Lethality, and Suicidal Intent', *British Journal of Psychiatry*, 147 (1985), pp. 655–9; and D. J. Pallis, J. S. Gibbons and D. W. Pierce, 'Estimating Suicide Risk among Attempted Suicides', *British Journal of Psychiatry*, 144 (1984), pp. 139–48.

3. K. Hawton, J. Fagg, S. Simkin, E. Bale and A. Bond, 'Attempted Suicide in Oxford, 1994', unpublished report from University Department of Psychiatry, Oxford.

4. For full details of the Canada data, see I. Sakinofsky, 'The Epidemiology of Suicide in Canada', in A. Leenaars, S. Wenckstern, I. Sakinofsky, M. Kral, R. Dyck and R. Bland (eds.), *Suicide in Canada*, University of Toronto, 1996.

5. E. K. Moscicki, P. O'Carroll, D. S. Rae, B. Z. Locke, A. Roy and D. A. Regier, 'Suicide Attempts in the Epidemiologic Catchment Area Study', *Yale Journal of Biology and Medicine*, 61 (1988), pp. 259–68.

6. R. D. Goldney, 'Suicidal Ideation in a Young Adult Population', *Acta Psychiatrica Scandinavica*, 79 (1989), pp. 481–9.

7. D. Buglass and J. Horton, 'A Scale for Predicting Subsequent Suicidal Behaviour', *British Journal of Psychiatry*, 124 (1974), pp. 573–8.

8. N. Kreitman and J. Foster, 'The Construction and Selection of Predictive Scales, with Special Reference to Parasuicide', *British Journal of Psychiatry*, 159 (1991), pp. 185–92.

9. J. Bancroft, K. Hawton, S. Simkin *et al.*, 'The Reasons People Give for Taking Overdoses', *British Journal of Medical Psychology*, 52 (1979), pp. 353–65.

10. A. T. Beck, A. W. Weissman, D. Lester and L. Trexler, 'The Assessment of Pessimism: the Hopelessness Scale', *Journal of Consulting and Clinical Psychology*, 42 (1974), pp. 861–5.

11. D. W. Pierce, 'Suicidal Intent in Self-injury', *British Journal of Psychiatry*, 130 (1977), pp. 377–85.

12. R. Plutchik, H. M. Van Praag, S. Picard and H. R. Conte *et al.*, 'Is There a Relationship between the Seriousness of Suicidal Intent and the Lethality of the Suicidal Attempt?', *Psychiatry Research*, 27 (1989), pp. 71–9.

13. D. W. Pierce, 'Predictive Validation of a Suicide Intent Scale', *British Journal of Psychiatry*, 139 (1981), pp. 445–6.

14. J. Suokas and J. Lonnqvist, 'Outcome of Attempted Suicide and Psychiatric Consultation: Risk Factors and Suicide Mortality during a Five-year Follow-up', *Acta Psychiatrica Scandinavica*, 84 (1991), pp. 545–9.

15. R. W. Beck, J. B. Morris and A. T. Beck, 'Cross-validation of the Suicidal Intent Scale', *Psychological Reports*, 34 (1974), pp. 445–6.

16. A. T. Beck and R. Steer, 'Clinical Predictors of Eventual Suicide: a 5–10-year Prospective Study of Suicide Attempters', *Journal of Affective Disorders*, 17 (1989), pp. 203–9; D. Lester, A. T. Beck and S. Narrett, 'Suicidal Intent in Successive Suicidal Actions', *Psychological Reports*, 43 (1978), p. 110.

CHAPTER 5: THE CAUSES OF ATTEMPTED SUICIDE

1. R. W. Maris, 'Deviance as Therapy: the Paradox of the Self-destructive Females', *Journal of Health and Social Behaviour*, 12 (1981), pp. 113–24.

2. See K. Hawton and J. Catalan, *Attempted Suicide*, second edition, Oxford University Press, 1987.

3. R. D. Goldney, 'Parental Representation in Young Women Who Attempt Suicide', *Acta Psychiatrica Scandinavica*, 72 (1985), pp. 230–32.

4. G. Parker, H. Tupling and L. B. Brown, 'A Parental Bonding Instrument', *British Journal of Medical Psychology*, 52 (1979), pp. 1–10.

5. M. van Egmond, N. Garnefski, D. Jonker and A. Kerkhov, 'The Relationship between Sexual Abuse and Female Suicidal Behavior', *Crisis*, 14 (1993), pp. 129–39.

6. Hawton and Catalan, *Attempted Suicide*.

7. S. Platt and N. Kreitman, 'Trends in Parasuicide and Unemployment among Men in Edinburgh, 1968–1982', *British Medical Journal*, 289 (1984), pp. 1029–32.

8. Hawton, Fagg, Simkin, Bale and Bond, 'Attempted Suicide in Oxford, 1994', unpublished report.

9. J. Bancroft, A. Skrimshire, J. Casson, O. Harvard-Watts and F. Reynolds, 'People Who Deliberately Poison Themselves: Their Problems and Their Contacts with Helping Agencies', *Psychological Medicine*, 7 (1977), pp. 289–303.

10. S. M. Davonport, 'Association between Parasuicide and

St Valentine's Day', *British Medical Journal*, 300 (1990), pp. 783−4.

11. For further discussion of these difficulties, see A. K. MacLeod, J. M. G. Williams and M. M. Linehan, 'New Developments in the Understanding and Treatment of Suicidal Behaviour', *Behavioural Psychotherapy*, 20 (1992), pp. 193−218.

12. J. J. Platt, G. Spivack and W. Bloom, *Manual for the Means−End Problem-solving Procedure (MEPS): A Measure of Interpersonal Problem-solving Skill*, Hahnemann Community MH/MR Center, Department of Mental Health Services, Hahnemann Medical College and Hospital, Philadelphia, 1987.

13. D. E. Schotte and G. A. Clum, 'Problem-solving Skills in Suicidal Psychiatric Patients', *Journal of Consulting and Clinical Psychology*, 55 (1987), pp. 49−54. Similarly poor problem-solving ability has also been found in younger suicidal people; see M. J. Rotheram-Borus, P. D. Trautman, S. C. Dopkins and P. E. Shrout, 'Cognitive Style and Pleasant Activities among Female Adolescent Suicide Attempters', *Journal of Consulting and Clinical Psychology*, 58 (1990), pp. 554−61.

14. M. M. Linehan, P. Camper, J. A. Chiles, K. Strohsal and E. N. Shearin, 'Inter-personal Problem Solving and Parasuicide', *Cognitive Therapy and Research*, 11 (1987), pp. 1−12.

15. I. Orbach, H. Bar-Joseph and N. Dror, 'Styles of Problem Solving in Suicidal Individuals', *Suicide and Life Threatening Behavior*, 20 (1990), pp. 56−64.

16. J. F. Simonds, T. McMahon and D. Armstrong, 'Young Suicide Attempters Compared with a Control Group', *Suicide and Life Threatening Behavior*, 21 (1991), pp. 134−51.

17. A. K. MacLeod, G. Rose and J. M. G. Williams, 'Components of Helplessness about the Future in Parasuicide', *Cognitive Therapy and Research*, 17 (1993), pp. 441−55.

18. A. T. Beck, G. Brown and R. A. Steer, 'Prediction of Eventual Suicide in Psychiatric Inpatients by Clinical Ratings of Helplessness', *Journal of Consulting and Clinical Psychology*, 57 (1989), pp. 309−10.

19. Beck, Weissman, Lester and Trexler, 'The Measurement of Pessimism'.

20. M. M. Linehan, J. L. Goodstein, S. L. Neilsen and J. A. Chiles, 'Reasons for Staying Alive when You Are Thinking of Killing Your-

self: the Reasons for Living Inventory', *Journal of Consulting and Clinical Psychology*, 51 (1983), pp. 276–86.

CHAPTER 6: RATIONAL SUICIDE, EUTHANASIA AND
MARTYRDOM

1. D. Humphry, 'Rational Suicide among the Elderly', *Suicide and Life Threatening Behavior*, 22 (1992), pp. 125–9, see p. 127; D. Humphry, *Final Exit: the Practicalities of Self-deliverance and Assisted Suicide*, Carol Publishing, Secaucus, NJ, 1991.
2. Humphry, 'Rational Suicide among the Elderly'.
3. Humphry, 'Rational Suicide among the Elderly', p. 126.
4. A. Koestler, *Arrow in the Blue*, Collins and Hamish Hamilton, London, 1952.
5. R. D. Goldney, 'Arthur Koestler: Was His Suicide Rational?', *Crisis*, 7 (1986), pp. 33–53.
6. J. Richman, 'A Rational Approach to Rational Suicide', *Suicide and Life Threatening Behavior*, 22 (1992), pp. 130–41.
7. Scott, 'Cancer Patients', in Scott, Williams and Beck (eds.), *Cognitive Theory in Clinical Practice*.
8. Richman, 'A Rational Approach to Rational Suicide'.

CHAPTER 7: PSYCHODYNAMICS, BIOLOGY AND GENETICS

1. S. Freud, *Mourning and Melancholia* (1917), Standard Edition, vol. 14, Hogarth Press, London, 1957.
2. Ibid.
3. S. Freud, *The Ego and the Id* (1923), Standard Edition, vol. 19, Hogarth Press, London, 1961.
4. For psychoanalytic observations on suicide as a 'reversible' and 'magical' act, see K. A. Menninger, 'Psychoanalytic Aspects of Suicide', *International Journal of Psychoanalysis*, 14 (1933), p. 376; C. W. Wahl, 'Suicide as a Magical Act', *Bulletin of the Menninger Clinic*, 21 (1957), p. 91.
5. M. Klein, 'A Contribution to the Psychogenesis of Manic-depressive States' (1935), in *Contributions to Psycho-Analysis 1921–1945: Melanie Klein*, Hogarth Press, London.

6. H. Guntrip, *Schizoid Phenomena, Object Relations and the Self*, Hogarth Press, London, 1968.

7. S. Asch, 'Suicide and the Hidden Executioner', *International Review of Psychoanalysis*, 7 (1980), pp. 51–60.

8. J. Bowlby, *Maternal Care and Mental Health*, Columbia University Press, 1951.

9. J. T. Maltsberger, *Suicide Risk: the Formulation of Clinical Judgment*, New York University Press, New York and London, 1986.

10. P. W. Gold, F. K. Goodwin and G. P. Chrousos, 'Clinical and Biochemical Manifestation of Depression', *New England Journal of Medicine*, 319 (1988), pp. 348–420.

11. M. Asberg, P. Thoren, L. Traskman *et al.*, 'Serotonin Depression: a Biochemical Subgroup within the Affective Disorders?', *Science*, 191 (1986), pp. 478–80.

12. See also E. F. Coccaro, L. J. Siever, H. M. Klar *et al.*, 'Serotonergic Studies in Patients with Affective and Personality Disorders', *Archives of General Psychiatry*, 46 (1989), pp. 587–99; K. M. Malone, E. M. Corbitt, L. Shuhua and L. Mann, 'Prolactin Response to Fenfluramine and Suicide Attempt Lethality in Major Depression', *British Journal of Psychiatry*, 168 (1996), pp. 324–9; G. N. Pandey, S. C. Pandey, Y. Dwivedi *et al.*, 'Platelet Serotonin-2A Receptors: a Potential Biological Marker for Suicidal Behavior', *American Journal of Psychiatry*, 152 (1995), pp. 850–55.

13. See R. M. Winchel, B. Stanley and M. Stanley, 'Biochemical Aspects of Suicide', in S. J. Blumenthal and D. J. Kupfer (eds.), *Suicide over the Life Cycle: Risk Factors, Assessment and Treatment of Suicidal Patients*, American Psychiatric Association Press, Washington, DC, 1990.

14. M. Linnoila, M. Virkkunen, M. Scheinin *et al.*, 'Low Cerebralspinal Fluid 5-HIAA Concentration Differentiates Impulsive from Nonimpulsive Violent Behavior', *Life Science*, 33, pp. 2609–14.

15. A. Roy, N. L. Segal, B. S. and Robinette Centerwall, 'Suicide in Twins', *Archives of General Psychiatry*, 48 (1991), pp. 29–32.

16. F. Schulsinger, S. S. Kety, D. Rosenthal and P. H. Wender, 'A Family Study of Suicide', in M. Schou and E. Stromgren (eds.), *Prevention and Treatment of Affective Disorders*, Academic Press, New York, 1979.

17. S. Kety, 'Genetic Factors in Suicide: Family, Twin and Adoption Studies', in Blumenthal and Kupfer (eds.), *Suicide over the Life Cycle*.

CHAPTER 8: THE EFFECT OF THE MEDIA

1. Durkheim, *Le Suicide*.
2. D. P. Phillips, 'The Influence of Suggestion on Suicide: Substantive and Theoretical Implications of the Werther Effect', *American Sociological Review*, 39 (1974), pp. 340–54.
3. B. Barraclough, D. Shepherd and C. Jennings, 'Two Newspaper Reports of Coroners' Inquests Incite People to Commit Suicide?', *British Journal of Psychiatry*, 131 (1977), pp. 528–32.
4. K. A. Bollen and D. P. Phillips, 'Imitative Suicides: a National Study of the Effects of Television News Stories', *American Sociological Review*, 47 (1982), pp. 802–9.
5. For evidence of suicide by burning as an imitative phenomenon, see J. R. Ashton and S. Donnan, 'Suicide by Burning as an Epidemic Phenomena [sic]: an Analysis of 82 Deaths and Inquests in England and Wales in 1978–9', *Psychological Medicine*, 11 (1981), pp. 735–9.
6. S. J. Ellis and S. Walsh, 'Soap May Seriously Damage Your Health' (letter), *Lancet* (1986), p. 686.
7. S. Platt, 'The Aftermath of Angie's Overdose: Is Soap (Opera) Damaging to Your Health?', *British Medical Journal*, 294 (1987), pp. 954–7; S. Platt, 'The Consequences of a Televised Soap Opera Drug Overdose: Is There a Mass Media Imitation Effect?', in R. F. W. Diekstra, R. W. Maris, S. D. Platt, A. Schmidtke and G. Sonneck (eds.), *Attitudinal Factors in Suicidal Behaviour and Its Prevention*, Swets & Zeitlinger, Brill, 1987.
8. J. M. G. Williams, C. Lawton, S. Ellis, S. Walsh and J. Reed, 'Imitative Parasuicide by Overdose', *Lancet*, 8550 (1987), pp. 102–3 (report of findings of research commissioned by the Independent Broadcasting Authority).
9. A. Schmidtke and H. Hafner, 'The Werther Effect after Television Films: New Evidence from an Old Hypothesis', *Psychological Medicine*, 18 (1988), pp. 665–76.
10. D. P. Phillips, 'The Impact of Fictional Television Stories on

American Adult Fatalities', *American Journal of Sociology*, 87 (1982), pp. 1340–59.

11. R. C. Kessler and H. Stipp, 'The Impact of Fictional Television Suicide Stories on US Fatalities: a Replication', *American Journal of Sociology*, 90 (1984), pp. 151–67.

12. J. N. Barron and P. C. Reiss, 'Mass Media and Violent Behavior', *American Sociological Review*, 131 (1985), pp. 528–32.

13. D. P. Phillips and L. L. Carstensen, 'Clustering Teenage Suicides after Television News Stories about Suicides', *New England Journal of Medicine*, 315 (1986), pp. 685–9.

14. M. Gould, 'Suicide Clusters and Media Exposure', in Blumenthal and Kupfer (eds.), *Suicide over the Life Span*.

CHAPTER 9: THE CRY OF PAIN

1. R. M. Post, 'Transduction of Psychosocial Stress into the Neurobiology of Recurrent Affective Disorder', *American Journal of Psychiatry*, 149 (1992), pp. 999–1010.

2. G. L. Engel, 'Anxiety and Depression-withdrawal: the Primary Effects of Unpleasure', *International Journal of Psychoanalysis*, 43 (1962), pp. 89–97.

3. R. D. Goldney, 'Attempted Suicide: an Ethological Perspective', *Suicide and Life Threatening Behavior*, 10 (1980), pp. 131–41.

4. E. S. Schneidman, 'Orientations towards Death: a Vital Aspect of the Study of Lives', *International Journal of Psychiatry*, 2 (1966), pp. 167–200.

5. P. Gilbert, J. Prince and S. Allan, 'Social Comparison, Social Attractiveness and Evolution: How Might They Be Related?', *New Ideas in Psychology*, 13 (1995), pp. 149–65.

6. M. J. Raleigh, M. T. McGuire, G. L. Brammer and A. Yuwiler, 'Social and Environmental Influences on Blood Serotonin Concentrations in Monkeys', *Archives of General Psychiatry*, 41 (1984), pp. 405–10.

7. S. Platt, 'Unemployment and Suicidal Behaviour: a Review of the Literature', *Social Science and Medicine*, 19 (1984), pp. 93–115.

8. R. G. Wilkinson, 'Income Distribution and Life Expectancy', *British Medical Journal*, 304 (1992), pp. 165–8.

9. P. Gilbert, *Depression: The Evolution of Powerlessness*, LEA, Hove, and Guilford, New York, 1992.

10. P. Gilbert, 'Defence and Safety: Their Function in Social Behaviour and Psychopathology', *British Journal of Clinical Psychology*, 32 (1993), pp. 131–54.

11. N. L. Farberow and E. S. Schneidman (eds.), *The Cry for Help*, McGraw-Hill, New York, 1961.

12. Stengel, *Suicide and Attempted Suicide*.

13. Schneidman, 'Orientations towards Death'.

14. N. Kessel, 'The Respectability of Self-poisoning and the Fashion of Survival', *Journal of Psychosomatic Research*, 10 (1966), pp. 29–36.

15. Alvarez, *Savage God*.

16. MacDonald and Murphy, *Sleepless Souls*.

CHAPTER 10: MEMORY TRAPS

1. J. D. Teasdale and S. J. Fogarty, 'Differential Effects of Induced Mood on Retrieval of Pleasant and Unpleasant Events from Episodic Memory', *Journal of Abnormal Psychology*, 88 (1979), pp. 248–57; G. G. Lloyd and W. A. Lishman, 'Effect of Depression on the Speed of Recall of Pleasant and Unpleasant Experiences', *Psychological Medicine*, 5 (1975), pp. 173–80.

2. J. M. G. Williams and K. Broadbent, 'Autobiographical Memory in Attempted Suicide Patients', *Journal of Abnormal Psychology*, 95 (1986), pp. 144–9; J. M. G. Williams and B. H. Dritschel, 'Emotional Disturbance and the Specificity of Autobiographical Memory', *Cognition and Emotion*, 2 (1988), pp. 221–34.

3. J. M. G. Williams, 'Depression and the Specificity of Autobiographical Memory', in D. C. Rubin (ed.), *Remembering Our Past: Studies in Autobiographical Memory*, Cambridge University Press, 1996.

4. R. G. Moore, F. N. Watts and J. M. G. Williams, 'The Specificity of Personal Memories in Depression', *British Journal of Clinical Psychology*, 27 (1988), pp. 275–6.

5. J. M. G. Williams and J. Scott, 'Autobiographical Memory in Depression', *Psychological Medicine*, 18 (1988), pp. 689–95.

6. A. Puffet, D. Jehin-Marchot, M. Timsit-Berthier and M. Timsit,

'Autobiographical Memory and Major Depressive States', *European Psychiatry*, 6 (1991), pp. 141–5.

7. K. Nelson, 'The Ontogeny of Memory for Real Events', in U. Neisser and C. E. Winograd (eds.), *Remembering Reconsidered: Ecological and Traditional Approaches to the Study of Memory*, Cambridge University Press, 1988, pp. 244–76.

8. J. Morton, 'The Development of Event Memory', *Psychologist*, 1 (1990), pp. 3–10.

9. W. Kuyken and C. R. Brewin, 'Autobiographical Memory Functioning in Depression and Reports of Early Abuse', *Journal of Abnormal Psychology*, 104 (1995), pp. 585–91.

10. J. Evans, J. M. G. Williams, S. O'Loughlin and K. Howells, 'Autobiographical Memory and Problem Solving Strategies of Parasuicide Patients', *Psychological Medicine*, 22 (1992), pp. 399–405.

11. E. M. Marx, J. M. G. Williams and G. S. Claridge, 'Depression and Social Problem-solving', *Journal of Abnormal Psychology*, 101 (1992), pp. 78–86.

12. For the work that led to these conclusions, see J. M. G. Williams, N. Ellis, C. Tyers, H. Healy, G. Rose and A. K. MacLeod, 'The Specificity of Autobiographical Memory and Imageability of the Future', *Memory and Cognition*, 24 (1996), pp. 116–25.

13. C. B. Traux and R. R. Carkhuff, 'Concreteness: a Neglected Variable in Research in Psychotherapy', unpublished MS, Psychotherapy Research Program, Universities of Kentucky and Wisconsin, 1967. For a similar observation, made in studies of young mothers who were having problems in relationships with their children, see R. G. Wahler and A. D. Afton, 'Attentional Processes in Insular and Non-insular Mothers: Some Differences in Their Summary Reports about Child Problem Behaviours', *Behaviour Therapy*, 2 (1980), pp. 25–41.

14. A. D. Brittlebank, J. Scott, J. M. G. Williams and I. N. Ferrier, 'Autobiographical Memory in Depression; State or Trait Marker?', *British Journal of Psychiatry*, 162 (1993), pp. 118–21.

CHAPTER 11: THE PRIMARY PREVENTION OF SUICIDAL
BEHAVIOUR

1. D. W. Coombs, H. L. Miller, R. Alarcon, C. Herlinhy, J. M. Lee and D. P. Morison, 'Presuicide Attempt Communications between Parasuicides and Consulted Caregivers', *Suicide and Life Threatening Behavior*, 22 (1992), pp. 289–302.

2. W. Rutz, L. von Knorring and J. Walinder, 'Frequency of Suicide on Gotland after Systematic Postgraduate Education of General Practitioners', *Acta Psychiatrica Scandinavica*, 80 (1989), pp. 151–4.

3. W. Rutz, L. von Knorring and J. Walinder, 'Long-term Effects of an Educational Program for General Practitioners Given by the Swedish Committee for the Prevention and Treatment of Depression', *Acta Psychiatrica Scandinavica*, 85 (1992), pp. 83–8.

4. A. MacDonald, 'The Myth of Suicide Prevention by General Practitioners', *British Journal of Psychiatry*, 162 (1993), p. 260.

5. As an Office of Population Census and Surveys report found, one in seven people in Britain between 16 and 64 has some sort of neurotic health problem at any one time; see H. Meltzer, B. Gill and M. Pettigrew, *OPCS Survey of Psychiatric Morbidity in Great Britain*, OPCS, London, 1994.

6. *Sensitivity* of a test is defined as the number of true positives divided by the sum of true positives plus false negatives, then multiplied by 100. The numerator is the 'positive hit rate' (suicides successfully predicted) and the denominator is the total number of such hits that are possible – the total number of actual suicides in the population being studied. *Specificity* of a test is defined as the number of true negatives divided by the sum of false positives and true negatives, then multiplied by 100. The numerator is the negative 'hit rate' (lack of suicide successfully predicted) and the denominator is the total number of such hits that are possible – the total number of people who do not commit suicide in the population being studied.

7. A. D. Pokorny, 'Prediction of Suicide in Psychiatric Patients: Report of a Prospective Study', in R. W. Maris, A. L. Berman, J. T. Maltsberger and R. I. Yufit (eds.), *Assessment and Prediction of Suicide*, Guilford Press, New York, 1992.

8. R. W. Maris, 'The Prediction of Suicide' in M. J. Kelleher (ed.), *Divergent Perspectives on Suicidal Behaviour*, Report of Fifth European Symposium on Suicide, Cork, 1994, pp. 28–41.

9. For further discussion of this work, see D. Lester, *Can We Prevent Suicide?*, AMS Press, New York, 1989.

10. D. I. R. Jones in *British Medical Journal*, 282 (1977), pp. 28–9.

11. S. Greer and M. Alderson, 'Samaritan Contact among 325 Parasuicide Patients', *British Journal of Psychiatry*, 135 (1979), pp. 263–8.

12. C. Jennings, B. M. Barraclough and J. R. Moss, 'Have the Samaritans Lowered the Suicide Rate: a Controlled Study', *Psychological Medicine*, 8 (1978), pp. 413–27.

13. D. Lester, 'The Effectiveness of Suicide Prevention Centres', *Suicide and Life Threatening Behavior*, 23 (1993), pp. 263–7.

14. For sceptical evaluations, see *Suicide and Parasuicide*, MRC Topic Review, Medical Research Council, London, 1995; D. Shaffer, M. A. Garland, M. Gould *et al.*, 'Preventing Teenage Suicide: a Critical Review', *Journal of the American Academy of Childhood and Adolescent Psychiatry*, 27 (1988), pp. 675–87.

15. D. Shaffer, A. Garland, V. Vieland *et al.*, 'The Impact of Curriculum-based Suicide Prevention Programs for Teenagers', *Journal of the American Academy of Childhood and Adolescent Psychiatry*, 30 (1991), pp. 588–96.

16. D. Gunnell, *The Potential for Preventing Suicide*, Health Care Evaluation Unit, University of Bristol, 1994.

CHAPTER 12: SECONDARY PREVENTION: THERAPY FOR SUICIDAL FEELINGS AND BEHAVIOUR

1. One of the best introductions to such an approach can be found in K. Hawton and J. Kirk, 'Problem Solving Treatment', in K. Hawton, D. Clark, P. Salkovskis and J. Kirk (eds.), *Cognitive Therapy for Adult Psychiatric Patients*, Oxford University Press, 1989.

2. T. J. D'Zurilla and M. R. Goldfried, 'Problem Solving and Behaviour Modification', *Journal of Abnormal Psychology*, 78 (1970), pp. 107–26; M. R. Goldfried and A. P. Goldfried, 'Cognitive Change

Methods', in F. H. Kanfer and A. P. Goldstein (eds.), *Helping People Change*, Academic Press, New York, 1975.

3. Hawton and Kirk, 'Problem Solving Treatment', in Hawton *et al.* (eds.), *Cognitive Therapy for Adult Psychiatric Patients*.

4. J. S. Gibbons, J. Butler, P. Urwin and J. L. Gibbons, 'Evaluation of a Social Work Service for Self-poisoning Patients', *British Journal of Psychiatry*, 133 (1978), pp. 111–18.

5. For two small-scale studies that have given provisionally more encouraging results, see B. C. McLeavey, R. J. Daly, J. W. Ludgate and C. M. Murray, 'Interpersonal Problem Solving Skills Training in the Treatment of Self Poisoning Patients', *Suicide and Life Threatening Behavior*, 24 (1994), pp. 382–94; P. M. Salkovskis, C. Atha and D. Storer, 'Cognitive-Behavioural Problem Solving in the Treatment of Patients Who Repeatedly Attempt Suicide', *British Journal of Psychiatry*, 157 (1990), pp. 871–6.

6. M. M. Linehan, H. E. Armstrong, A. Suarez, D. Allmond and H. L. Heard, 'Behavioural Treatment of Chronically Parasuicidal Borderline Patients', *Archives of General Psychiatry*, 48 (1991), pp. 1060–64.

7. M. M. Linehan, H. L. Heard and H. E. Armstrong, 'Naturalistic Follow-up of a Behavioural Treatment for Chronically Parasuicidal Borderline Clients', *Archives of General Psychiatry*, 50 (1993), pp. 971–4.

8. Evans, Williams, O'Loughlin and Howells, 'Autobiographical Memory and Problem Solving Strategies'.

9. H. G. Morgan, E. M. Jones and J. H. Owen, 'Secondary Prevention of Non-fatal Deliberate Self-Harm: the Green Card Study', *British Journal of Psychiatry*, 163 (1993), pp. 111–12.

CHAPTER 13: FINAL THOUGHTS

1. P. Levi, *The Drowned and the Saved*, Michael Joseph, London, 1988.
2. D. M. Shepherd and B. M. Barraclough, 'The Aftermath of Parental Suicide for Children', *British Journal of Psychiatry*, 129 (1976), pp. 267–76.
3. N. L. Farberow, 'Adult Survivors after Suicide: Research Prob-

lems and Needs', in A. A. Leenaars (ed.), *Life Span Perspectives of Suicide*, Plenum Press, New York, 1991.

4. A. Sucitto, in *Peace and Kindness*, Amaravasti Publications, Hemel Hempstead, 1990.

INDEX

Numbers in italics refer to figures; those in bold refer to tables.

Protestants, 33
psychiatric illness
  as an explanation for suicide,
    11–13, 38
  Durkheim's view of psychiatric
    causation, 56–7
  evidence for psychiatric illness as a
    cause of suicide, 51–5
  gender and age effects not
    explained by, 55–6
  non compos mentis verdicts, 4, 5, 6, 7,
    11–12
  and the risk of suicide, 39–40
  statistics of suicides, 2, 50
psychiatric intervention
  and probability of suicidal
    behaviour, 2, 197
psychoanalytic perspectives, 118–21
psychological autopsy, 51
psychosis, 59
psychotherapy, 18, 62, 156, 174, 211
Puerto Rico (rates of depression), *48*
Pythagoras, 2, 103

Raleigh, Michael, 144
Ramesey, William, 12
rational suicide, 111–13, 117
  renewed fascination with, xi
Reasons for Living Inventory, 95
religious affiliation, 33–4, 41, **61**
Renaissance, 7, 9
renal dialysis, 38
Resource Holding Potential (RHP),
  145–6, 147
Richman, Joseph, 112
RNA (ribonucleic acid), 141
Rose, Gillian, 94
Roy, A., 126, 127
rural areas, 36, 60
Rutz, W., 179

sadism, 120
St Bartholomew's Hospital, 133
Samaritans, 77, 193–4
Savage God (Alvarez), 67, 188
Scandinavia, 39
schizoid suicide, 121

schizophrenia
  and DBT, 210
  external stresses, 65
  and genetic influences, 127–8
  and low levels of 5-HIAA, 125
  and maniacal suicide, 56
  risk of suicide, 39, 51, **52**, 54–5, 65,
    66
  and suicidal behaviour, 125
  symptoms, 54, 64, 65
  and uncontrolled limbs, 7
Schmidtke, Arnold, 134, 135, 136
Schneidman, E. S., 143, 150
school-based intervention, 195–6
Schulsinger, F., 127
Scotland, *26*
Scott, Jan, 167, 174
Second World War, 21
secondary prevention of suicidal
    behaviour, 197–217
  assessing suicidal intent and the
    probability of repetition,
    199–200
  Dialectical Behaviour Therapy
    (DBT), 208–10
  evaluation of problem-solving
    approaches, 207–8
  follow-up of DBT for suicidal
    behaviour, 210–13
  a framework for therapy, 199
  the future of secondary prevention
    research, 216–17
  problem-solving therapy, 201–7
  psychological mechanisms
    underlying therapeutic change,
    213–16
  some common problems, 200–201
  vigilance for suicidal expression,
    197–9
*Secretary's Task Force on Youth Suicide,
    The* (US Department of Health
    and Human Services), 33
secularization of suicide, 7, 8
sedatives, 71, 73, *75*, 180, 189, 191, *192*
selective abstraction, 198
self-deliverance *see* rational suicide
self-neglect, **52**